KNOWLEDGE CONTRIBUTORS

Edited by

VINCENT F. HENDRICKS
Roskilde University,
Denmark

KLAUS FROVIN JØRGENSEN
Roskilde University,
Denmark

and

STIG ANDUR PEDERSEN
Roskilde University,
Denmark

KLUWER ACADEMIC PUBLISHERS
DORDRECHT / BOSTON / LONDON

A C.I.P. Catalogue record for this book is available from the Library of Congress.

ISBN 1-4020-1747-2

Published by Kluwer Academic Publishers,
P.O. Box 17, 3300 AA Dordrecht, The Netherlands.

Sold and distributed in North, Central and South America
by Kluwer Academic Publishers,
101 Philip Drive, Norwell, MA 02061, U.S.A.

In all other countries, sold and distributed
by Kluwer Academic Publishers,
P.O. Box 322, 3300 AH Dordrecht, The Netherlands.

Printed on acid-free paper

Printed in the Netherlands.

CONTENTS

PREFACE

In the 1950's Georg von Wright provided the first surveys in epistemic logic. Roughly 10 years later Jaakko Hintikka published his seminal work on the logic of knowledge and belief. Epistemic and doxastic logics have since then grown into mature disciplines enjoying many important applications in philosophy, computer science, game theory, economics and linguistics to mention of few fields of applications.

Knowledge Contributors is based on the *Dimensions in Epistemic Logic* conference hosted by ΦLOG—*The Danish Network for Philosophical Logic and Its Applications* in May 2002 at Roskilde University, Denmark. The conference featured lectures by such recognized experts in epistemic logic as Joseph Y. Halpern (Cornell University, USA), Jaakko Hintikka (Boston University, USA), Wiebe van der Hoek (University of Liverpool, UK), Wolfgang Lenzen (University of Osnabrück, DE), Hans Rott (University of Regensburg, DE), Krister Segerberg (Uppsala University, SE), John F. Sowa (USA), Moshe Y. Vardi (Rice University, USA) and Ryszard Wójcicki (Polish Academy of Sciences, PL).

The conference had three aims which are reflected in the current volume and its organization of the contributions: (1) To track the history of epistemic logic, (2) to consider important applications of epistemic logic in a variety of fields and (3) to discuss future directions of research in epistemic logic with particular emphasis on 'active agenthood' and multimodal systems. The editors would like to thank the invited speakers, and their co-authors, for contributing, in the most lucid and inspiring way, to the fulfillment of the conference aims and for making their contributions available for publication.

The editors would also like to extend their gratitude to ΦLOG's organizational committee consisting of Torben Braüner, Henning Christiansen (Roskilde University), Jan Riis Flor (University of Copenhagen), Cynthia M. Grund (University of Southern Denmark), Lars Bo Gundersen (Aarhus University), Per Hasle (University of Southern Denmark), K. Hvidtfeldt Nielsen (Aarhus University), Peter Øhrstrøm (Aalborg University) and ΦLOG's secretary Pelle Guldborg Hansen (Roskilde University). ΦLOG is only made possible by a research grant from the *Danish Research Council for the Humanities* for which the editors and the network remain grateful. The editors would like to thank Lise Sonne-Hansen for her careful BIBTEX'ing of the manuscript. Finally we would like to extend our gratitude to Kluwer Academic Publishers and in particular acquisition editor Floor Oosting for taking on this project.

Vincent F. Hendricks   Klaus Frovin Jørgensen
Stig Andur Pedersen

September 2003

V.F. HENDRICKS, K.F. JØRGENSEN AND S.A. PEDERSEN

INTRODUCTION

The study of epistemic attitudes – in particular knowledge and belief – dates at least back to the Scholaticism of the Middles Ages. The formal study of the same attitudes was then largely initiated by von Wright's seminal paper from the 1950's (37). The formal systematic study of knowledge and belief saw the light of day by Hintikka's book by the same name *Knowledge and Belief: An Introduction to the Logic of the Two Notions* from 1962 (16). Hardly a publication in epistemic logic has surfaced since without reference to this ground-breaking investigation. More recent monographs dedicated to epistemic and/or doxastic logic[1] include notably Lenzen (22), Schlesinger (25), Boh (3), Knuuttila (19), Meyer and van der Hoek (35), Fagin et al. (6), Sowa (30), Hendricks (12), (14), and Halpern (11).

The contemporary logics of knowledge and belief are advanced and sophisticated. Epistemic and doxastics logics for single agents have been catalogued; logics for multi-agent systems have been catalogued; epistemic modalities have been combined with temporal and alethic modalities, etc. These advances make the way for multiple epistemic operators, multiple doxastic operators, common knowledge operators, alethic and temporal operators, mono-modal systems, multi-modal systems, dynamic epistemic/doxastic systems, belief revision features and agents equipped with learning mechanisms. This is not an exhaustive list. There is a vast fan of important applications and models utilizing these powerful logics of knowledge and belief. Examples range from robots on assembly lines, social and coalitional interactions, card games, 'live' situations in economics, miscellaneous linguistic practices and so on.

It is not the purpose of this introduction to review epistemic logic from its date of birth to this day and age in detail.[2] Certain distinctive developmental features stand out as particularly pertinent to both the research progression and direction as well as the general epistemological and applicational relevance of epistemic logic. These may be subsumed under 'agent and system', 'active agenthood', 'multiple active agents', 'multi-modalites' and constitute the features with respect to which this introduction and the contributions in this volume are organized.

1. AGENT AND SYSTEM

The formal systematic surveys of epistemic and doxastic logics were early on largely influenced by the advances in (alethic) modal logic. Standard systems of modal logic were furnished with epistemic interpretations, and some fundamental results of epistemic logic could then be extracted.

Syntactically, the language of propositional epistemic logic is obtained by augmenting the language of propositional logic with a unary epistemic

V.F. Hendricks, K.F. Jørgensen and S.A. Pedersen (eds.), Knowledge Contributors, 1–15.

operator K_Ξ such that

$$K_\Xi A \quad \text{reads} \quad \text{'Agent } \Xi \text{ knows } A\text{'}$$

and similarly for belief

$$B_\Xi A \quad \text{reads} \quad \text{'Agent } \Xi \text{ believes } A\text{'}$$

for some arbitrary proposition A. These formalizations may be viewed as interpretations of $\Box A$ in alethic logic reading 'It is necessary that A'. Interpreting modal logic epistemically is crudely a reading of modal formulae as epistemic statements expressing attitudes like knowledge, belief or conviction of certain agents towards certain propositions.

The semantics of modal logic is likewise given a novel interpretation. Hintikka came up with a semantic interpretation of epistemic and doxastic operators respectively which in terms of standard possible world semantics may be rendered accordingly (16):

$K_\Xi A$: *in all possible worlds compatible with what* Ξ *knows it is the case that* A

$B_\Xi A$: *in all possible worlds compatible with what* Ξ *believes it is the case that* A

The basic assumption is that any ascription of propositional attitudes like knowledge and belief, requires partitioning the set of possible worlds into two compartments: The compartment consisting of possible worlds compatible with the attitude in question and the compartment of worlds incompatible with it. Based on the partition the agent is capable of constructing different 'world-models' using the epistemic modal language. The agent is not necessarily required to know which one of the world-models constructed is the real world-model. Be that as it may, the agent does not consider all these world-models equally possible or accessible from his current point of view. Some world-models may be incommensurable with his current information state or other background assumptions. These incompatible world-models are excluded from the compatibility partition.[3]

The set of worlds considered accessible by an agent depends on the actual world, or the agent's actual state of information. It is possible to capture this dependency by introducing a relation of accessibility, R, on the set of compatible possible worlds. To express the idea that for agent Ξ, the world w' is compatible with his information state, or accessible from the possible world w which Ξ is currently in, it is required that R holds between w and w'. This relation is written Rww' and reads 'world w' is accessible from w'. The world w' is said to be an *epistemic* or *doxastic alternative* to world w for agent Ξ depending on whether knowledge or belief is the considered attitude. Given the above semantical interpretation, if a proposition A is true in all worlds which agent Ξ considers possible then Ξ knows A and similarly for belief.

A possible world semantics for a propositional epistemic logic with a single agent then consists of a *frame* $\mathcal{F}$ which in turn is a pair (W, R) such that W is a non-empty set of possible worlds and R is a binary accessibility relation on W. A *model* $\mathbb{M}$ for an epistemic system consists of a frame and a denotation function φ assigning sets of worlds to atomic propositional formulae. Propositions are taken to be sets of possible worlds; namely the set of possible worlds in which they are true. Let *atom* be the set of atomic propositional formulae, then $\varphi : atom \longrightarrow P(W)$ where P denotes the powerset operation. The model $\mathbb{M} = \langle W, R, \varphi \rangle$ is called a Kripke-model and the resulting semantics Kripke-semantics (20): An atomic propositional formulae, $\mathbf{a}$, is said to be true in a world w (in $\mathbb{M}$), written $\mathbb{M}, w \models \mathbf{a}$, iff w is in the set of possible worlds assigned to $\mathbf{a}$, i. e. $\mathbb{M}, w \models \mathbf{a}$ iff $w \in \varphi(\mathbf{a})$ for all $\mathbf{a} \in atom$. The formula $K_\Xi A$ is true in a world w, i.e. $\mathbb{M}, w \models K_\Xi A$, iff $\forall w' \in W$: if Rww', then $\mathbb{M}, w' \models A$. The semantics for the Boolean connectives follows the usual recursive recipe. A modal formula is said to be *valid* in a frame iff the formula is true for all possible assignments in all worlds admitted by the frame.

Similar semantics may be formulated for the belief operator. Since a belief is not necessarily true but rather probable, possible, or likely to be true belief may for instance be modelled by assigning a sufficiently high degree of probability to the proposition in question and determining the doxastic alternatives accordingly. The truth-conditions for the doxastic operator are defined in a way similar to that of the knowledge operator and the model may also be expanded to accommodate the two operators simultanously.

A nice feature of possible world semantics is that many common epistemic axioms correspond to certain algebraic properties of the frame in the following sense: A modal axiom is valid in a frame if and only if the accessibility relation satisfies some algebraic condition. For an example, the axiom expressing the veridicality property that if a proposition is known by Ξ, then A is true,

(1) $$K_\Xi A \rightarrow A,$$

is valid in all frames in which the accessibility relation is *reflexive* in the sense that

$$\forall w \in W : Rww.$$

Every possible world is accessible from itself. Similarly if the accessibility relation satisfies the condition that

$$\forall w, w', w'' \in W : Rww' \wedge Rw'w'' \rightarrow Rww''$$

then the axiom reflecting the idea that the agent knows that he knows A if he does,

(2) $$K_\Xi A \rightarrow K_\Xi K_\Xi A,$$

is valid in all *transitive* frames. Other axioms of epistemic import require yet other rational properties to be met in order to be valid in all frames.

A nomenclature due to Lemmon (21) and later refined by Bull and Segerberg (4) is helpful while cataloguing the axioms typically considered interesting for epistemic logic (Table 1).

K	$K_\Xi(A \rightarrow A') \rightarrow (K_\Xi A \rightarrow K_\Xi A')$
D	$K_\Xi A \rightarrow \neg K_\Xi \neg A$
T	$K_\Xi A \rightarrow A$
4	$K_\Xi A \rightarrow K_\Xi K_\Xi A$
5	$\neg K_\Xi A \rightarrow K_\Xi \neg K_\Xi A$
.2	$\neg K_\Xi \neg K_\Xi A \rightarrow K_\Xi \neg K_\Xi \neg A.$
.3	$K_\Xi(K_\Xi A \rightarrow K_\Xi A') \vee K_\Xi(K_\Xi A' \rightarrow K_\Xi A)$
.4	$A \rightarrow (\neg K_\Xi \neg K_\Xi A \rightarrow K_\Xi A)$

TABLE 1. Common epistemic axioms

- Axiom K, also called the *axiom of deductive cogency*: If the agent Ξ knows $A \rightarrow A'$, then if Ξ knows A, Ξ also knows A'. The axiom maintains that knowledge is closed under material implication.
- Axiom D, also referred to as the *axiom of consistency* requires Ξ to have consistency in his knowledge: If an agent knows A, he does not simultaneously know its negation.[4]
- Axiom T, also called the *axiom of truth* or *axiom of veridicality*, says that if A is known by Ξ, then A is true.
- Axiom 4 is also known as the *axiom of self-awareness*, *positive introspection* or *KK-thesis*. They all refer to the idea that an agent has knowledge of his knowledge of A if he has knowledge of A.
- Axiom 5 is also known as the *axiom of wisdom*. It is the stronger thesis that an agent has knowledge of his own ignorance: If Ξ does not know A, he knows that he doesn't know A. The axiom is sometimes referred to as the *axiom of negative introspection*.
- Axiom .2 reveals that if Ξ does not know that he does not know A, then Ξ knows that he does not know not A.
- Axiom .3 maintains that either Ξ knows that his knowledge of A implies his knowledge of A' or he knows that his knowledge of A' implies his knowledge of A.
- Axiom .4 amounts to the claim that any true proposition *per se* constitutes knowledge and is sometimes referred to as *axiom of true (strong) belief*.

These axioms in proper combinations make up epistemic modal systems of varying strength depending on the modal formulae valid in the respective systems given the algebraic properties assumed for the accessibility relation.

The weakest system of epistemic interest is usually considered to be system **T**. The system includes T and K as valid axioms where K is valid in all Kripke-models. Additional modal strength may be obtained by extending **T** with other axioms drawn from the above pool altering the frame semantics to validate the additional axioms. By way of example, while $K_{\Xi}A \rightarrow A$ is valid in **T**, $K_{\Xi}A \rightarrow A$, $K_{\Xi}A \rightarrow K_{\Xi}K_{\Xi}A$ and $\neg K_{\Xi}A \rightarrow K_{\Xi}\neg K_{\Xi}A$ are all valid in **S5** but not in **T**. System **T** has a reflexive accessibility relation, **S5** has an equivalence relation of accessibility. The arrows in table 2 symbolize that the system to which the arrow is pointing is included in the system from which the arrow originates and hence reflect relative strength. Then **S5** is the strongest and **S4** the weakest of the ones listed.

Epistemic Systems			
KT4	=	**S4**	
KT4 + .2	=	**S4.2**	↑
KT4 + .3	=	**S4.3**	↑
KT4 + .4	=	**S4.4**	↑
KT5	=	**S5**	↑

TABLE 2. Relative strength of epistemic systems between **S4** and **S5**

One of the important tasks of epistemic logic have been, and still is, to map the possible complete systems of such logics hopefully allowing for a picking of the most 'appropriate' ones even though this appropriateness may be highly context-dependent as Halpern has noted (10). These 'appropriate' logics often range from **S4** over the intermediate systems **S4.2-S4.4** to **S5**. By way of example, Hintikka settled for **S4** (16), Kutschera argued for **S4.4** (36) , van der Hoek has proposed to strengthen knowledge according to system **S4.3** (34). In their contribution to this collection van Ditmarsch, van der Hoek and Kooi together with Fagin, Halpern, Moses and Vardi (6) assume knowledge to be **S5** valid.

In his contribution to this volume 'Knowledge, Belief, and Subjective Probability: Outlines of a Unified System of Epistemic/Doxastic Logic', Wolfgang Lenzen studies a range of axioms with respect to knowledge and two other attitudes expressing respectively conviction and belief, their formal properties and relations, philosophical implications and eventually concludes that:

> Summing up one may say that the logic of knowledge is isomorphic to an alethic modal system at least as strong as S4.2 and at most as strong as S4.4.

Conviction and belief are on the other hand weaker cognitive commitments than knowledge according to Lenzen. Even if the agent assigns probability 1 to the proposition in question and determines the set of alternatives accordingly this still does not suffice for validating the axiom of veridicality. The story is the same for belief as belief is considered weaker than conviction. For belief a proposition is considered likely or probable and the alternatives are considered doxastically accessible if the lower bound of subjective probability is greater than or equal .5 with respect to the proposition for the agent. Both conviction and belief imply a margin of error: The fact that Ξ is either convinced or believes A does not necessarily imply that A is true. Accordingly axiom T is dropped for conviction and belief and replaced by the consistency axiom D

$$B_{\Xi}A \rightarrow \neg B_{\Xi}\neg A \tag{3}$$

characterizing the consistency among convictions or beliefs. Lenzen then goes on to scrutinize additional axioms and systems appropriate for the two attitudes.[5]

One thing is to determine such approriate systems yet another is to determine appropriate or rational conditions of utterability for epistemic attitudes. Partially based on Grice's conversational maxims Lenzen formulates a number of pragmatic rules designed for the rational use of knowledge, belief and conviction governed statements. Lenzen provides a number of interesting philosophical insights in particular pertaining to the combined use of such commitments.

2. ACTIVE AGENTHOOD

A significant difference between alethic logic and epistemic logic is the addition of the agent Ξ to the syntax. One may legitimately question the roles assigned to the agents in epistemic logic. In the beginning they primarily served as indices on the accessibility relation between possible worlds. Epistemic-logical principles or axioms building up modal systems, however, are relative to an agent whom may or may not validate these principles. Being indices on accessibility relations will hardly suffice for epistemological and cognitive significance since there is nothing particularly epistemic about being indices.

Epistemic logics should accordingly observe the knower much more explicitly. An agent may have knowledge which is **S4.3** valid thereby obtaining a certain epistemic strength. An important set of questions seem to be *how* the agent has to *behave* in order to gain the epistemic strength that he has. To make epistemic logic pertinent to epistemology, computer science, artificial intelligence and cognitive psychology the agents must be activated. The original symbolic notation of a knowing agent also suggests this: An agent should be inside the scope of the knowledge operator—not outside as Hintikka notes in his contribution to this collection and elsewhere (17). Inquiring agents are agents who read data, change their minds, interact or have common knowledge, act according to strategies and play games, have memory and act upon it, follow various methodological rules, expand, contract or revise their knowledge bases, etc. all in the pursuit of knowledge. Inquiring agents are *active agents* (13).

The realization that the agents of epistemic logic should play an active role in the knowledge acquisition, validation, maintenance and potential interaction processes is discussed in Jaakko Hintikka's contribution to this volume 'A Second Generation Epistemic Logic and Its General Significance' as it in particular relates to his interrogative theory of inquiry developed here and elsewhere. Hintikka observes the obligation of active agenthood by emphasizing the strategies for his new application of epistemic logic as a logic of questions and answers and the search for the best questions to ask. Answers to questions are in essence requests for knowledge, information or epistemic imperatives in a strategic way inviting game-theoretical considerations:

> Another main requirement that can be addressed to the interrogative approach – and indeed to the theory of any goal-directed activity – is that it must do justice to the strategic aspects of inquiry. This requirement can be handled most naturally by doing what Plato already did to the Socratic *elenchus* and by construing knowledge-seeking by questioning as a game that pits the questioner against the answerer. Then the study of those strategies of knowledge acquisition becomes another application of the mathematical theory of games ...

Game theory is about strategies for winning games—and it is an agent whom may or may not have a winning strategy among other agents. van Benthem, Fagin, Halpern, Moses and Vardi, Aumann, Stalnaker and others studying game theory have demonstrated how logical epistemology uncovers important features of *agent rationality*. They also show how game theory adds to the general understanding of notions like knowledge, belief and belief revision.[6] Baltag, Moss, Solecki combine epistemic logic with belief revision theory to study actions and belief updates in games (2).

Mixing the theory of belief change and epistemic logic furnishes an illustrative example of active agents. The idea dates back to the mid 1990's. Alchourrón, Gärdenfors and Makinson's seminal belief revision theory (AGM) from the 1980's is a theory about the rational change of beliefs for expansions, contractions and revisions in light of new (possibly conflicting) evidence (1), (8). In 1994 de Rijke showed that the AGM-axioms governing expansion and revision may be translated into the object language of dynamic modal logic (5). Segerberg about the same time demonstrated how the entire theory of belief revision could be formulated in a modal logic.

A bit before but especially around the turn of the millennium Segerberg merged the static doxastic logic with the dynamics of belief change into 'dynamic doxastic logic' (27). Doxastic operators in the logic of belief like $B_\Xi A$ may be captured by AGM in the sense that 'A is in Ξ's belief-set T', or $\neg B_\Xi \neg A$ becomes '$\neg A$ is not in Ξ's belief-set T'. Similarly for other combinations of the belief operator with negation. An immediate difference between the two paradigms is that while AGM can express dynamic operations on belief-sets like expansions ('A is in Ξ's belief-set T expanded by D', i.e. $A \in T + D$), revisions ('A is in Ξ's belief-set T revised by D', i.e. $A \in T * D$), and contractions ('A is in Ξ's belief-set T contracted by D', i.e. $A \in T - D$), no such dynamics are immediately expressible in the standard language of doxastic logic. On the other hand, action languages include operators like $[\nu]$ and $\langle\nu\rangle$ which prefixed to a well-formed formula A, $[\nu]A$, respectively $\langle\nu\rangle A$ on Segerberg's interpretation mean that 'after $[every]$ $\langle some \rangle$ way of performing action ν it is the case that A'. By introducing three new operators $[+]$, $[*]$, and $[-]$ into the doxastic language the three dynamic operations on belief-sets may be rendered as $[+D]B_\Xi A$, $[*D]B_\Xi A$ and $[-D]B_\Xi A$.

After revising the original belief revision theory such that changes of beliefs happen in 'hypertheories' or concentric spheres enumerated according to entrenchment Segerberg has provided several axiomatizations of the dynamic doxastic logic together with soundness and completeness results (29), (28). The dynamic doxastic logic paradigm may also be extended to iterated belief revision[7] as studied by Lindström and Rabinowicz in (23) and accommodate various forms of agent introspection (24).

The AGM proposal for the rational change of beliefs has dominated the literature since its first formulation. In 'Economics and Economy in the Theory of Belief Revision' Hans Rott addresses the question of whether actual ecomomical principles and economic patterns have played any significant roles in the development of belief revision theory. Addressing this question requires a distinction between what Rott refers to as 'economic' behavior as opposed to 'economical' behavior. The former has close shaves with *economics* in terms of rationality and profit while the latter is more biased towards *economy* in the sense of thrifty or frugal. Tracing the history and motivation for the theory of belief revision Rott considers the extent to which these two different perspectives as they relate to cognitive changes and transformations have formed integral parts of the very formulation of AGM. His conclusion is striking and quite surprising:

So belief revision theory has as a matter of fact not focussed on *economy*, and the idea of *economical* belief revisions has very limited normative force, too. Regarding economic belief revision, our findings are more encouraging. It is possible to reconstruct large parts of belief revision in terms of rational choice theory. As a matter of fact, ideas combining economics have prevailed in the AGM paradigm and related approaches.

3. MULTIPLE ACTIVE AGENTS

The logics of knowledge have been described with a single agent as the object so far. Active agenthood applies to multiple possibly interacting and coordinating agents and the formal framework considered may be expanded to a multi-agent setup.

Following Fagin, Halpern, Moses and Vardi (6) the idea is to syntactically augment the language of propositional logic with n knowledge operators, one for each agent involved in the group of agents under consideration. The primary difference between the semantics given for a mono-agent and a multi-agent semantics is roughly that n accessibility relations are introduced. A modal system for n agents is obtained by joining together n modal logics where for simplicity it may be assumed that the agents are homogenous in the sense that they may all be described by the same logical system. An epistemic logic for n agents consists of n copies of a certain modal logic. In such an extended epistemic logic it is possible to express that some agent in the group knows a certain fact, that an agent knows that another agent knows a fact etc. It is possible to develop the logic even further: Not only may an agent know that another agent knows a fact, but they may all know this fact simultaneously. From here it is possible to express that everyone knows that everyone knows that everyone knows, that ... . That is *common knowledge*.

A convention would hardly be looked upon as a convention if it was not for common knowledge among the agents to observe it as such Lewis once noted. Other norms, social and linguistic practices, agent interactions and games presuppose a concept of common knowledge. A relatively simple way of defining common knowledge is not to partition the group of agents into subsets with different common 'knowledges' but only to define common knowledge for the entire group of agents. Once multiple agents have been added to the syntax, the language is augmented with an additional operator C. CA is then interpreted as 'It is common knowledge among the agents that A'. Well-formed formulas follow the standard recursive recipe with a few, but obvious, modifications taking into account the multiple agents. An auxiliary operator E is also introduced such that EA means 'Everyone knows that A'. EA is defined as the conjunction $K_1A \wedge K_2A \wedge ... \wedge K_nA$.

To semantically interpret n knowledge operators, binary accessibility relations $R_{1,\ldots,}R_n$ are defined over the set of possible worlds W. A special accessibility relation, R°, is introduced to interpret the operator of common knowledge. The relation must be flexible enough to express the relationship between individual and common knowledge. The idea is to let the accessibility relation for C be the transitive closure of the union of the accessibility relations corresponding to the singular knowledge operators. The model $\mathbb{M}$ for an epistemic system with n agents and common knowledge is accordingly a structure $\mathbb{M} = \langle W, R_1, R_2, ..., R_n, R^\circ, \varphi \rangle$ where W is a non-empty space of possible worlds, $R_1, R_2, ..., R_n, R^\circ$ are accessibility relations on W for which $R^\circ = (R_1 \cup R_2 \cup ... \cup R_n)^\circ$ where '$^\circ$' denotes the transitive closure and φ again is the denotation function assigning worlds to atomic propositional formula $\varphi : atom \longrightarrow P(W)$. The semantics for the Boolean connectives remain intact. The formula $K_i A$ is true in a world w, i.e. $\mathbb{M}, w \models K_i A$, iff $\forall w' \in W$: if $R_i ww'$, then $\mathbb{M}, w' \models A$. The formula CA is true in a world w, i.e. $\mathbb{M}, w \models CA$, iff $R^\circ ww'$ implies $\mathbb{M}, w' \models A$. Varying the properties of the accessibility relations $R_1, R_2, ..., R_n$ as described above results in different epistemic logics. For instance system **K** with common knowledge is determined by all frames while system **S4** with common knowledge is determined by all reflexive and transitive frames. Similar results are possible to obtain for the remaining epistemic logics (6).

Common knowledge is not an unproblematic type of knowledge for interacting agents. In 'Common Knowledge Revisited', Ron Fagin, Joseph Halpern, Yoram Moses and Moshe Vardi consider a paradox arising in the context of common knowledge. On the one hand it seems that common knowledge among agents is a precondition for agreement and coordinated efforts of various kinds, and yet on the other such knowledge among agents in a certain group is actually impossible to obtain due to problems related to simultaneity and temporal imprecision:

> This puts us in a somewhat paradoxical situation, in that we claim both that common knowledge is a prerequisite for agreement and coordinated action and that it cannot be attained. We discuss two answers to this paradox: (1) modelling the world with coarser granularity, and (2) relaxing the requirements for coordination.

Active agenthood is also realizable directly on the agent level. One may also choose to endow the agents with *epistemic capacities* facilitating special epistemic behaviors. Fagin, Halpern, Moses and Vardi have for instance considered 'perfect recall' (6): Interacting agents' knowledge in the dynamic system may increase as time goes by but the agents may still store old information. The agent's current local state is an encoding of all events that have happened so far in the run. Perfect recall is sort of a methodological recommendation telling the agent to remember his earlier epistemic states.

There are other structural properties of agents being studied in the literature of dynamic epistemic logics. In an epistemic logic suited for modelling various games of imperfect information van Benthem refers to such properties as 'styles of playing' (31). Properties like 'bounded memory', various 'mechanisms for information updates' and 'uniform strategies' are analyzed in (32).[8]

In 'Concurrent Dynamic Epistemic Logic' Hans van Ditmarsch, Wiebe van der Hoek and Barteld Kooi study 'perfect recall' and 'no learning' as they relate to the change of knowledge over time given the execution of certain plans adding actions to the language of epistemic logic. For this new active and dynamic epistemic logic both soundness and completeness results are proved with the following broad perspective:

> Our work fits in approaches that not only dynamize the epistemics, but also epistemize the dynamics: the actions that (groups of) agents perform are epistemic actions. Different agents may have different information about which action is taking place, including higher-order information. This rather recent tradition treats all of knowledge, higher-order knowledge, and its dynamics on the same foot.

The epistemic logics of this day and age incorporate other modalities than the epistemic ones – in particular tense and temporal operators. Temporal imprecision is responsible for the common knowledge paradox as Fagin, Halpern, Moses and Vardi points out and have added temporal structure to the language of epistemic logic. van Ditmarsch, van der Hoek and Kooi make extensive use of tense as it relates to the transformation of knowledge, and adding actions to the language is yet another way of expanding the expressiveness of epistemic logic for both obtaining important epistemological and practical results using multi-modalities.

4. MULTI-MODALITIES

There are various ways in which multi-modalities may be realized in epistemic logic. One prevalent way is to follow Fagin et al. in reinpreting agents as well as possible worlds relative to entire system of agents (6).[9]

In a system of agents each individual agent is considered to being in some 'local state'. The whole system – as the sum of the local agents – is accordingly in some 'global state'. The dynamics may be modelled by defining what is referred to as a 'run' over the system which is a function from time to global states. The run may be construed as an account of the behavior of the system for possible executions. This gives rise to 'points' which are pairs of runs and times. For every time, the system is in some global state as a function of the particular time. The system may be thought of as series of runs rather than agents. What is being modelled are the possible behaviors of the system over a collection of executions. A system like this defines a Kripke-structure with an equivalence relation over points. The accessibility relation is specified with respect to possible points such that some point w' is accessible from the current point w if the agent is in the same local state at w and w'. Knowledge is defined with respect to the agents' local states. Truth of a formula is given with respect to a point. If truth is relative to a point then there is a question of *when* which opens up for the introduction of temporal operators. One may for instance define a universal future-tense operator such that a formula is true relative to the current point and all later points. The mixture of epistemic and temporal operators can handle claims about the temporal development of knowledge in the system.

In 'Laws, Facts and Contexts: Foundations of Multi-Modal Reasoning' John Sowa suggests an alternate route to embody multi-modalities. The idea is to drop possible worlds simpliciter and replace them with a concept of contexts elegantly represented by existential graphs derived from the works of notably Peirce and McCarthy. Possible world semantics are substituted for Dunn's semantics where a possible world is replaced by an ordered pair of laws and facts. Modality is now dependent on the choice of laws rather than on possible worlds and primitive accessibility relations between such often abstract entities. Based on these and additional prerequisites Sowa finally introduces 'nested graph models' which constitute a general formal framework with sufficient expressive power to handle multi-modalities and represent a variety of other semantics:

> [...] Dunn's semantics can use the axioms of an ontology as the laws that define the accessibility relations: Peirce-Kamp-McCarthy contexts combined with Tarski's metalevels can support metalevel reasoning about the selection of laws and facts; the outside-in evaluation method of Peirce's endoporeutic or Hintikka's game-theoretical semantics can accommodate the discourse constraints of dynamic semantics; and nested graph models are flexible enough to represent all of the above.

A different step in the direction of reinterpreting possible worlds for the sake of enhanced expressiveness is to follow Ryszard Wójcicki in his 'Referential Semantics' where possible worlds are understood as 'reference points'. Reference points may be construed as collections of agents using the same language and sharing or subscribing to the same criteria of truth. Such an interpretation has the advantage of dropping the metaphysical baggage that possible worlds tend to bring along and at the same time facillitates an alternative perspective on the concept of knowledge as a cross-referential phenomenon:

> Knowledge develops through critical assessment of alternative points of views, alternative often also in the sense that they are expressed in "different languages" meant to be languages based on different criteria of truth. ...

5. CONCLUSION

In the 1970's Scott noted that a mistake of modal logic was the focus on systems with only one modal operator (26). This narrow concentration is considered an obstacle for the extraction of pertinent results. For instance, if the epistemic operators are not combined with temporal operators little may be said about the change or development of knowledge and other epistemic states. The modern epistemic logic has come a long way since Scott's relevant concern. Active agenthood and multi-modalities have among other features added to the importance of (dynamic) epistemic logical modelling.

It is the hope that *Knowledge Contributors* will both shed light on the development of epistemic logic and demonstrate its relevance for applications in philosophy, computer science, game theory and other disciplines utilizing the means and methods of epistemic logic.

Department of Philosophy and Science Studies
Roskilde University
Denmark

NOTES

[1]To avoid tedious repetition the term 'epistemic logic' will occassionally be used to denote both the logic of knowledge and the logic of belief. Where the distinction is needed, the distinction is made.

[2]For excellent overviews of epistemic logic and its key issues refer to Gribomont and Gochet (9) and van Benthem (33).

[3]The epistemological significance of this partitioning is examined in (13) under the rubric of 'forcing'.

[4]This axiom also has a deontic motivation since if an agent is obligated to do whatever A prescribes, he is not at the same time obligated to do $\neg A$.

[5]Belief is often axiomatized between system $\mathsf{KD4}$ and $\mathsf{KD45}$.

[6]van Benthem has also pointed out that there is an epistemic logic 'hidden' in game-theory (31).

[7]A change in beliefs may either occur once in which case it is a one-shot revision or multiple changes may successively occur in which case it is an iterated revision.

[8]Agents as explcitly learning mechanims are also integral parts of Kelly's computational epistemology (18) and a related approach called modal operator epistemology (12), (14).

[9]A topological reconstruction of possible worlds furnishing the entities with enough formal structure to reason about them alethically, temporally and epistemically may be found in (12), (14).

REFERENCES

[1] C.E. Alchourrón, P. Gärdenfors, and D. Makinson. On the Logic of Theory Change. *Journal of Symbolic Logic*, 50:510–530, 1985.

[2] A. Baltag, L.S. Moss, and S. Solecki. The Logic of Public Annoucements, Common Knowledge, and Private Suspicion. *Presented at TARK98.* Accepted for publication in *Annals of Pure and Applied Logic*, 2002, 1998.

[3] I. Boh. *Epistemic Logic in the Middle Ages.* Routledge, 1993.

[4] R. Bull and K. Segerberg. Basic Modal Logic. in ((7)): 1–88, 1984.

[5] M. de Rijke. Meeting Some Neighbours: A Dynamic Modal Logic Meets Theories of Change and Knowledge Representation. in *Logic and Information Flow*, Eijck, J.v and Visser, A. (eds.). Cambridge: MIT Press, 1994.

[6] R. Fagin, J. Y. Halpern, Y. Moses, and M. Y. Vardi. *Reasoning about Knowledge.* MIT Press, Cambridge, 1995.

[7] D. Gabbay and F. Guenthner. *Handbook of Philosophical Logic.* vol. II: *Extensions of Classical Logic.* Dordrecht: D. Reidel Publishing Company, 1984.

[8] P. Gärdenfors. *Knowledge in Flux—Modelling the Dynamics of Epistemic States.* MIT Press, Cambridge, 1988.

[9] P. Gochet and P. Gribomont. Epistemic Logic. forthcoming in *Handbook of the History and Philosophy of Logic*, edited by Gabbay, D.M. and Woods, J. Amsterdam: Elsevier Science, 2003.

[10] J. Y. Halpern. Should Knowledge Entail Belief? *Journal of Philosophical Logic*, 25:483–494, 1995.

[11] J.Y. Halpern. *Reasoning about Uncertainty.* MIT Press, Cambridge, 2003.

[12] V. F. Hendricks. *The Convergence of Scientific Knowledge — a view from the limit.* Trends in Logic: Studia Logica Library Series. Kluwer Academic Publishers, 2001.

[13] V. F. Hendricks. Active Agents. ΦNEWS (2002), vol. **2**: 5–40. A revised version of the paper is published in a special volume of the *Journal of Logic, Language and Information*, van Benthem, J. and van Rooy, R. (eds.). (2003), 2003.

[14] V. F. Hendricks. *Forcing Epistemology.* in press, 2003.

[15] V. F. Hendricks and J. Malinowski, editors. *Trends in Logic: 50 Years of Studia Logica.* Trends in Logic: Studia Logica Library Series. Kluwer Academic Publishers, 2003. Contributions from J. van Benthem, W. Buszkowski, M.L. Dalla Chiara, M. Fitting, J.M. Font, R. Giuntini, R. Goldblatt, V. Marra, D. Mundici, R. Leporini, S.P. Odintsow, H. Ono, G. Priest and H. Wansing.

[16] J. Hintikka. *Knowledge and Belief: An Introduction to the Logic of the Two Notions.* Cornell University Press, Cornell, 1962.

[17] J. Hintikka and I. Halonen. Epistemic Logic. *Routledge Encyclopedia of Philosophy*, volume 1, 1998.

[18] K. Kelly. *The Logic of Reliable Inquiry.* Oxford University Press, New York, 1996.

[19] S. Knuuttila. *Modal Logic in the Middle Ages.* Routledge, 1993.

[20] S. Kripke. Semantical Analysis of Modal Logic. *Zeitschrift für Matematische Logik und Grundlagen der Matematik*, 9:67–96, 1963.

[21] E. J. Lemmon. *An Introduction to Modal Logic*. Basil Blackwell Publishers, Oxford, 1977. in collaboration with D. Scott.

[22] W. Lenzen. Recent Work in Epistemic Logic. *Acta Philosophica Fennica*, 30:1–219, 1978.

[23] S. Lindström and W. Rabinowicz. Extending Dynamic Logic: Accommodating Iterated Beliefs and Ramsey Conditionals within DLL. in *For Good Measure*, Lindahl, L., Needham, P. and Sliwinski, R. (eds.). *Uppsala Philosophical Studies* **46**: 123–153, 1997.

[24] S. Lindström and W. Rabinowicz. DDL Unlimited: Dynamic Doxastic Logic for Introspective Agents. *Erkenntnis*, 50:353–385, 1999.

[25] G. N. Schlesinger. *The Range of Epistemic Logic*. Aberdeen University Press, 1985.

[26] D. Scott. Advice on Modal Logic. in *Philosophical Problems in Logic*, Lambert, K. (ed.). Dordrecht: D. Reidel Publishing Company: 143–173, 1970.

[27] K. Segerberg. Belief Revision from the Point of View of Doxastic Logic. *Bulletin of the IGPL*, 3:535–553, 1995.

[28] K. Segerberg. A Completeness Proof in Full DDL. in *Philosophical Crumbs: Essays Dedicated to Ann-Mari Henschen-Dahlqvist on the Occasion of her Seventyfifth Birthday*, Sliwinski, R. (ed.). *Uppsala Philosophical Studies* **49**: 195-207, 1999.

[29] K. Segerberg. The Basic Dynamic Doxastic Logic of AGM. *Uppsala Prints and Preprints in Philosophy*, 1, 1999.

[30] John F. Sowa. *Knowledge Representation:*. Logical, Philosophical, and Computational Foundations. Brooks/Cole, Pacific Grove, California, 2000.

[31] J.F.A.K. v. Benthem. Logic and Game Theory—close encounters of the third kind. in *Prooceedings of LLC99*, Loon, I.v., Mints, G. and Muskens, R. (eds). CSLI Publications, 2000.

[32] J.F.A.K. v. Benthem. Dynamic-Epistemic Logic of Games. to appear in *Prooceedings of LOFT4*, Bonanno, G. (ed.), *Bulletin of Economic Research*, 2001.

[33] J.F.A.K. v. Benthem. Fifty Years: Changes and Constants in Logic. in (15): 35-56, 2003.

[34] W. van der Hoek. Systems for Knowledge and Belief. *Journal of Logic and Computation*, 3(2):173–195, 1996.

[35] W. van der Hoek and J.-J.Ch. Meyer. *Epistemic Logic for AI and Computer Science*, volume 41 of *Cambridge Tracts in Theoretical Computer Science*. Cambridge University Press, Cambridge, 1995.

[36] F. von Kutschera. *Einführung in die intensional Semantik*. W. de Gruyter, Berlin, 1976.

[37] H. G. Von Wright. *An Essay on Modal Logic*. North-Holland Publishing Company, Amsterdam, 1951.

WOLFGANG LENZEN

KNOWLEDGE, BELIEF, AND SUBJECTIVE PROBABILITY: OUTLINES OF A UNIFIED SYSTEM OF EPISTEMIC/DOXASTIC LOGIC

FOREWORD

The aims of this paper are (i) to summarize the *semantics* of (the propositional part of) a unified epistemic/doxastic logic as it has been developed at greater length in (48) and (ii) to use some of these principles for the development of a semi-formal *pragmatics* of epistemic sentences. While a semantic investigation of epistemic attitudes has to elaborate the truth-conditions for, and the analytically true relations between, the fundamental notions of belief, knowledge, and conviction, a pragmatic investigation instead has to analyse the specific conditions of rational utterance or utterability of epistemic sentences. Some people might think that both tasks coincide. According to Wittgenstein, e.g., the *meaning* of a word or a phrase is nothing else but its *use* (say, within a certain community of speakers). Therefore the pragmatic conditions of utterance of words or sentences are assumed to determine the meaning of the corresponding expressions. One point I wish to make here, however, is that one may elaborate the meaning of epistemic expressions in a way that is largely independent of – and, indeed, even partly incompatible with – the pragmatic conditions of utterability. Furthermore, the crucial differences between the pragmatics and the semantics of epistemic expressions can satisfactorily be explained by means of some general principles of *communication.* In the first three sections of this paper the logic (or semantics) of the epistemic attitudes *belief*, *knowledge*, and *conviction* will be sketched. In the fourth section the basic idea of a general pragmatics will be developed which can then be applied to epistemic utterances in particular.

1. THE LOGIC OF CONVICTION

Let '$C(a,p)$' abbreviate the fact that person a is firmly convinced that p, i.e. that a considers the proposition p (or, equivalently, the state of affairs expressed by that proposition) as absolutely certain; in other words, p has maximal likelihood or probability for a. Using 'Prob' as a symbol for subjective probability functions, this idea can be formalized by the requirement:

(PROB-C) $\quad C(a,p) \leftrightarrow \mathrm{Prob}(a,p) = 1$

Within the framework of standard possible-worlds semantics $\langle I, R, V \rangle$, $C(a,p)$ would have to be interpreted by the following condition:

(POSS-C) $\quad V(i, C(a,p)) = \mathrm{t} \leftrightarrow \forall j(iRj \rightarrow V(j,p) = \mathrm{t})$

V.F. Hendricks, K.F. Jørgensen and S.A. Pedersen (eds.), Knowledge Contributors, 17–31.

Here I is a non-empty set of (indices of) possible worlds; R is a binary relation on I such that iRj holds iff, in world i, a considers world j as possible; and V is a valuation-function assigning to each proposition p relative to each world i a truth-value $V(i,p) \in \{\text{t,f}\}$. Thus $C(a,p)$ is true (in world $i \in I$) iff p itself is true in every possible world j which is considered by a as possible (relative to i).

The probabilistic 'definition' **POSS-C** together with some elementary theorems of the theory of subjective probability immediately entails the validity of the subsequent laws of conjunction and non-contradiction. If a is convinced both of p and of q, then a must also be convinced that p and q:

(C1) $C(a,p) \wedge C(a,q) \rightarrow C(a,p \wedge q)$

For if both $\text{Prob}(a,p)$ and $\text{Prob}(a,q)$ are equal to 1, then it follows that $\text{Prob}(a,p \wedge q) = 1$, too. Furthermore, if a is convinced that p (is true), a cannot be convinced that $\neg p$, i.e. that p is false:

(C2) $C(a,p) \rightarrow \neg C(a,\neg p)$

For if $\text{Prob}(a,p) = 1$, then $\text{Prob}(a,\neg p) = 0$, and hence $\text{Prob}(a,\neg p) \neq 1$. Just like the alethic modal operators of possibility, $\Diamond$, and necessity, $\Box$, are linked by the relation $\Diamond p \leftrightarrow \neg\Box\neg p$, so also the doxastic modalities of thinking p to be possible – formally: $P(a,p)$ – and of being convinced that p, $C(a,p)$, satisfy the relation

(Def. P) $P(a,p) \leftrightarrow \neg C(a,\neg p)$

Thus, from the probabilistic point of view, $P(a,p)$ holds iff a assigns to the proposition p (or to the event expressed by that proposition) a likelihood greater than 0:

(PROB-P) $V(P(a,p)) = \text{t} \leftrightarrow \text{Prob}(a,p) > 0$

Within the framework of possible-worlds semantics, one obtains the following condition:

(POSS-P) $V(i,P(a,p)) = \text{t} \leftrightarrow \exists j(iRj \wedge V(j,p) = \text{t})$,

according to which $P(a,p)$ is true in world i iff there is at least one possible world j – i.e. a world j accessible from i – in which p is true.

In view of **Def P**, the former principle of consistency, **C2**, can be paraphrased by saying that whenever a is firmly convinced that p, a will a fortiori consider p as possible. However, considering p as possible does not conversely entail being convinced that p. In general there will be many propositions p such that a considers both p and $\neg p$ as possible. Such a situation, where $P(a,p) \wedge P(a,\neg p)$, makes clear that unlike the operator C, P does not satisfy a principle of conjunction analogous to **C1**. However, the converse entailment

(C3) $P(a,p \wedge q) \rightarrow P(a,p) \wedge P(a,q)$

and its counterpart

(C4) $C(a, p \wedge q) \to C(a, p) \wedge C(a, q)$

clearly are valid, because the probabilities of the single propositions p or q always are at least as great as the probability of the conjunction $(p \wedge q)$. Similarly, since the probability of a disjunction $(p \vee q)$ is always at least as great as the probabilities of the single disjuncts p and q, it follows that both operators C and P satisfy the following principles of disjunction:

(C5) $C(a, p) \vee C(a, q) \to C(a, p \vee q)$

(C6) $P(a, p) \vee P(a, q) \to P(a, p \vee q)$

Now the probabilistic 'proofs' of such principles are not without problems. Since its early foundations by De Finetti (38), the theory of subjective probability has always been formulated in terms of *events,* while in the framework of philosophical logic, attitudes like $C(a, p)$ are traditionally formulated in terms of *sentences.* So if one wants to apply the laws of the theory of subjective probability to the fields of cognitive attitudes, one has to presuppose (i) that for every event X there corresponds exactly one proposition p, and (ii) that the cognitive attitudes really are 'propositional' attitudes in the sense that their truth is independent of the specific linguistic representation of the event X. That is, whenever two sentences p and q are logically equivalent and thus describe one and the same event X, then $C(a, p)$ holds iff $C(a, q)$ holds as well. This requirement can be formalized by the following rule:

(C7) $p \leftrightarrow q \vdash C(a, p) \leftrightarrow C(a, q)$

This principle further entails that everybody must be convinced of everything that logically follows from his own convictions:

(C8) $p \to q \vdash C(a, p) \to C(a, q)$

For if p logically implies q, then p is logically equivalent to $p \wedge q$; thus $C(a, p)$ entails $C(a, p \wedge q)$ (by **C7**) which in turn entails $C(a, q)$ by **C4**.

There has been a long discussion (still going on in the literature) whether and to which extent the cognitive attitudes of real subjects actually are *deductively closed.* In view of man's almost unlimited fallibility in matters of logic, some authors have come to argue that **C8** should be restricted to very elementary instances like **C4** or **C5** or to some other so-called 'surface tautologies.'[1] Which option one favours will strongly depend on the methodological role that one wants to assign to epistemic logic. If epistemic logic is conceived of as a *descriptive system* of people's factual beliefs, then not even the validity of elementary principles like **C4** seems warranted. If, however, epistemic logic is viewed as a *normative* system of *rational* belief, then even the strong condition of full deductive closure, **C8**, appears perfectly acceptable. Incidentally, if one presupposes that everybody has at least one conviction – an assumption which is logically guaranteed by some of the subsequent iteration-principles[2] – **C8** entails the further rule

(C9) $p \vdash C(a, p)$,

according to which everybody is convinced of every tautological proposition (or state of affairs) p.

To round off our exposition of the logic of conviction, let us consider some laws for *iterated* epistemic attitudes. According to the thesis of the 'privileged access' to our own mental states, whenever some person a is convinced of p, a knows that she has this conviction. Similarly, if a is not convinced that p, i.e. if she considers p as possible, then again she knows that she considers p as possible:

(E1) $C(a, p) \rightarrow K(a, C(a, p))$

(E2) $\neg C(a, p) \rightarrow K(a, \neg C(a, p))$

Here '$K(a, q)$' abbreviates the fact that a *knows* that q. Now, clearly a knows that q only if in particular a is convinced that q:

(E3) $K(a, p) \rightarrow C(a, p)$

Hence **E1** and **E2** immediately entail the following purely doxastic iteration-principles:

(C10) $C(a, p) \rightarrow C(a, C(a, p))$

(C11) $\neg C(a, p) \rightarrow C(a, \neg C(a, p))$

It is easy to verify that the implications **C10** and **C11** may be strengthened into equivalences. Hence iterated doxastic operators (or 'modalities') are always reducible to simple expressions of the type $C(a, p)$ or $\neg C(a, q)$, where p and q contain no further doxastic expressions. As was proven in theorem **MT 15** of (48), iterated doxastic *propositions* of arbitrary complexity can be reduced to simple, non-iterated propositions. Technically speaking, the logic of conviction turns out to be structurally isomorphic to the 'deontic' calculus **DE4** of (44) which differs from the better-known alethic calculus **S5** only in that it does not contain the truth-axiom $\Box p \rightarrow p$. Given the intended doxastic interpretation of necessity as *subjective* necessity or certainty, the failure of $C(a, p) \rightarrow p$ comes as no surprise. After all, humans are not infallible; therefore someone's conviction that p – however firm it may be – can never logically guarantee that p is in fact the case.

2. THE LOGIC OF KNOWLEDGE

Although, then, a's conviction that p is logically compatible with p's actually being false, it is a truism since Plato's early epistemological investigations in the *Theaitetos* that a cannot *know* that p unless p is in fact true. This first ('objective') condition of knowledge can be formalized as:

(K1) $K(a,p) \rightarrow p$

Another (subjective) condition of knowledge has already been stated in the preceding section. **E3** says that person a cannot know that p unless she is convinced that p. This is a refinement of Plato's insight that knowledge requires belief—*viz.*, belief of the strongest form possible. Plato had discussed yet a third condition of knowledge which is somewhat harder to grasp. In order really to constitute an item of *knowledge*, a's true belief must be 'justified' or 'well-founded.' One might think of explicating this requirement by postulating the existence of certain proposition $q_1, ..., q_n$ which justify a's belief that p by logically entailing p. But which epistemological status should be accorded to these justifying propositions? If it were only required that the q_i must all be true and that a is convinced of their truth, then the third condition of knowledge would become redundant and each true belief would by itself be justified.[3] On the other hand one cannot require that the q_i are *known* by a to be true, because then Plato's definition of knowledge as justified true belief would become circular.

Therefore one will either treat 'knowledge' as a primitive, indefinable notion which is characterized only partially by the necessary conditions **K1** and **E3**. Or one takes the conjunction of these two conditions as already *sufficient* for a's knowing that p—an option favoured, e.g., by Kutschera (52). Let us refer to this simple concept of knowledge as 'knowledge*' or 'K^*'. If one thus defines:

(Def. K*) $K^*(a,p) \leftrightarrow C(a,p) \wedge p,$

the logic of knowledge* can entirely be derived from the logic of conviction. The former conjunction-principle **C1** immediately entails the corresponding principle

$$K^*(a,p) \wedge K^*(a,q) \rightarrow K^*(a,p \wedge q),$$

but conjunctivity seems to be valid also for the more demanding concept of knowledge along Plato's lines:

(K2) $K(a,p) \wedge K(a,q) \rightarrow K(a,p \wedge q)$

For if one assumes that a's single beliefs that p and that q are justified, then a's belief that $(p \wedge q)$ would be justified as well. Furthermore, the rules of deductive closure of conviction, **C7** - **C9**, directly entail corresponding rules for K^* which, again, seem to be valid also for the more ambitious concept K:

(K3) $p \leftrightarrow q \vdash K(a,p) \leftrightarrow K(a,q)$

(K4) $p \rightarrow q \vdash K(a,p) \rightarrow K(a,q)$

(K5) $p \vdash K(a,p)$

Provided that epistemic logic is taken as a *normative* theory of *rational* (or 'implicit') attitudes, these rules are just as acceptable as their doxastic counterparts.

It is easy to verify that **Def. K*** together with **E1** or **C10** entails the iteration law $K^*(a,p) \rightarrow K^*(a,K^*(a,p))$. The corresponding so-called 'KK-thesis' (formulated for the general concept of knowledge, K) says that whenever a knows that p, a knows that he (or she) knows that p:

(K6) $K(a,p) \rightarrow K(a,K(a,p))$

In the literature surveyed in (46), several 'counter-examples' have been constructed to show that someone may know something without knowing that he knows. For instance, assume that during an examination candidate a answers the question in which year Leibniz was born by saying: 'In 1646'. The fact that a *gave* the correct answer usually is taken as sufficient to conclude that a *knew* the correct answer. But a may not have known at all that he knew it; in fact he may have thought he was just guessing. Such examples typically play on the ambiguity of the English verb 'to know' which has the meaning both of the German 'wissen' and of 'kennen'. In the former case, 'to know' is followed by a that-clause and then expresses a *propositional attitude*; while in the latter case, 'to know' is part of a direct object construction ('to know the answer'; 'to know the way to the railway station'; 'to know London'; etc) and then expresses no such attitude. Therefore the above 'counter-example' fails to refute **K6** since a's 'knowing' the correct answer, or his knowing the year in which Leibniz was born, does not represent a propositional attitude as would be required by **K6**. According to the premises of the story, a did *not* know *that* Leibniz was born in 1646 because she was not at all certain of the date. If a person really *knows* that Leibniz was born in 1646 (i.e., by **E3**, if a in particular is *convinced* that Leibniz was born in 1646), then a can never *believe that she does not know* that Leibniz was born in 1646.

The argument contained in the preceding passage contains an application of another important principle which establishes an epistemic logical connection between all the three basic notions of knowledge, belief, and conviction. In its general form, it would have to be put as follows: Whenever person a is *convinced* that p, she will *believe* that she *knows* that p. With '$B(a,p)$' abbreviating 'a believes that p', this principle takes the symbolic form:

(E4) $C(a,p) \rightarrow B(a,K(a,p))$

In view of certain iteration laws discussed earlier in this paper, **E4** can be strengthened into the statement that when a is convinced that p, she must be convinced that she knows that p.

(E5) $C(a,p) \rightarrow C(a,K(a,p))$

As was kindly pointed out to me by Vincent F. Hendricks, Lamarre/Shoham (43) and other recent authors refer to **E5** as 'Moore's Principle' because the basic idea that being certain entails being certain that one knows is thought to have first been put forward in (50).[4] Incidentally, the implications **E4** and **E5** might further be strengthened into equivalences, and because of **C10** also the following law becomes provable:

(E6) $C(a,C(a,p)) \leftrightarrow C(a,K(a,p))$

E6 shows that knowledge and conviction are *subjectively* indiscernible in the sense that person a cannot tell apart whether she is "only" convinced that p or whether she really knows that p. This observation does not remove, however, the *objective* difference between a's being convinced that p and a's knowing that p; only the latter but not the former attitude entails the truth of p. Therefore it is always (objectively) possible that a is convinced of something which as a matter of fact is not true; but person a herself can never think this to be possible.

Because of the objective possibility of $C(a,p) \wedge \neg p$, the K-analogue of the doxastic iteration principle **C11**, i.e. $\neg K(a,p) \rightarrow K(a,\neg K(a,p))$, fails to hold. From the assumption that *a does not know* that p one cannot infer that she *knows* that she does not know that p. For if *a mistakenly* believes that she knows that p, i.e. if $C(a,p) \wedge \neg p$, one has $\neg K(a,p)$ (because of **K1**) and yet a does not know of her mistake, because in view of **E4** a believes that she *does* know that p; hence she is far from believing (or even knowing) that she does *not* know that p.

Technically speaking the logic of knowledge is isomorphic to a modal calculus at least as strong as but weaker than **S5**. Now there is a very large – indeed, as shown in (39), an *infinite* – variety of modal systems between **S4** and **S5**. E.g., so-called system **S4.2** is characterized by an axiom which – with 'necessity' interpreted as 'knowledge' – takes the form:

(K7) $\neg K(a,\neg K(a,p)) \rightarrow K(a,\neg K(a,\neg K(a,p)))$

Another calculus **S4.4** is axiomatized by (the $\Box$-counterpart of):

(K8) $p \wedge \neg K(a,\neg K(a,p)) \rightarrow K(a,p))$

However, the meaning or validity of these principles is not at all evident because common sense says little or nothing about the epistemic counterpart of the alethic modality $\Diamond\Box p$, i.e. $\neg K(a,\neg K(a,p))$. Fortunately, the laws of epistemic logic developed earlier in this paper give us a clue how to understand this complex term. It can be proven that person a is *convinced* that p iff she does *not know that she does not know* that p:

(E7/K9) $\neg K(a, \neg K(a,p)) \leftrightarrow C(a,p)$

One the one hand, $C(a,p)$ entails $C(a, K(a,p))$ (by **E5**) and a fortiori $\neg C(a, \neg K(a,p))$ (by **C2**) and thus also $\neg K(a, \neg K(a,p))$ (by **E3**); on the other hand $\neg C(a,p)$ implies $K(a, \neg C(a,p))$ (by **E2**) and hence also $K(a, \neg K(a,p))$ (by rule **K4** in conjunction with **E3**).

In view of **K9**, then, the **S4.2**-like principle **K7** amounts to saying that when person a is convinced that p, she knows that she is convinced that p—this is exactly the contents of our earlier principle **E1**. Similarly, **S4.4**-like principle **K8** states that when p is true and when a is convinced that p, then a already knows that p. This holds true only of the simple concept of knowledge as true conviction, but not of Plato's more demanding conception of knowledge as justified true conviction. Summing up one may say that the logic of knowledge is isomorphic to an alethic modal system *at least as strong as* **S4.2** *and at most as strong as* **S4.4**.[5]

To conclude our discussion of the logic of knowledge, let it just be pointed out that a possible-worlds semantics for K can be given along the following lines:

(POSS-K) $V(i, K(a,p)) = \mathrm{t} \leftrightarrow \forall j(iSj \rightarrow V(j,p) = \mathrm{t})$

Here 'S' denotes an accessibility relation between worlds which obtain iff world j is compatible with (or possible according to) all that a knows in world i.

3. THE LOGIC OF ('WEAK') BELIEF

The concept of *conviction*, $C(a,p)$, has been defined above to obtain only if person a is absolutely *certain* that p. The more general concept of *belief*, $B(a,p)$, will be satisfied by the much weaker requirement that person a considers p as *likely* or as *probable*, where the lower bound of (subjective) probability may reasonably be taken to be .5, i.e. person a will not believe that p unless she considers p as more likely than not:

(PROB-B) $B(a,p) \leftrightarrow \mathrm{Prob}(a,p) > 1/2$

The notion of 'weak' belief also satisfies the principle of non-contradiction analogous to **C2**:

(B1) $B(a,p) \rightarrow \neg B(a, \neg p)$

Clearly, if p has a probability greater than $1/2$, then $\neg p$ must have a probability less than $1/2$. On the other hand, $B(a,p)$ does not satisfy the counterpart of conjunction principle **C1**, because even if two single propositions p and q both have a probability $> .5$, it may well happen that $\mathrm{Prob}(a, p \wedge q)$ is as small as the product $\mathrm{Prob}(a,p) \cdot \mathrm{Prob}(a,q)$ and hence $< .5$. For instance, let an urn contain two black balls and one white ball where one of the black balls is made of metal while the white ball and the other black ball is made of wood. Now if just one ball is drawn from the urn at random, the probability of $p =$ 'The ball is black' equals 2/3 and is thus $> 1/2$; also the probability of $q =$ 'The ball is made of wood' is $2/3 > 1/2$. But the probability of the joint proposition $(p \wedge q) =$ 'The ball is made of wood and is black' only is 1/3.

It follows from the theory of probability that conjunctivity of belief is warranted only in the special case where one of the two propositions is *certain*:

(E8) $B(a,p) \wedge C(a,q) \rightarrow B(a,p \wedge q)$

Here certainty may be said to represent a special instance of belief in the sense of:

(E9) $C(a,p) \rightarrow B(a,p)$

The validity of this principle derives from the fact that each proposition p with maximal probability 1 a fortiori has a probability greater than .5! Thus, *semantically* speaking, a's believing that p is entirely compatible with a's being absolutely certain that p, although from a *pragmatic* point of view when person a says 'I believe that p', she thereby expresses that she is *not convinced* that p.

The epistemological thesis of the privileged access to (or privileged knowledge of) our own mental states mentioned earlier in connection with principles **E1** and **E2** evidently applies not only to the particular doxastic attitude $C(a,p)$, but to the more general notion $B(a,p)$ as well. Thus, whenever person a believes that p, a knows that she believes that p; and, conversely, if she does not believe that p, she knows that she does not believe that p:

(E10) $B(a,p) \rightarrow K(a, B(a,p))$

(E11) $\neg B(a,p) \rightarrow K(a, \neg B(a,p))$

In view of **E3** and **E8** one immediately obtains the following pure iteration-laws:

(B2) $B(a,p) \rightarrow B(a, B(a,p))$

(B3) $\neg B(a,p) \rightarrow B(a, \neg B(a,p))$.

Furthermore the rules of deductive closure of belief:

(B4) $p \leftrightarrow q \vdash B(a,p) \leftrightarrow B(a,q)$

(B5) $p \rightarrow q \vdash B(a,p) \rightarrow B(a,q)$

(B6) $p \vdash B(a,p)$

can be justified in strictly the same way as the corresponding principles for conviction or for knowledge.

In order to obtain a complete axiomatization of the logic of ('weak') belief, one first has to introduce the relation of 'strict implication' between *sets of propositions* $\{p_1, ..., p_n\}$ and $\{q_1, ..., q_n\}$ $(n \geq 2)$. Let this generalization of the ordinary relation of logical implication be symbolized by $\{p_1, ..., p_n\} \Rightarrow \{q_1, ..., q_n\}$. This relation has been defined by Segerberg (51) to hold iff, for logical reasons, at least as many propositions from the set $\{q_1, ..., q_n\}$ must be true as there are true propositions in the set $\{p_1, ..., p_n\}$. Now, just like the logical implication between p and q guarantees that the probability of q is at least as great as the probability of p, so also the strict implication between $\{p_1, ..., p_n\}$ and $\{q_1, ..., q_n\}$ entails that the *sum* of the probabilities of the q_i is at least as great as the corresponding sum $\sum_{i \leq n} \text{Prob}(a, p_i)$. Therefore, if at least one proposition from $\{p_1, ..., p_n\}$ is believed by a to be true (and hence has a probability $> .5$) and if all the other p_i are not believed by a to be false (and hence have a probability $\geq .5$), so that in sum $\sum_{i \leq n} \text{Prob}(a, p_i) > n \cdot 1/2$, it follows that also $\sum_{i \leq n} \text{Prob}(a, q_i) > n/2$, and thus at least one of the q_i must be believed by a to be true:

(B7)
$$\{p_1, ..., p_n\} \Rightarrow \{q_1, ..., q_n\} \vdash B(a, p_1) \wedge$$
$$\neg B(a, \neg p_2) \wedge ... \wedge \neg B(a, \neg p_n) \rightarrow B(a, q_1) \vee ... \vee B(a, q_n)$$

4. THE PRAGMATICS OF EPISTEMIC SENTENCES

The foregoing sketch of the logics of knowledge, belief, and conviction may be considered as an investigation into the *truth-conditions* of epistemic attitudes. Let us now turn to the *conditions of utterance* (or utterability) of corresponding sentences. This investigation is meant to explain, among others, why sentences of the type 'a mistakenly believes that p' or 'a is convinced that p, but a does not know that p' can only be reasonably maintained by a speaker $b \neq a$. Also we want to explain why statements of the form 'I think it possible that p' or 'I believe that p' are normally understood to mean (in addition to what is explicitly asserted) that, in the first case, the speaker does not believe that p, or, in the second case, that the speaker is not convinced that p. These particular aspects of the pragmatics of *epistemic* sentences shall not be given ad hoc, however, but rather be derived from a general theory of utterances of arbitrary sentences. Such a general pragmatics will rely on certain maxims of (rational) communication or conversation, which in turn has to be rendered precise by means of epistemic logical principles.

As a first, very elementary principle of rational communication consider the so-called 'maxim of quality' which was formulated in the classical study (41, p. 46) as follows: 'Do not say what you believe to be false!.' This maxim is in need of some modifications. First, instead of requiring 'Do not *say* what you believe to be false' it would be more adequate to demand 'Do not *assert* what you believe to be false', because when people are using language, e.g., in an ironic way they often *say* p in order to *assert* $\neg p$. Second, it would be better to transform Grice's doubly negated maxim ('not ... false') into the positive maxim 'Only assert what you believe to be true!'. Otherwise, if p is a proposition such that person a neither believes that p nor believes that $\neg p$, (e.g., p = 'Throwing this coin will show up heads') it would count as rational for a to assert both p and $\neg p$. Third, the question arises in which sense or to which degree a has to believe that p in order to be entitled to rationally assert p. Is it sufficient that a just believes p in the ordinary, weak sense of $B(a,p)$, or should it be required that a must strongly believe p in the sense of $C(a,p)$?

Our communicative practice in everyday life shows that the hearer in general takes it for granted that the speaker is certain or convinced of what he asserts. Gazdar (40, p. 46) suggested an even stronger variant of the maxim of quality: 'Say only that which you *know*.' But this requirement is too demanding because, for epistemic-logical reasons, the speaker could never know whether he really satisfies it. Therefore it appears reasonable to demand only that the speaker must always *think* or *believe* to know that what he asserts is true. Using '$A(a,p)$' to abbreviate 'a asserts that p', this version of the maxim of quality can be formalized as follows:

(QUAL) $A(a,p) \rightarrow_p C(a,p)$

In contrast to the symbol '$\rightarrow$' for ordinary logical implication, the new sign '$\rightarrow_p$' is meant to symbolize a relation of *pragmatic* implication which should be understood in some such way that **QUAL** reads as follows: 'If a asserts p, a thereby shows (or indicates) that he is convinced that p'; or 'The fact that a asserts p entitles the hearer to infer that a is certain that p'; or also 'By the maxims of (rational) conversation, a is entitled to assert p only if a is convinced that p', etc.

Grice (41, p. 45) has put forward another important maxim (called the 'maxim of quantity') which says: 'Make your contribution as informative as is required (for the current purposes of the exchange).' This principle also is in need of some clarifications and modifications. First it should be observed that the maxim of quantity may be incompatible with the maxim of quality 'Say only that which you believe to know.' The recommendation to make your contribution as informative as is required has to be restricted by the clause 'as far as you can.' We often face situations where the others expect us to say more than we know (or, more precisely, more than we believe to know). Second, even if we have the desired knowledge at hand, it is not always clear *how informative* our contributions should be and to which extent the others want to be informed about details of the matter. Unfortunately, there does not appear to exist a meaningful *quantitative* notion of (the degree of) information. Indeed, unlike in the case of probabilistic concepts, we do not even have a clear *classificatory* concept of informational content at hand. At best we have some intuitions about a *comparative* concept of information. Thus it is plausible to assume that p is more informative than q only if p has greater logical content than q, i.e. only if p logically entails q. Conversely, however, p's logically entailing q does not always mean that p is (in any *relevant* aspect) more informative than q, for the extra content by which p surpasses q may be entirely irrelevant for the purposes of the conversation. Since there is no clear and immediate logical definition of informational content in sight, let us presuppose the relation 'p is (relevantly) more informative than q' as primitive here, and let it be symbolized by '$p >_i q$'.

The basic idea of Grice's maxim of quantity can now be rendered more precise in the following way. If the speaker a has the choice between two assertions p and q, where the former is relevantly more informative than the latter, then a is conversationally obliged to make the more informative assertion p provided this is not in conflict with the maxim of quality. In other words, a is conversationally allowed to make the less informative assertion q only if a is *not certain* that p. To put it formally:

(**QUAN**) If $(p >_i q)$, then $A(a,q) \rightarrow_p \neg C(a,p)$

This pragmatic implication may be combined with the former **QUAL** so as to yield the following *main principle of pragmatics*: By making the weaker or less informative assertion q, the speaker pragmatically implies or indicates that while she is convinced that q, she is not certain that (and hence does not know whether) the more informative p also is the case:

(**PRAG 1**) If $(p >_i q)$, then $A(a,q) \rightarrow_p C(a,q) \wedge \neg C(a,p)$

Let us now apply this general pragmatic principle to utterances of certain *epistemic* propositions p and q in particular and assume that the logical relations existing between the epistemic attitudes of some person b correlate with corresponding degrees of (relevant) informational content. Thus, e.g., sentence $K(b,p)$ may be taken to be more informative than $C(b,p)$ which in turn is $>_i B(b,p)$, and again $B(b,p) >_i P(b,p)$. One thus obtains the following corollaries:

(**PRAG 2**) $A(a,P(b,p)) \rightarrow_p C(a,P(b,p)) \wedge \neg C(a,B(b,p))$

(**PRAG 3**) $A(a,B(b,p)) \rightarrow_p C(a,B(b,p)) \wedge \neg C(a,C(b,p))$

(**PRAG 4**) $A(a,C(b,p)) \rightarrow_p C(a,C(b,p)) \wedge \neg C(a,K(b,p))$

Now consider the special instances where speaker a makes assertions about his own epistemic attitudes. Setting $b = a$ in **PRAG 2** we obtain that if a asserts that he considers it possible that p, he pragmatically implies $C(a,P(a,p)) \wedge \neg C(a,B(a,p))$. In view of the earlier laws for iterated doxastic attitudes, this may be simplified as follows:

(**PRAG 5**) $A(a,P(a,p)) \rightarrow_p P(a,p) \wedge \neg B(a,p)$

By asserting that he considers it possible that p, a indicates that he does not believe that p (and a fortiori that he does not know that p). In this sense a's *utterance* of $P(a,p)$ is *pragmatically* incompatible with his (weakly or strongly) believing that p or with his knowing that p, even though – as we have seen above – the state of affairs $P(a,p)$ is *semantically* (or also objectively) compatible with $B(a,p)$, $C(a,p)$, and $K(a,p)$.

Similarly it follows from **PRAG 3** that if a asserts that he believes that p, he thereby pragmatically implies that he is not convinced that p:

(**PRAG 6**) $A(a, B(b,p)) \rightarrow_p B(a,p) \wedge \neg C(a,p)$

Many controversies in the literature concerning the validity of epistemic-logical laws – and especially a great part of the discussion of the so-called 'Entailment-thesis' $K(a,p) \rightarrow B(a,p))$ – suffer from not sufficiently distinguishing between semantic and pragmatic implications. Once this distinction is made, one not only obtains a perfectly consistent theory of propositional attitudes but actually one in which the semantic laws serve to *explain* the pragmatic ones.

Turning now to **PRAG 4** we face a problem, however. If one would just substitute b for a in **PRAG 4,** one would obtain the principle

$$A(a, C(a,p)) \rightarrow_p C(a, C(a,p)) \wedge \neg C(a, K(a,p))$$

which is intuitively unacceptable. It says that if person a asserts that she is certain that p, a thereby pragmatically implies not only (as desired) $C(a, C(a,p))$, i.e. $C(a,p)$, but also $\neg C(a, K(a,p))$, i.e., in view of **E5**, $\neg C(a,p)$. In other words, a person who asserts 'I am certain that p' would imply that she does not know that p and hence that she is *not* certain that p, after all.

To solve this problem, observe that **PRAG 4** is based on the premise that asserting 'b knows that p' is more informative than asserting 'b is convinced that p'. This assumption certainly is justified in the general case where $b \neq a$. Since $K(b,p)$ unlike $C(b,p)$ semantically entails p, a's assertion of 'b *knows* that p' is more informative than a's assertion of 'b is *convinced* that p' because the former pragmatically entails not only $C(a, C(b,p))$ but in addition also $C(a,p)$. Thus by asserting 'b *knows* that p' person a indicates that she herself is convinced that p, too. However, in the special case $b = a$, the corresponding assertion of 'a knows that p' (or, more idiomatically, 'I know that p') is no longer more informative than 'I am certain that p' (and, incidentally, no more informative than the simple assertion of p, either). In view of **QUAN** both $A(a,p) \rightarrow_p C(a,p)$, and $A(a, C(a,p)) \rightarrow_p C(a, C(a,p))$, and also $A(a, K(a,p)) \rightarrow_p C(a, K(a,p))$; but for epistemic logical reasons the respective pragmatic consequents $C(a,p), C(a, C(a,p))$, and $C(a, K(a,p))$ are all *equivalent* to each other. Thus no matter whether one simply asserts 'p', or 'I am convinced that p' or 'I know that p', the pragmatic effects on the hearer h will always be the same: h may take it for granted that speaker a is convinced that p, but this cannot logically warrant that p actually is the case. Therefore the premise $K(a,p) >_i C(a,p)$ does not hold when a's own utterances are at stake, and so in the case $a = b$ the maxim **QUAL** must not be applied.

The pragmatic principles developed above may further be used to explain several phenomena that have been observed in connection with epistemic utterances. So-called Moore's paradox consists in the fact that one cannot rationally assert, e.g., 'It is raining, but I do not believe that'. The reason of the *pragmatic inconsistency* of this assertion (which, when analyzed from a semantic points of view, describes a fully self-consistent state of affairs) lies in principle **QUAN**. By asserting '$p \wedge \neg B(a,p)$', person a pragmatically implies $C(a, p \wedge \neg B(a,p))$ which is epistemic-logically equivalent to $C(a,p) \wedge C(a, \neg B(a,p))$, i.e. to $C(a,p) \wedge \neg B(a,p)$, in flat contradiction to principle **E9**. The solution of the so-called 'Surprise-Examination' or 'Hangman-Paradox' also crucially depends on the pragmatic implications of epistemic sentences, but it requires a much subtler analysis that cannot be given in the framework of this paper.[6]

Department of Philosophy
University of Osnabrück
FB 2 - Philosophie
D-49069 Osnabrück
Germany

NOTES

[1]Cf., e.g., (42).

[2]Clearly, since $C(a,p) \vee \neg C(a,p)$ holds tautologically, **C10** and **C11** entail that $C(a, C(a,p)) \vee C(a, \neg C(a,p))$ is epistemic-logically true. So either way there exists a q such that $C(a,q)$.

[3]Clearly, if $C(a,p) \wedge p$, then there exist some $q_1, ..., q_n$ such that the q_i are true and $C(a, q_i)$ and $\{q_1, ..., q_n\}$ logically entail p, *viz.*, $q_1 = q_n = p$!

[4]A careful analysis of Moore's paper doesn't, however, fully confirm this assumption. Although 'Certainty' contains a lot of interesting epistemological observations, Moore all too often appears to conflate the (semantic) truth-conditions for $C(a,p)$ and $K(a,p)$ on the one hand and the pragmatic conditions for the utterability of the corresponding assertions: 'I am certain that p' and 'I know that p' on the other hand. Similar comments apply to Wittgenstein's detailed commentary on Moore in (53). Cf. (49).

[5]A discussion of further candidates for the logic of knowledge may be found in (47).

[6]Cf., e.g., (45) and ch. 5 of (48).

REFERENCES

[38] Bruno de Finetti. Foresight: Its Logical Laws, Its Subjective Sources. In H.E. Kyburg & H.E. Smokler (eds.), *Studies in Subjective Probability*, Huntington, N.Y.: R.E. Krieger, 53 - 118, 1964.

[39] Kit Fine. An Ascending Chain of **S4**-logics. *Theoria*, 40:110 – 116, 1974.

[40] Gerald Gazdar. *Pragmatics - Implicature, Presupposition, and Logical Form.* Academic Press, New York, 1979.

[41] H. Paul Grice. Logic and Conversation. In P. Cole & J.L. Morgan (eds.), *Syntax and Semantics* Vol. 3, New York: Academic Press, 41 - 58, 1975.

[42] Jaako Hintikka. Knowledge, Belief, and Logical Consequence. *Ajatus*, 32:32 – 47, 1970.

[43] P. Lamarre and Y.O. Shoham. Knowledge, belief and conditionalization. In J. Doyle, E. Sandewall & P. Torraso (eds.), *Principles of Knowledge Representation and Reasoning*, San Mateo, CA: Morgan Kaufman, 1994.

[44] E. J. Lemmon. *An Introduction to Modal Logic.* Blackwell, Oxford, 1977.

[45] Wolfgang Lenzen. Die Paradoxie der überraschenden Übung - Logische, epistemologische und pragmatische Aspekte. *Logique et Analyse*, 19:267 – 284, 1976.

[46] Wolfgang Lenzen. *Recent Work in Epistemic Logic.* North Holland Publishing Company, Amsterdam, 1978.

[47] Wolfgang Lenzen. Epistemologische Betrachtungen zu [**S4**, **S5**]. *Erkenntnis*, 14:33 – 56, 1979.

[48] Wolfgang Lenzen. *Glauben, Wissen und Wahrscheinlichkeit.* Springer Verlag, Wien, 1980.

[49] Wolfgang Lenzen. Wittgensteins zweifel über wissen und gewissheit. *Grazer Philosophische Studien*, 10:43–52, 1980.

[50] G. E. Moore. Certainty. In G. E. Moore, *Philosophical Papers*, London: George Allen and Unwin, 227-251, 1959.

[51] Krister Segerberg. Qualitative Probability in a Modal Setting. In J. Fenstad (ed.), *Proceedings of the 2nd Scandinavian Logic Symposium*, Amsterdam: North Holland Publishing Company, 341-352, 1971.

[52] Franz von Kutschera. *Einführung in die intensionale Semantik.* de Gruyter, Berlin, 1976.

[53] L. Wittgenstein. *Über Gewissheit. On Certainty.* Blackwell, Oxford, 1969. Ed. by G.E.M. Anscombe & G. H. von Wright.

JAAKKO HINTIKKA

A SECOND GENERATION EPISTEMIC LOGIC AND ITS GENERAL SIGNIFICANCE

1. THE PRIMA FACIE CONUNDRUM OF EPISTEMIC LOGIC

Epistemic logic was practiced already in the middle ages (see (56), (70)). It was thrust to the awareness of contemporary philosophers by von Wright in his *An Essay on Modal Logic* ((79), see chapter 4). In this paper, I will consider epistemic logic primarily in relation to its epistemological applications. Surely any satisfactory epistemic logic ought to be able to prove its mettle as an epistemo-logic, to coin a phrase. From this perspective, the half-century long career of epistemic logic presents us with something of a paradox. Epistemic logic was created by philosophers for philosophical purposes. It is one of the core areas in what is (misleadingly) known as philosophical logic. Yet its most promising philosophical suggestions were put forward relatively late, and even then they have received but lukewarm attention on the part of philosophers. These potential philosophical applications are in my judgment incomparably more interesting and significant than the technicalities of epistemic logic that routinely receive the lion's share of attention in books and papers on epistemic logic. In typical surveys of epistemic logic (cf. (72), (74)), little attention is paid to the epistemological perspectives opened by epistemic logic.

There are several partial explanations of this paradoxical state of affairs. Reasoning about knowledge has become an important subject in such branches of computer science as AI and data base theory. Epistemic logic has been harnessed to the service of such studies, which has encouraged work on the more computation-oriented aspects and hence more technical aspects of the subject. Furthermore, since epistemic logic provides a refutation of Kripke's so-called New Theory of Reference (see (68) and cf. below), the uncritical acceptance of this 'theory' has discouraged serious interest in epistemic logic.

Even more generally, in spite of a nearly unanimous professed rejection of formalistic philosophy of logic and mathematics by contemporary philosophers, their argumentative practice exhibits a formalist bias. They tend to feel safest in discussing the formal behavior of different notions. When they venture on the uncharted seas of interpretational questions, their ideas are far too often arbitrary and myopic. A simple example may illustrate what I am saying. I understand perfectly what kind of reasoning the logicians have in mind when they speak of reasoning in terms of 'arbitrary individuals', but the notion of such an individual has by itself no explanatory value. I have never seen, heard, smelled, touched or kissed an arbitrary individual. Reifying logicians' jargon into such chancy entities seems to me entirely, well, arbitrary.

V.F. Hendricks, K.F. Jørgensen and S.A. Pedersen (eds.), Knowledge Contributors, 33–55.

Nevertheless, it seem to me that there are—or perhaps I should say there were—valid reasons for philosophers' suspicion of the promised philosophical applications of epistemic logic. In this paper, I propose to outline, first, what the promises were, second, why they did not at first pan out and, third, how those reasons for disregarding the philosophical implications of epistemic logic can be removed by means of important new ideas which can be said to launch a new generation of epistemic logics.

But, first, what was the old first-generation epistemic logic like? Syntactically, all that we need is to add to a suitable many-sorted but otherwise ordinary first-order language epistemic operators of the form K_a, to correspond roughly to the English expression *a knows that*. Often the identity of the knower does not matter. Then we can drop the knower indicator and read K as *it is known that*. This notation may not be entirely self-explanatory. For one thing, it hides the fact that the knower indicator a is semantically speaking outside the scope of the epistemic operator. Further clarifications are made in the following when we proceed.

Many of the basic properties of epistemic logic emerge already in application in which we have only one epistemic operator.

But what is the semantics of such an epistemic language? In order to answer this question, it is useful to raise the question of the pragmatic role of our notion of knowledge. Why do we have this notion in our conceptual repertoire? Suppose I am some morning considering how to prepare for the trials and tribulations of the impending day. Should I carry my raincoat and my umbrella? Should I don a suit in order to impress my boss? Then I learn from the weather forecast that the day will be sunny and warm and from my trusted secretary that my boss will be out of town. How does this enhanced knowledge affect my behavior? I do not have to tell you. I leave my raincoat and umbrella at home and instead of the uncomfortable suit don a comfortable blazer. What has happened? What has happened that I have been able, because of my newly acquired knowledge, to leave out certain possibilities as to what might happen during the day out of my planning and other considerations.

This shows the general conceptual role of the notion of knowledge. In order to speak of what a certain person a knows and does not know, we have to assume a class ('space') of possibilities. These possibilities will be called scenarios. Philosophers typically call them possible worlds. This usage is a symptom of intellectual megalomania. In most applications 'possible worlds' are not literally worlds in the sense of universes but merely 'small worlds', that is, so many applications of the language in question, typically applications to some relatively small nook and corner of our four-dimensional world. Such a space of scenarios is essentially the same as what probability theorists mean by sample space. It might be called the epistemic space. Depending on the application, the elements of that space can be states of affairs or sequences of events. What the concept of knowledge accomplishes in any case is a dichotomy (relative to the knower) of the elements of the epistemic space into those that are ruled out by a's knowledge and those that are compatible with everything he or she (or it, if we are dealing with a computer) knows in a given scenario. Its abstract semantical manifestation is relation $R(a, w_1, w_2)$ between a knower a in the scenario w_1 and those scenarios w_2 that are compatible with everything a knows in w_1. It is then true that a knows in w_1 that S if and only if it is true that S in all the scenarios w^* such that $R(a, w_1, w^*)$. These scenarios w^* are called the epistemic a-alternatives to w_1 or more loosely a's knowledge-worlds in w_1.

Thus the epistemic operator K_a is a kind of quantifier, viz. a universal quantifier ranging over a's knowledge-worlds. Much of the logic and semantics of epistemic notions can be considered as implications of this simple insight.

This pragmatic motivation of epistemic logic calls for several comments. For one thing, in order to be considered seriously for the purposes of acting (or of being acted on), the possibilities that I have called scenarios must be in some sense real (concrete) possibilities. Hence it is not realistic (pace the likes of Chalmers) to introduce a separate dimension of epistemic possibilities different from real or metaphysical ones.

Furthermore, what has been said does not separate the notion of knowledge from those of information or even true belief. All of them have a similar role in guiding our actions. All of them induce similar dichotomies of the epistemic space, and all of them have therefore a similar logic. One difference is that in the case of knowledge the rejection of excluded scenarios must be justified. However, much of the logic of knowledge is independent of the precise nature of this justification. For this reason, it need not be discussed here.

Another difference is that it is usually required that whatever is known must be true. This requirement is not discussed here, either. It is impossible to implement in many real-life applications of epistemic notions. For this reason, it might in fact be more appropriate to speak of the logic of information than of the logic of knowledge. Unfortunately the term 'information' has other misleading overtones. But fortunately this issue does not affect what will be done in this paper.

Another problem area which I will not deal with fully in this paper is the behavior of identity. One reason why it would need a longer discussion is that the received approaches are seriously off the mark. The source of the problem is the fact that in epistemic and other intensional context we have to consider individuals as potential members of several scenarios. This is true in particular of individuals considered as values of bound variables. Hence we must have—or, rather, there must be implicit in the semantics of our language—criteria of identity for denizens of different scenarios. They are sometimes called criteria of cross-identification. How are we to deal with them? Many philosophers and linguists have approached this problem by means of the notion or reference. This is especially true of Kripke and his acolytes. Kripke postulates a special kind of direct or rigid reference to explain the identity in question. This 'new theory of reference' nevertheless offers us merely a good analogue of Karl Kraus's dictum about psychoanalysis. The so-called new theory of reference embodies the very problem it is supposed to be a solution to. What a system of reference does is to provide criteria which tell us what the references of our expressions are in each of the different possible scenarios we might want to approach by means of our language. Hence, almost by definition, such a system does not tell anything about the identities of individuals (or of objects of a higher type) in different scenarios. For this purpose, we need another system—or rather, there is another system embedded in our working conceptual system—governing such identities. This system might be called the identification system. It turns out to be largely independent of the reference system. Hence what is wrong about the new theory of reference in the first place is hence that it is a theory of reference.

Epistemic logic plays an interesting role here in that it provides specific examples of the failure of the 'new theory of reference' . For in whatever way the reference of (say) a singular term be is determined, it always makes sense to ask, 'Does b know what a is?' The answer cannot turn on the grammatical or logical category of 'a' above. It is always a factual question.

Of course a full treatment would here involve discussing the alleged mechanisms of creating direct reference that Kripke and others have proposed. Suffice it here merely to put Kripke's idea of dubbing into a historical perspective. Kripke's idea is but a dramatized version of the old alarm that it is ostension that provides the basic semantical links between language and reality. Wittgenstein held it for a while—for rather a long while, if I am right. However, he eventually came to reject it, for reasons that at least prima facie apply quite as well against Kripke.

To put the same point in different terms, to say that 'a' behaves like a rigid designation in b's knowledge worlds is to say that

$$(\exists x)\ K_b\ (a = x) \tag{4}$$

But what this expresses is the fact that b knows what a is. (Cf. below.) And this cannot be guaranteed by the meaning of 'a' alone. Whether or not (4) is true depends crucially on the identification system one is relying on.

In this sense epistemic logic provides strong evidence against any theory of direct reference. No wonder, therefore, that the new theorists of reference have studiously neglected it, in spite of its importance for applications of logic.

2. THE PROMISES

Now what are the promises of such an epistemic logic? What questions does it help us to answer? Well, what questions are we likely to ask in epistemology? One of the first concerns surely the objects of knowledge. When one knows something, what is the knowledge about? Interesting prima facie distinctions are codified in the syntax of ordinary language. We speak of knowing truths, propositions and facts. Such knowledge is expressed by the *knows that* construction which is incorporated in our epistemic logic. But how can we express what might be called knowledge of objects, that is, the kind of knowledge expressed in English by what is known as simple *wh*-constructions such as *knowing who, what, where, when* etc. In the simplest cases, the answer seems obvious. If K expresses it is known that and the variable x ranges over persons, then the sentence

(5) It is known who murdered Roger Ackroyd

can be expressed by

(6) $(\exists x)\ K\ (x \text{ murdered Roger Ackroyd})$

which has the form

(7) $(\exists x)\ K\ M(x, r)$

For what else could be meant by *knowing who* did the dastardly deed than *knowing of some particular individual* x that x did it?

Indeed, this is a viable analysis of simple *wh*-knowledge. The simplest case of such simple knowledge is knowing the identity of an individual. *It is known who* b is can be expressed by

(8) $(\exists x)\ K\ (b = x)$

All that is presupposed by such analyses is some systematization of the logic and semantics of the logic of knowledge along the lines indicated above. What this amounts to is some version of what is known as possible-worlds semantics for epistemic logic, including a system of reference and a separate system of cross-identification. (If you share my distaste of the 'possible worlds' terminology, you may speak of possible scenarios instead.)

Knowing what an entity of a higher type is can likewise be expressed in terms of K, but now we have to quantify over higher-order entities. For instance, *knowing which function* $g(x)$ is can be expressed by

(9) $(\exists f)\ K\ (\forall x)(g(x) = f(x))$

where f is a function variable. This might be abbreviated as

(10) $(\exists f)\ K\ (g = f)$

which brings out the parallelism between (10) and (8).

Unfortunately, this analysis of what it means to know the identity of a function is in terms of higher-order quantification (quantification over functions). Such quantification promptly leads to an avalanche of difficult problems. Which higher-order entities exist? If we know and answer to that question, we could decide what axioms to posit in set theory. What does it mean for a higher-order entity to exist, anyway? We would obviously be much wiser if we could dispense with higher-order quantification.

The distinction between knowledge of propositions (or truths) and knowledge of entities has many intriguing applications. Here I will mention only one. It is obvious that intuitionistic mathematics is calculated to deal, not so much with mathematical truths, as with our knowledge of mathematics. But if this knowledge is assumed to be propositional very little seems to be accomplished. Indeed, S is provable in the usual epistemic logics if and only if KS is provable.

The real novelty is, I have argued, that intuitionists (the original ones, not the soi-disant ones of our day and age) were not concerned with our knowledge of mathematical propositions, but with our knowledge of mathematical objects. Consider, for example, the axiom of choice. Does a choice set always exist? You can consider this question till you are blue in the face without finding an easy answer. In contrast, it is easy for anyone to admit that we do not always know what a choice function would be. I will not pursue this matter here, and use it only to illustrate the tremendous interest of the distinction between knowledge of truths (propositions) and knowledge of objects (entities).

This distinction between the knowledge of propositions and knowledge of entities is thus of considerable philosophical and other theoretical interest. For another application, it shows that at least in the simplest cases we can analyze knowledge of objects in terms of knowledge of propositions. This is shown by expressions like (8) (or perhaps also (5)-(7)), in that the only epistemic element they contain is the *knowing that* operator K.

More generally speaking, one thing that epistemic logic seems to promise is an analysis of different kinds of knowledge in terms of the single operator K. This project can be carried out in some cases, in addition to the analysis of simple *wh*-knowledge just outlined. For instance, why- and how-knowledge are obviously more complex conceptually, but can be brought within the scope of such analysis. (See e.g. (66)) Most importantly, an insight into the possibility (and indeed presence in our actual discourse) of the different modes of identification opens up possibilities of analyzing different types of knowledge by acquaintance, that is, of the kind of knowledge that is in natural languages expressed by a direct (grammatical) object construction. (cf. (63), chapters 3-4, and 1990.)

Such analyses have a philosophical interest that goes way beyond whatever logico-linguistic relevance they may have. For instance, the fact that the only epistemic operator we need is the *knows that* operator suggests strongly that propositional knowledge can be thought of as the only basic kind of knowledge. This meshes well with the initial observations above concerning the pragmatic function of the notion of knowledge.

For another thing, it is obvious on the basis of the model theoretical meaning of propositions like (7) that they express what in the current jargon is called *de re* knowledge. The possibility of a uniform analysis in terms of a single epistemic operator shows that there is no irreducible *de re* knowledge. Such a notion is a figment of certain philosophers' imagination—or so it seems on the basis of our observations so far. And since the postulation of such direct reference is the kingpin of the so-called 'New Theory of Reference', this theory is thus seen to involve a serious confusion.

Likewise, the possibility of an analysis of the kinds of knowledge that rely on different modes of identification by reference to a single epistemic operator shows that what is involved in acquaintance-type knowledge is not a different kind of *knowledge*, but a different mode of identification. This difference in identification manifests itself in the form of a difference between the (correlated pairs of) quantifiers involved, not in the form of a difference in the kind of information (knowledge). This particular insight turns out to be relevant even for neuroscientific theorizing, as is shown in Hintikka and Symons (forthcoming).

Unfortunately, it is not immediately obvious that such analyses can always be carried out. Thus the promises I have described threaten to remain only promises. For instance, the analysis exemplified by (6)-(5) works naturally only in the case of simple *wh*-knowledge. For how can we analyze more complex types of knowledge in the same spirit? How can we represent knowledge statements like the following?

(11) Mary knows whose advice every young mother should trust.

(12) It is known how the observed variable y depends on the controlled variable x in such-and-such experimental situation.

Needless to say, we understand (11) in the sense in which prima facie answers to it have the form 'her mother' rather than 'Dr. Spock' . In view of this explication, one might try to express the logical form of (11) as follows:

(13) $$(\forall x)(M(x) \rightarrow (\exists y)K_{Mary}T(x, y))$$

But (13) does not say the same as (11). In (11) Mary's knowledge is about all actual young mothers all of whom must therefore be known to her in order for (13) to be true. This is not implied by (11).

This point is important enough to be elaborated by means of further examples and explanations. For one thing, if (13) were equivalent with

(11), the latter would imply

(14) If Celia is a young mother,
Mary knows whose advice Celia should trust.

But this may very well be false, viz. if Mary does not know Celia.

In general, we might say that knowing something about each individual (as in 13) is different from knowing the same thing about all individuals (as in (11)). Aristotle already knew better than to assimilate the two to each other; see *An. Post.* *A*1,71a25-b9.

On a purely linguistic level, Elisabeth Engdahl already in 1986 argued that the logical form of sentences like (11)-(12) cannot be represented on the first-order level.

Semantically speaking, the reason for all this can be said to be that when we 'quantify into' a construction governed by an epistemic operator, the values of variables must be the same in all of the relevant knowledge-words, in other words, such values must be known to the agent in question. A solution might seem to be to make explicit the dependence of the trusty advisor on the young mother in question, perhaps as follows:

(15) $$(\exists f)K_{Mary}(\forall x)(M(x) \to T(x, f(x))$$

This is obviously a much better reading. For Mary's knowledge amounts to picking out an advisor for each young mother, and of course such picking out is mathematically speaking precisely what a function does. However, it now sounds strange to say that the object of Mary's knowledge is a certain function, not certain advisors. In other words, it is puzzling that no first-order translation of (11) into the language of epistemic logic seems to be possible.

Obviously an analysis which dispenses with quantification over higher-order entities would be preferable. For one thing, such an analysis would be free of all the difficult problems which are associated with questions of existence of higher order entities. All told, it is not clear how our distinction between different types of knowledge can be made general.

Similar difficulties emerge with the other philosophical and other conceptual insights promised by the original 'first-generation' epistemic logic. Many of these promises concerned the application of epistemic logic to the theory of questions and answers. This theory can be made virtually a part of epistemic logic by construing a direct question as a request to bring about a certain epistemic state. (There will be restrictions on how this state of affairs is to be brought about.)

A specification of this epistemic state is called the *desideratum* of the direct question in question. It ought to be representable by means of a satisfactory epistemic logic. Much of the logical theory of questions and answers can be formulated in terms of the desiderata of questions.

For instance, (6) is the desideratum of the direct question

(16) Who murdered Roger Ackroyd?

Likewise, the first-person version of (11), viz.

(17) I know whom every young mother should trust

expresses the desideratum of the direct question

(18) Whom should every young mother trust most?

For simple *wh*-questions epistemic logic enables us to define some of the most important concepts in the theory of questions and their answers. In particular we can define the presupposition of a simple *wh*-question. In the case of (16) it is obviously

(19) $$K\ (\exists x)\ M(x, r)$$

But it is not obvious how this notion could be defined more generally.

Furthermore, the all-important question-answer relationship can be formulated for simple *wh*-questions. Suppose the addressee of the question (16) responds by offering a singular term, say 'b', as the hoped for answer. Assuming that the reply is true and accepted by the questioner, he, or she (or, it, if the inquirer is a computer) can now say

(20) I know that b murdered Roger Ackroyd

in brief

(21) $$K_I\ M(b, r)$$

When does this satisfy the questioner? When is it a true or *conclusive* answer, as I will call it? Not always, for the questioner might fail to know who b is. In view of the meaning of the desideratum of a question, the answer is if and only if it implies the desideratum of the question, in this case if and only if it implies

(22) $$(\exists x)\ K_I\ (b = x)$$

When does this implication hold, then? The semantics of epistemic logic described above yields the answer: If and only if it is the case that

(23) $$(\exists x)\ K_I\ (b = x)$$

In other words, (23) must be available as an extra premise. Our semantical common sense agrees with this diagnosis.

In brief the 'reply' (21)

$$K_I\ M(b, r)$$

entails the desideratum

(24) $$(\exists x) K_I\ M(x, r)$$

only in conjunction with the extra conclusiveness condition (23).

In the case of simple *wh*-questions, we can thus characterize explicitly the relation of questions to their (conclusive) answers.

This result opens a highly interesting epistemological perspective. The question (16) is a factual question. Answering it requires providing the questioner with the factual information codified in (24). It also requires providing the questioner with the conclusiveness condition (23). Now what (23) expresses is not purely factual knowledge. It involves also conceptual (in this case, lexical) knowledge, viz. knowledge of who it is that is being referred to.

This is especially clear when '*b*' is a proper name. (It can be one, as pointed out above.) There the knowledge expressed by the conclusiveness condition is purely conceptual, viz. knowledge of the meaning of the proper name '*b*' .

Such conceptual knowledge is a priori as far as the usual factual discourse is concerned. Hence we have located a role for a priori knowledge smack in the middle of empirical questioning and *a fortiori* empirical inquiry. A priori knowledge is needed to secure the conclusiveness conditions, in effect to convert arbitrary responses to genuine answers. I find it hard to think of a more interesting perspective into the epistemology of empirical inquiry.

But, alas, an attempt to generalize these observations to all kinds of questions and *ergo* all kinds of inquiry face the same problems as were discussed in connection with different kinds of knowledge.

These observations illustrate and reinforce what was said earlier by way of criticizing philosophers' *de dicto* vs *de re* distinction. In what was just discovered there is implicit an interesting logico-semantical insight. In a reply like (21) to a simple *wh*-question, one is clearly speaking of *b* *de dicto*, as this term is currently used. Otherwise no collateral conclusiveness condition (23) would be needed. Indeed, according to the usual terminology, in the desideratum like (24) of a simple *wh*-question, the kind of knowledge required is *de re* knowledge. But when the conclusiveness condition (23) is adjoined to (21), the knowledge involved in (23) is transmuted to a *de re* knowledge. This naturally does not affect the kind of knowledge or the kind of reference involved in (21). What this shows is that there are no such things as irreducibly *de re* or *de dicto* knowledge or even *de re* or *de dicto* reference in the case of simple *wh*-questions. However, it is not obvious how this striking result can be extended to all epistemic contexts.

Other epistemological applications of epistemic logic seem to fall to the same category of interesting but unfulfilled promises. One general novelty is to try to model knowledge-seeking in general by construing it as a questioning process. Of course such an approach is in a sense no novelty for it goes back to the very first explicit model of reasoning in Western philosophy, that is, to the Socratic method of questioning or *elenchus*. In the briefest possible terms, this method amounts to modeling all inquiry as a questioning process. In fact, Aristotle already suggested that all the first principles of science can be obtained by such a questioning process.

The same Aristotle in effect refined this model by noting that the answers to certain questions are predictable independently of the particular answerer. They are the answers that from one perspective are logically implied by earlier answers. Such logical inference steps can be separated from the (true) interrogative steps. They are governed by the rules of inference of deductive logic.

When we are recording the successive steps of interrogative inquiry on paper (or on a computer disk), logical inference steps and interrogative steps look rather similar. The former are steps from a premise (or number of premises) to a conclusion; the latter are steps from the presupposition(s) of a question to its answer.

There are even closer analogies between some of the most important types of logical and interrogative steps. For one thing, in an application of the rule of existential instantiation we move from a sentence of the form

(25) $$K\ (\exists x)\ F[x]$$

or perhaps

(26) $$K\ (\exists x)\ F[x]$$

to an instance of theirs of the form

(27) $$F[\alpha]$$

or perhaps

(28) $$K\ F[\alpha]$$

where α is a new individual constant, in some treatments a member of a special class of individual constants called dummy names. Their m.o. is very much the same as the John Does and the Jane Roes of legal parlance.

In a comparable interrogative step, the inquirer moves from the presupposition of a simple *wh*-question, which is of the form (25) or (26) to an answer of the form

(29) $$F[a]$$

or perhaps

(30) $$K\ F[a]$$

If this is to be a genuine answer, there must also be available the conclusiveness condition

(31) $$(\exists x)\ K\ (a = x)$$

The main function of (31) is merely to make a available as a substitution-value of various future steps of logical inference.

Now these two kinds of steps do not only look alike. There is a deeper connection between them. This connection can be seen best by raising two important general questions that turn out to be interrelated. One of them concerns the role of logic in inquiry in general. At first sight, it might seem that the last word on question was put forward by Aristotle when he separated the necessitated answers, that is, logical inference steps, form the unnecessitated ones, that is, from interrogative steps. In Aristotle's terminology, the former can be judged *ad argumentum* without considering the answerer whereas the latter can be fully evaluated only *ad hominem*. It might seem that Aristotle was seriously biased in weighting the two kinds of answers, in that he devoted most of his attention to syllogistically construed logical inference steps. Even though this impression may not be entirely correct historically, the fact remains that in actual real-life inquiry the most important job is done by interrogative steps. Only in them does new factual information enter into the inquirer's line of thought.

Accordingly, deductive logic seems to play a rather modest role in inquiry in general. And this result seems to belie the widespread popular image of logic as the 'secret' of all good reasoning. This view is epitomized by the stories of the clever 'deductions' of real or fictional sleuths like the proverbial Sherlock Holmes. We might in fact call this suspect perspective the Sherlock Holmes view of reasoning. The Sherlock Holmes view on the role of logic in inquiry can be said to be mistaken only as long as we do not consider strategies of inquiry and inference. Such strategies manifest themselves in the form of answers to the problem as to what to do next in the course of actual inquiry. The normal situation is that the inquirer has reached a number of propositions that he, she or it can use as premises of logical inferences or also as presuppositions of questions. Indeed, we have two separate strategic questions here depending on whether the inquirer is restricted to purely deductive means or whether the inquirer is trying to find the best questions to ask. In other words, the one problem is to locate the best deductive premise, the other one to find the best presupposition for the question to be asked next.

It can be shown that in neither case can we find an effective (computable) rule which would provide the correct answer in all cases. So is there anything concrete and constructive that can be said about the strategies of inquiry in general? Even though neither of the two questions just mentioned is mechanically answerable in general, there is a most remarkable thing than can be said of their answers. Subject to certain conditions to be explained, *the answer is the same for both questions*. Or, rather, this is what is suggested by the parallelism just mentioned. (Compare here (27)-(28) and (29)-(30).) The two outcomes of the next step differ only in having a different individual constant in the same position. This usually makes little difference to the rest of the inquiry. Hence if the best way to shorten the rest of a deductive inquiry is to reach (27) through a logical inference step, the best way of shortening it by means of an interrogative step is to use the same sentence as the presupposition of the question that would yield (29).

This interesting strategic parallelism between deduction and interrogation requires explanations and qualifications. Some of the qualifications needed here are inessential. For one thing, it might make a difference to the rest of the inquiry if the individual a obtained in the answer to the inquirer's question is not new but identical with one of the individuals already considered. But if the inquirer must ask a question here, he, she or it does not usually know sight unseen whether that is the case. Hence the inquirer has in his or her strategic thinking taken into account the possibility that the answer individual is a new one.

Most importantly, the parallelism is complete only if the inquirer never has to reject ('bracket') one of the answers he, she or it receives. Hence that has been said applies only to types of inquiry in which we are dealing with what in the traditional jargon would be called contexts of (pure) discovery. However, this important qualification does not reduce the interest of our results.

The parallelism between question-answer steps and deductive steps can be extended to propositional questions and the deductive rule for disjunctions. Consider, for example, the propositional question

Is it the case that S_1 or is it the case that S_2?

Its presupposition is obviously

(32) $$(S_1 \vee S_2)$$

(possibly prefixed by K). Its desideratum is

(33) $$(K\ S_1 \vee K\ S_2)$$

A deductive rule for disjunctions splits the argument into two branches initiated by S_1 and S_2, respectively.

An answer introduces here either S_1 or S_2 into the inquirer's line of reasoning. In other words, the rest of the inquiry is the same as in the case of a deductive step except that in the case of an answer the inquirer can dispense with one of the two branches. But since the inquirer did not in general know ahead of time which branch he or she could disregard, the inquirer would have to consider in a strategic context both possibilities. Thus we find here the same kind of parallelism as in the case of existential instantation.

But what about questions that do not have nonvacuous presuppositions? Now what are such questions like? They are of course yes-or-no questions. (The term yes-or-no has to be taken in the logical rather than grammatical sense here.) But in the same way as in the case of propositional questions, a yes-or-not question 'Is it the case that S?' corresponds to a tautology introduction rule in deductive logic, that is, to the introduction of $(S_1 \vee \neg S_2)$. This starts two branches (lines of thought) in the way illustrated by the tree method. Only one of them corresponds to the rest of the inquiry initiated by an answer to the yes-or-no question, but in the inquirer's strategic planning (prior to the answer) he or she has to consider both possible answers, thus creating an analogue to the deductive situation

However, the parallelism that has just been discussed apparently cannot be generalized. It is not even clear in general what answers to more complex questions will look like logically, nor is it clear what their presuppositions might be. And even if there were answers to these questions available, there apparently are no rules of logical inference that could parallel the relevant complex question-answer steps. This might seem to jeopardize the entire strategic analogy deduction and interrogative inquiry.

Other limitations are likewise conspicuous. Perhaps the most important shortcoming of first-generation epistemic logic confronts us when we begin to emulate Socrates and Aristotle and model all inquiry as a questioning process. Such a model is straightforward to implement as long as the inquirer is given a fixed conclusion that it to be established through an interrogative process starting from given initial premises. This may be enough to answer why-questions through a questioning process. However, there does not seem to be any way of analyzing similarly the all-important method of answering questions, that is, initial 'big' or principal questions, by means of a number of 'small' or operative questions. This would be a serious limitation to any application of the logic of questions and answers to epistemology.

In view of such applicational shortcomings of first-generation epistemic logic, it might in fact look as if the philosophical community might perhaps have been excused even though it has so far turned a deaf ear to the interesting and important philosophical vistas suggested by the observations so far described.

3. PROMISES FULFILLED BY MEANS OF THE NOTION OF INDEPENDENCE

I have so far been telling a story which is partly historical, partly systematic. That story has led us to a tantalizing impasse. On the one hand, by considering simple examples we can discover highly interesting philosophical suggestions apparently implicit in our epistemic logic. On the other hand, these suggestions apparently cannot be generalized from the simple cases in which they are more or less obvious to more complex cases. Sometimes such an extension can apparently be accomplished only by appealing to higher-order entities which lead us to problems which are at least as recalcitrant as the ones we were trying to overcome. What are we to do?

The most popular response in this day and age seems to be to throw up our hands and claim that conceptual realities in epistemology are just too complex and too context-dependent to be captured by the clumsy tools of epistemic logic. Apparently it would be politically correct in this situation to evoke such phrases as 'family resemblance' or 'fuzzy logic' .

Alternatively, some philosophers might propose to evoke more examples and to develop ever so much more detailed taxonomy and other theory for them, in the style of empirical linguists.

The main message of my paper is that both reactions would be dead wrong. Not only can all the difficulties I have described be solved; they can be solved in one fell swoop. This swoop is provided by the same approach that has prompted a revolution in the foundations of ordinary nonepistemic first-order logic. It is usually referred to as game-theoretical semantics, but what is important in it is not the use of game-theoretical ideas *per se*. Rather, the crucial insight is that the dependence of real-life variables on each other is expressed in a logical notation by the formal dependence of the quantifiers on each other to which they are bound. This insight motivates a change even in the notation of first-order logic. In the usual notation, the dependencies between quantifiers are indicated by the nesting of their scopes. But such a nesting relation is of a rather special kind. Among other things it is transitive and asymmetrical. Hence not all patterns of dependence and independence can be expressed by its means. Hence the received logical notation does not do its job adequately, and hence it has to be made more flexible. Since the problem is to enable us to structure our formulas more freely, it could in principle be solved without introducing any new notation and merely relaxing the scope rules, that is, the formation rules for the pairs of parentheses that indicate the dependence relations between quantifiers. In practice, it is more perspicuous to introduce instead a special independence indicator (Q_2y/Q_1x) which expresses the independence of the quantifier Q_2y of the quantifier Q_1x. Game theory comes in in that such independence can be modeled in game-theoretical semantics by the informational independence of the move mandated by (Q_2y) of the move mandated by (Q_1x), in the general game-theoretical sense of informational independence. The systematic use of this notation results in the first place in what is known as independence-friendly (IF) first-order logic.

The use of the slash (independence) notation is not restricted to the usual extensional first-order logic, however. One remarkable thing here is that this notion of independence applies to all semantically active ingredients of a sentence whose semantics can be formulated in terms of a semantical game rule. The epistemic operator K_a is a case in point in that it mandates a choice by the falsifier of one of a's knowledge worlds with respect to which a semantical game is to be continued. Accordingly, the slash notation makes sense also in epistemic logic.

How, then, does it help us? Consider, in order to answer this question, the sentence (7)

$$(\exists x)\ K\ M(x, r)$$

It expresses its intended meaning 'it is known who murdered Roger Ackroyd' because the 'witness individual' value of x must be chosen before the choice of a possible world (scenario) mandated by K. Hence this individual must be the same in all of them.

But for this purpose the value of x must not necessarily be chosen in a semantical game *before* the choice of the scenario (possible world) connected with K. It suffices to make the choice *independently of* the scenario choice. Hence (7) says the same as

(34) $$K\ (\exists x/K)\ M(x, r).$$

Likewise in (17) the choice of the witness individual (the trusted person) depends on the mother in question but not on the choice of the possible world prompted by K_I. Hence the right logical form of (17) is

(35) $$K\ (\forall x)(\exists y/K)\ T(x, y)$$

As can be seen, this is a sentence of IF first-order epistemic logic, and hence independent of all the problems connected with higher-order quantification.

It is easily seen that (35) and its analogues do not reduce to a slash-free notation. Hence the criticisms reported earlier are valid, albeit only as long as the IF notation is not used. But as soon as this notation is available, we can solve one of the problems posed in section 2 above, viz. the problem of expressing the desiderata of complex *wh*-questions on that first-order level.

The same notation can be extended to propositional connectives. For instance, we can write

(36) $$K(S_1\ (\vee/K)\ S_2)$$

This is readily seen to be equivalent with

(37) $$(K\ S_1 \vee K\ S_2)$$

In more complex examples, however, the slash notation is not dispensable. An example is offered by

(38) $$K\ (\forall x)(F_1(x)(\vee/K)\ F_2(x))$$

In general we can take any sentence of the form

(39) $$K\ S$$

where S is a first-order sentence in a negation normal form. If in (39) we replace one or more existential quantifiers $(\exists x)$ by $(\exists x/K)$ and/or one or more disjunctions $(F_1 \vee F_2)$ by $(F_1(\vee/K)F_2)$, we obtain an epistemic sentence which can serve as the desideratum of a (usually multiple) question.

The possibility that there are several slashes in the desideratum means the possibility of dealing with multiple questions. Their behavior in natural language turns out to be a most instructive chapter of epistemic logic, as documented in (64). In this paper, I will not deal with sentences with multiple K's, i.e. with iterated questions.

Thus the received terminology already embodies a mistake. What happens in quantified epistemic logic is not 'quantifying into' an opaque context, but to quantify *independently of* an epistemic operator and the moves it mandates.

The resulting logic of K-sentences can be considered a second-generation epistemic logic (or a fragment of such a logic). In that logic, the most important concepts relating to questions and answers can be defined for all different kinds of questions. For one thing, if the desideratum of a question is (39), its presupposition is obtained by dropping all the slashes $/K$. A reply to such a question brings about the truth of a sentence in which each slashed existential quantifier subformula

(40) $$(\exists x/K)\ F[x]$$

is replaced by

(41) $$F[g(y_1, y_2, \ldots)]$$

where $(Qy_1), (Qy_2), \ldots$ are all the quantifiers on which the quantifier $(\exists x/K)$ in (40) depends in (39). Likewise, each disjunction $(F_1(\vee/K)F_2)$ occurring as a subformula of (39) is replaced by

(42) $$((g(y_1, y_2, \ldots) = 0 \wedge F_1) \vee (g(y_1, y_2, \ldots) \neq 0 \wedge F_2))$$

where $(Qy_1), (Qy_2), \ldots$ are all the quantifiers on which the disjunction in question depends in (39).

This reply amounts to an answer if and only if the conclusiveness conditions of the form

(43) $$K\ (\exists f/K)(g = f)$$

are satisfied. Instead of (43) we could write

(44) $$K\ (\forall y_1)(\forall y_2)\ldots(\exists z/K)(g(y_1, y_2, \ldots) = z)$$

Whenever there are no quantifiers $(Qy_1), (Qy_2), \ldots$ the function term $g(y_1, y_2, \ldots)$ is replaced by an individual constant.

This shows also how knowing the identity of a function can be expressed on the first-order level, thus removing one of the limitations of the first-generation epistemic logic.

This generalizes the notion of presupposition, desideratum, conclusiveness condition and the question-answer relation to all questions, with the partial exception of *why*- and *how*-questions, which have to be dealt with separately. With this qualification, it can be said that we have reached the first fully explicit and general logic of questions and answers. This generality is of considerable interest for the purposes of both philosophers and linguists. For philosophers, one of the many interesting things about this second-generation epistemic logic is that it is a *first-order* logic. All quantification is over individuals, thus avoiding all the difficult problems concerning the existence of higher-order entities.

Linguists might be interested in the fact that in the framework of semantic representation provided by epistemic logic, the slash / is the embodiment of the question ingredient. Applied to disjunctions (as in $(\vee/-)$), it creates propositional questions, and applied to the existential quantifiers (as in $(\exists x/-)$), it creates *wh*-questions. This throws indirectly light also on the semantics of the question ingredient in natural languages.

The independence notation has further uses. For one thing, it enables us to express what is commonly referred to as common knowledge. In the case of knowledge common to two agents, a and b, it means that they not only share the same information, but that each of them knows that the other one knows it, and that he or she knows that the other one knows, etc. This is achieved by making the order of the initial K's irrelevant and also using as the *wh*-ingredient $(—/K_aK_b)$. For instance, the following sentence expresses that it is common knowledge between a and b whether it is the case that S:

$$K_a(K_b/K_a)(S(\vee/K_aK_b)\neg S)$$

This shows that in order to express common knowledge in general, we have to make sure that the relevant knowledge operators are on a par in the slashes and not only when they are prefixed to a sentence. And if so, we can see that common knowledge could not have been formulated in general terms in the first generation epistemic logic.

The result of this liberalization of epistemic logic is a simple but powerful logic of knowledge, including a logic of questions and answers. This second-generation epistemic logic fulfills the promises that the first-generation suggested but did not deliver. By its means, we can carry out the promised analyses of all different kinds of knowledge and all different kinds of questions, using as the only epistemic ingredient the *knows that* operator K.

Thus for instance, knowledge *de dicto* and knowledge *de re* are but different variants of the same basic notion of knowledge. Moreover, the important difference between two different modes of identification can be seen not to imply any differences in the kind of information (knowledge) involved in them. This fact turns out to have interesting consequences even outside logic and philosophy in neuroscience, where it helps to understand the two visual cognition systems sometimes known as the *where*-system and the *what*-system. (See Hintikka and Symons, forthcoming.)

The notion of independence also enables us to deepen the analysis of the *de dicto* vs *de re* contrast sketched earlier. It is possible to assume that in a semantical game the nonlogical constants are not initially interpreted by the participants. Instead, the references that are assigned to them are chosen by the verifier as a move in the game. In fact, (67) have shown that this assumption serves to throw light on certain regularities in the semantics of ordinary language. It is perhaps not obvious that such mileage can be obtained from the assumption, for there is clearly only one choice that can win, viz. to assign to the constants their linguistically determined references. The extra mileage is nevertheless real, for once there is a game rule for the interpretation (i.e. assignment of references), applications of this rule may or may not be independent of other moves in the game. (This is the opening utilized by (67).) In particular, the choice of the reference of b in a sentence like (21) may or may not be independent of the choice of the scenario prompted by K_I. Above, it was assumed to be dependent on the choice of the scenario. It can be made independent notationally by replacing (21) by

(45) $$K_I M((b/K), r)$$

This is obviously what is meant by taking b to be *de re*. Almost equally obviously, (45) is logically equivalent with the conjunction of (21) and (23).

General terms can be treated in the same way. This possibility is perhaps somewhat more conspicuous in the case of belief than of knowledge, but this is merely a matter of degree. For instance, consider the statement

(46) $$K_a(P/K)(b)$$

It says that a knows that b is one of the individuals who or what in fact are P. It does not require that *a knows* that they and only they have the property P.

These extensions of the independence notation show several interesting things. It reinforces my earlier result concerning the definability of the *de dicto* vs *de re* contrast. It also shows that this contrast is not restricted to singular terms. Furthermore, we can now see that the familiar contrast between the referential and predicative uses of singular terms like definite descriptors is not an irreducible one but is rather a matter of different construction in terms of the same basic notions.

An especially interesting generalization of earlier insights that is now brought out to the open is the partly conceptual character of the conclusiveness conditions of all *wh*-questions, simple and complex. For instance, a reply to an experimental question whose desideratum is of the form (12) is a function-in-extension, that is to say, a mere correlation of argument-values and functions-values like a curve on graph paper. Such a reply does not qualify as an answer because the questioner might not know which function is represented by the correlation or by the graph. Knowing its identity is conceptual, in this case mathematical, knowledge. This throws into a strikingly sharp profile the role of mathematics in experimental (and hence presumably empirical) science and even the indispensability of mathematics in science in general. Likewise, the partial strategic parallelism between deduction and questioning can now be generalized. As the first step, we can epistemologize the questioning processes in the following way:

(i) Every initial premise S is replaced by $K_I S$.
(ii) Every answer A is replaced by $K_I(A \wedge C(A))$, where $C(A)$ is the conjunction of all the conclusiveness conditions for A.

This does not yet generalize the parallelism between question-answer steps and logical (deductive) steps which suggested a strategic near-identity of interrogation and deduction. We have generalized the rule for question-answer steps in inquiry, but we do not have any rule of deductive inference that would match it. Such a parallel rule can be obtained by generalizing the rules of purely deductive reasoning. The original analogy was between existential instantiation and simply *wh*-questions. The existential quantifier whose variable is instantiated must occur sentence-initially in the received rule applications of existential instantiation. Why cannot we instantiate also inside a larger formula? (Surely an existential quantifier expresses there, too, the availability of truth-making individuals.) The answer is that the 'witness individual' in question will then depend on certain other individuals. Hence the instantiating term must be a function of those individuals. Formally speaking, we can extend the rule of existential generalization so as to allow to replace a subformula of the form

(47) $$(\exists x)F[x]$$

of a larger formula by a formula of the form (41) except that now g must be a new function symbol or a 'dummy function symbol', if they are used as a separate category of symbols. Some people might want to call them names of 'arbitrary functions', in analogy with 'arbitrary individuals.'

This clearly serves to extend the parallelism between deduction and questioning discussed earlier. In a context of pure discovery, the optimal strategies of questioning parallel the optimal strategies of deductive inference, in the sense explained. Even though deductive steps and interrogative steps in inquiry are different from each other, they are in the case of pure discovery governed by the same rules. As I sometimes put it, Sherlock Holmes was right: all good thinking is logical thinking. More cautiously speaking, we have located one important role of deductive logic in inquiry, viz. the role of providing strategic advice for reasoning in general.

Along the same lines, we can also at once remove the most important limitation to the applicability of the logic of questions and answers and hence of the applicability of epistemic logic. We can now reconstruct the process of answering principal questions by means of operative questions. How can we do it? Simply using the desideratum of the principal question as the target proposition to be established by the interrogative process. Naturally, this involves making the epistemic element explicit throughout, as indicated above. For instance, the initial premises are not now first-order sentences $T_1, T_2, \dots$, but their epistemic forms $KT_1, KT_2, \dots$ answers to questions will likewise all begin with K, as in examples like the resulting logic is, as we may put it, the first general reconstruction of the *elenchus* of the Platonic Socrates who was already trying to cope with large-scale principal questions ('What is knowledge?', 'What is piety?') by means of putting small questions to his interlocutor. This opens up the possibility of constructing a genuine epistemology of knowledge seeking over and above the epistemology of knowledge justification, which what current epistemology almost entirely is.

Thus the second-generation epistemic logic serves to carry out all the major philosophical promises that were made but not fulfilled by the first-generation version. The crucial concept in this generational jump is the notion of informational independence, which thus emerges as the key idea in the logic of knowledge. It is clearly impossible to develop a general logic of knowledge without the help of the notion of independence. This role of the notion of independence has some methodological interest of its own. It turns epistemic logic into an ally in the revolution in ordinary nonepistemic logic that has been instigated by the same notion of independence. This notion is in turn possible to formulate only if we are using some form of game-theoretical semantics. Whatever successes the second-generation epistemic logic can score therefore provide evidence of the usefulness of game-theoretical concepts in logic. At the same time, the second-generation epistemic logic provides evidence of the importance of the notion of independence in general, including its prevalence in the semantics of an actual 'ordinary' working language.

Last but not least, we have in epistemic logic a vivid reminder of the aptness of the Wittgensteinean wonder at how much metaphysics can be condensed in a drop of logic (Wittgenstein called it grammar).

In the spirit of Wittgenstein's dictum, perhaps I can conclude with a list of some of the drops of insights which the original epistemic-logic promised but which were delivered only by the second-generation one.

1. Distinction between propositional knowledge and knowledge of objects (entities).
2. Uniform analysis of all different kinds of knowledge in terms of a single *knows that* operator.
    (a) The basic kind of knowledge is propositional.
    (b) There is no irreducible *de re* knowledge.
3. An analysis of the basic notions concerning questions and answers, including the notion of presupposition and the question-answer relation.

4. Answers (conclusive answers) to empirical questions often require a priori conceptual knowledge (e.g. mathematical knowledge).
5. A method of answering (principal) questions by means of (operative) questions.
6. A partial strategic parallelism between questioning and deduction. ('Sherlock Holmes vindicated.')

Department of Philosophy
Boston University
745 Commonwealth Avenue
Boston, Massachusetts 02215
USA

REFERENCES

[54] Aristotle. *Posterior Analytics.* Clarendon Press, Oxford, 2. edition, 1994. Translated with a commentary by Jonathan Barnes.

[55] Stephen E. Boër and William G. Lycan. *Knowing Who.* MIT Press, Cambridge, 1986.

[56] Ivan Boh. *Epistemic Logic in the Latter Middle Ages.* Routledge, London, 1993.

[57] Axel Bühler. *Die Logik kognitiver Sätze.* Duncker and Humblot, Berlin, 1983.

[58] Elisabet Engdahl. *Constituent Questions: The Syntax and Semantics of Questions with Special Reference to Swedish.* D. Reidel Publishing Co, Dordrecht, 1986.

[59] R. Fagin, J.Y. Halpern, Y. Moses, and M.Y. Vardi. *Reasoning about Knowledge.* MIT Press, Cambridge, 1995.

[60] Dov Gabbay and John Woods, editors. *Handbook of the History and Philosophy of Logic.* North Holland (Elsevier), Amsterdam, 2003.

[61] Paul Gochet and P. Gribomont. Epistemic logic. In (60).

[62] Jaakko Hintikka. *Knowledge and Belief: An Introduction to the Logic of Two Notions.* Cornell University Press, Ithaca, New York, 1962.

[63] Jaakko Hintikka. *The Intentions of Intentionality.* D. Reidel, Dordrecht, 1975.

[64] Jaakko Hintikka. The semantics of questions and the questions of semantics. *Acta Philosophica Fennica*, 28(4), 1976.

[65] Jaakko Hintikka. Cartesian cogito, epistemic logic and neuroscience. *Synthese*, 83(1):199–157, 1990.

[66] Jaakko Hintikka and Ilpo Halonen. Semantics and pragmatics for why-questions. *The Journal of Philosophy*, 92:636–657, 1995.

[67] Jaakko Hintikka and Jack Kulas. *Anaphora and Definite Descriptions.* D. Reidel, Dordrecht, 1985.

[68] Jaakko Hintikka and Gabriel Sandu. The fallacies of the 'new theory of reference. *Synthese*, 104:245–283, 1995.

[69] Jaakko Hintikka and John Symons. Systems of visual identification in neuroscience: Lessons from epistemic logic. Forthcoming.

[70] Simo Knuuttila. *Modalities in Medieval Philosophy.* Routledge, 1993.

[71] Armin Laux and Heinrich Wansing, editors. *Knowledge and Belief in Philosophy and Artificial Intelligence.* Akademie-Verlag, Berlin, 1995.

[72] Wolfgang Lenzen. Recent work in epistemic logic. *Acta Philosophica Fennica*, 30(1), 1978. Societas Philosophica Fennica, Helsinki.

[73] Wolfgang Lenzen. Epistemologische Betrachtungen zu [s4, s5]. *Erkenntnis*, 14:33–56, 1979.

[74] Wolfgang Lenzen. *Glauben, Wissen und Wahrscheinlickkeit: Systeme der epistemische Logik.* Springer-Verlag, Berlin, 1980.

[75] François Lepage and Serge Lapierre. *Logique partielle et savoir: Essai de philosophie formelle.* Bellarmin Vrin, Montréal/Paris, 2000.

[76] J.-J.Ch. Meyer and W. van der Hoek. *Epistemic Logic for AI and Computer Science.* Cambridge University Press, Cambridge, 1995.

[77] Werner Stelzner. *Epistemische Logik.* Akademic-Verlag, Berlin, 1984.

[78] Wiebe van der Hoek. Systems for knowledge and belief. *Journal of Logic and Computation*, 3:173–195, 1993.

[79] G.H. von Wright. *An Essay in Modal Logic.* North Holland, Amsterdam, 1951.

[80] Timothy Williamson. *Knowledge and its Limits.* Oxford University Press, Oxford, 2000.

HANS ROTT

ECONOMICS AND ECONOMY IN THE THEORY OF BELIEF REVISION

1. INTRODUCTION

Plato laboured hard to characterize the difference between genuine knowledge and mere belief. He may be read as having claimed the knowledge is *justified true belief* (*Meno* 97e–98a, *Theaetetus* 201c–202d). This account became the standard analysis of knowledge for more than two millennia. Since knowledge entails belief on the standard account,[1] any attempt to fathom out the foundations of knowledge must include an analysis of belief. After Edmund Gettier (99) shook the standard account, many philosophers argued that the characteristic tripartite definition of knowledge needs to be supplemented by a fourth condition. One particular prominent avenue was to take the stability or indefeasibility of a belief under criticism as a necessary condition for it to qualify as knowledge – an idea that can also be traced back to Plato's *Meno*. This suggests that it is not only the set of current beliefs but also the potential development of the agent's beliefs that is relevant to knowledge.

Aristotle opened his *Metaphysics* with the statement that all men by nature desire to know (*Met.* 980a). How can this objective be pursued? If knowledge is (or implies) justified true belief then the agent has to check for justification, truth and belief. Ideally, from a first-person perspective, everything one believes appears to be justified, so this criterion is not helpful for the agent. Truth, on the other hand, is not transparent to an agent (it can only be judged from a third-person perspective). Again ideally, belief is transparent to the agent. As a matter of internal control, there is one thing that an agent can do in the pursuit of truth. Since knowledge entails truth and since contradictions cannot be true, the agent has to eliminate contradictions from his beliefs in order to avoid falsehoods.[2]

What is the role played by logic (deduction and induction) in the acquisition of knowledge? Deductive logic serves as a standard against which to measure whether potential belief sets are free of contradictions or not. Inductive reasoning always involves decisions as to which sentences to adopt. *Logic in a narrow sense* refers to formal models of deductive reasoning, axiomatic systems which should preferably come together with some semantic underpinning. *Logic in a wider sense* is the theory of good reasoning, providing us not only with the means to check candidate belief sets for consistency but also with a methodology for deciding which of the candidate belief sets to adopt. The choice of a belief set is based on *extralogical* considerations, but only if we refer to the narrow conception of logic. I will in this paper proceed on the assumption that logic does include rules that are relevant for processes of belief formation and transformation (which may be seen as a kind of inductive reasoning, see Spohn

V.F. Hendricks, K.F. Jørgensen and S.A. Pedersen (eds.), Knowledge Contributors, 57–86.

(135)). We shall see that we can clearly distinguish an idea of *economical* behaviour (behaviour dictated by considerations of *economy*) from *economic* behaviour (behaviour as recommended by *economics*). We will ask to what extent the two ideas have as a matter of historical fact become embodied in formal models for belief formation and transformation, and we will address the question to what extent they *should* be respected in these models.

In this paper, I want to have a look at the role that economic or economical considerations may play within logic broadly conceived. In order to do this, I make extensive use of material that is discussed in more technical detail in other publications of mine ((128)–(131)). While I hope that the present paper affords a convenient survey of previous work, it may unfortunately not be readily accessible to people without any prior knowledge of the belief revision literature. Such readers are invited to check with the literature to which I refer. The first thing to do for us now, however, is to get an idea of what economics and economy are all about.

2. WHAT IS ECONOMICS?

One way of finding out what a term means is to look at the science that is supposed to study it. For the word 'economic', this seems to be an easy task. We just have to look at what economics is about. Dictionaries define 'economics' as the scientific study of the production, distribution and consumption of goods, services and wealth, or more concretely, the study of the system of trade, industry, money etc. But we want to dig deeper. According to Francis Y. Edgeworth ((92), p. 16), "[t]he first principle of Economics is that every agent is actuated only by self-interest." This restriction to a completely selfish attitude has long been removed. The formal part of Edgeworth's idea, however, remains valid. In the words of Herbert Simon: "The rational man of economics is a maximiser, who will settle for nothing less than the best."[3] This still seems to be the dominant view, as is shown by a few more recent statements. Hausman (104) (Sections 1 and 2) gives the following summary of the dominant school in the 20th century:

> The main 'orthodox', 'neoclassical', or 'neo-Walrasian' school models economic outcomes as equilibria in which individuals have done as well for themselves as they could given their preferences and the constraints on their choices. ... Agents are rational in the sense that their choices are determined by their preferences, which are complete and transitive. ... contemporary theoretical economics is largely a theory of rational choice. This may seem surprising, since economics is supposed to be an explanatory and predictive science of the actual interactions among people rather than a normative discipline studying how people ought rationally to choose, but it is indeed a fact.

In another handbook article, Rosenberg (125) tells us about the "assumptions of the 'economic man': that all agents have complete and transitive cardinal or ordinal utility rankings or preference orders and that they always choose that available option which maximises their utility or preferences". Earlier the same author characterised economics as guided (or misguided) by an "extremal intentional research programme", (124).[4] And what is being maximised is utility. According to Broome (88), pp. 21–22: " 'utility' acquired the meaning: *the value of a function that represents a person's preferences.* ... The first principle of economics is ... utility theory, ... modern, axiomatic utility theory ... "

What is common to these very abstract formulations of the basic tenets of modern economics is that economic agents are viewed as having definite preferences, and that when choosing actions or commodities, they aim at satisfying their preferences as well as the circumstances allow. It is important to note that not just any kind of preference is considered to be appropriate. Preferences have to be transitive and complete (technically speaking, they must be *pre-ordering* or *weak orderings*), in order to be representable by a suitably chosen utility function. Ties in preferences are permitted, of course, but incomparabilities are ruled out.[5] With a little exaggeration, one can say that economics is based on (or even: is an elaboration of) the theory of rational choice. Here, *choice* is called *rational* or *coherent* if and only if it is representable by a preference relation, and a *preference relation* in turn is considered to be *rational* if and only if it is representable by a *utility function*.[6]

Economics, then, is about *rational* rather than the *actual* behaviour of individuals.[7] The laws of economics should not be expected to be empirically adequate, they are valid only as idealisations, or as norms. Economics is based on a formalised variant of common-place folk psychology with individual-level explanation of free agents. It is essential to the research program of economics proper that processes pertaining to whole societies or economies are to be explained by, or reduced to, the behaviour of egocentric, maximising agents.[8] Usually, it is assumed that comparability of preferences or aggregability of utilities across different individuals does not make sense. It is important, however, that the possibility of comparison and aggregation is taken for granted across different "attributes" or "criteria" of goods, as well as across different situations in which the same goods are available (in varying amounts). This is part of ordinal and expected utility theory, and I suspect that this may ultimately be the reason for the economists' insistence on a person's preferences being representable by a utility function.

In order to find out whether there is anything economic (referring to economics in this abstract standard sense) about belief revision, we will have to look for patterns of rational choice, i.e., choice that is maximising with respect to some underlying preferences, or more exactly, to some weak ordering which can in turn be represented by a utility function.

3. ACTING ECONOMICALLY, A SECOND VIEW: "INFORMATIONAL ECONOMY"

There is an alternative and perhaps more intuitive concept of "acting economically". In the English language, there is a division of labour between the adjectives "economic" and "economical". The former is closely tied to the noun "economics" and means either "of or referring to economics", and has "profitable", "remunerative" and "gainful" as potential synonyms. The adjective "economical", on the other hand, is closely tied to the noun "economy" and means essentially the same as "thrifty", "frugal" or "not wasteful". This particular difference of meanings turns out to be useful for our discussion.

The 1980s saw the development of a variety of logical models that explicitly addressed the problem of maintaining consistency in beliefs. The prototypical problem dealt with is the one when an agent meets with new information that contradicts what he has believed to be true, as, e.g., when a scientific theory is falsified by an experiment. I am referring to *belief revision theory*, which is also known as the *theory of theory change*.[9] The theory has been limited to some extent, because it stipulates that contradictions are always resolved in such a way that the new piece of information is accepted. However, this restriction seems to me of minor importance, one that does not invalidate the discussion below and that has recently been rectified anyway.[10]

It was often proclaimed that the particular way of choosing among consistent successor belief sets was guided by an economy principle. The process of belief revision is often thought to require *economical* behaviour rather than *economic* behaviour. This perspective was forcefully taken in Peter Gärdenfors's influential book *Knowledge in Flux* (97). A glance at the index of the book makes it immediately clear that the *criterion of informational economy* is employed to motivate the essential parts of the formal modellings of Gärdenfors and his collaborators Carlos Alchourrón and David Makinson. Gärdenfors refers to this criterion for the motivation of belief expansions (p. 49), belief revisions (pp. 53, 58) and belief contractions (p. 61).[11] Basically, the criterion is taken to be identical with the idea of *minimal change* (p. 53) and the *conservativity principle* (p. 67). According to Gärdenfors,

> The key idea is that, when we change our beliefs, we want to retain as much as possible of our old beliefs – information is in general not gratuitous, and unnecessary losses of information are therefore to be avoided. ((97), p. 49, similarly on pp. 16, 157)

Ever since the appearance of Gärdenfors's book, the criterion of informational economy has been taken to be a "hallmark" of the research paradigm created by Alchourrón, Gärdenfors and Makinson (henceforth, AGM).[12]

There is, however, reason for asking why exactly a rational person should be conservative. Gärdenfors's argument that information is not gratuitous does not seem to be sufficient, because information, even if costly, may be wrong, and even if it is correct, it may be misleading. Spelled out a little more explicitly, the argument for conservatism seems to be this:

You shouldn't give away what is valuable
What you have is valuable
———
You shouldn't give away what you have

The first premise is hardly controversial, it might even be called analytically true as a prescription of economic rationality.[13] The second premise, on the other hand, is much harder to justify. Its truth (or at least our feeling that it is true) may have evolutionary reasons – probably the human species would long have been extinct if too many of the sentences we accept as true were wrong. Therefore, it is at least likely that many of the sentences that we happen to hold true have some survival value.[14]

But the argument for conservatism is a far cry from waterproof. Problems are not hard to come by. Isn't it all too obvious that what we have is not always best? So why should we care to preserve it? It is true that we lose *information* or *content* when we give up some sentences of our belief set, but it is not clear whether we lose some *truths*, and no-one should object to losing falsities. Notice that there is a basic tension here between the economical and the economic precept for belief dynamics: The former tends to recommend leaving everything as it is, while the latter recommends striving for the best.

4. ECONOMIC AND ECONOMICAL CONSIDERATIONS IN BELIEF REVISION THEORY

In asking what is economic about belief change, we have to keep in mind two different aspects. Besides the choice-preference-utility line of thinking that we sketched in Section 2, we have found a second type of idea in the thrifty clinging to the sentences one has accepted. (Notice that thrift in itself does not play a prominent role in the science of economics.)

In the work of AGM, it is comparatively easy to recognise the criterion of informational economy at work in expansions of belief sets by sentences that do *not* contradict the prior belief set. In such cases, AGM recommend simply to add the new sentence to the prior beliefs and take the deductive closure of everything taken together.[15] However, as we shall see, there are no traces of this criterion for the belief-contravening case which, after all, is the case for which logical models of belief change have primarily been devised.

But Gärdenfors's argument for conservatism can be generalised. In my view, it is one of the most important philosophical insights of belief revision theory in the 1990s that *belief states* cannot be represented properly by *belief sets* only. Something else has to be added, namely, some structure that encodes how the agent is to revise his belief set in response to surprising information. Typically there is a mechanism exploiting some sort of selection function or preference relation.[16] Let us use a neutral name and call the structure exploited by the mechanism a *belief-revision guiding structure*.[17] It turns out that if the new information is inconsistent with the presently accepted belief set, it is impossible to apply the pure idea of informational economy on the level of sentences. However, the idea can be applied on the level of revision-guiding structures. This at the same time defines a form of conservatism that is usable for iterated belief change.

Fig. 1 gives a representation of the various senses that "economic" and "economical" can take in belief revision contexts. The branch at the left indicates the idea that economic agents may be conceived of as rational or coherent choosers. Though this has not been the principal motivation of belief revision models, we will later see that exactly this idea casts a long shadow in the realm of belief formation.[18] On the right-hand branch, we represent the idea of informational economy that has always been advertised as the prime driving force of belief revision theory. In the next four sections, we will trace a few important distinctions within the principle of informational economy, also known as principle of minimal change or conservatism. The principle of informational economy *as applied to sentences* tells us: "Don't give away your beliefs beyond necessity!" The principle of informational economy *as applied to revision-guiding structures* tells us: "Don't change your doxastic preferences beyond necessity!" These two maxims can further be distinguished as to whether they concern the belief-contravening case (the one for which belief revision models have primarily been invented) or only to the case where the new information is consistent with the agent's belief set.

Fig. 2 gives a different representation of the situation in terms of various dimensions of coherence. At the bottom there are six dots standing for options of belief base revision, where *belief bases* are sets of sentences that need not obey the static coherence constraint of logical closure. We will not be concerned with this approach in this paper,[19] but instead focus on methods of changing belief sets that are presumed to be logically closed – i.e., on the upper six dots. *Basic changes* represent options that recognise neither economical constraints of minimal change nor economic constraints concerning the rationality of choices. Moving from left to right in the lattice of the six dots adds economical constraints of minimal change, moving

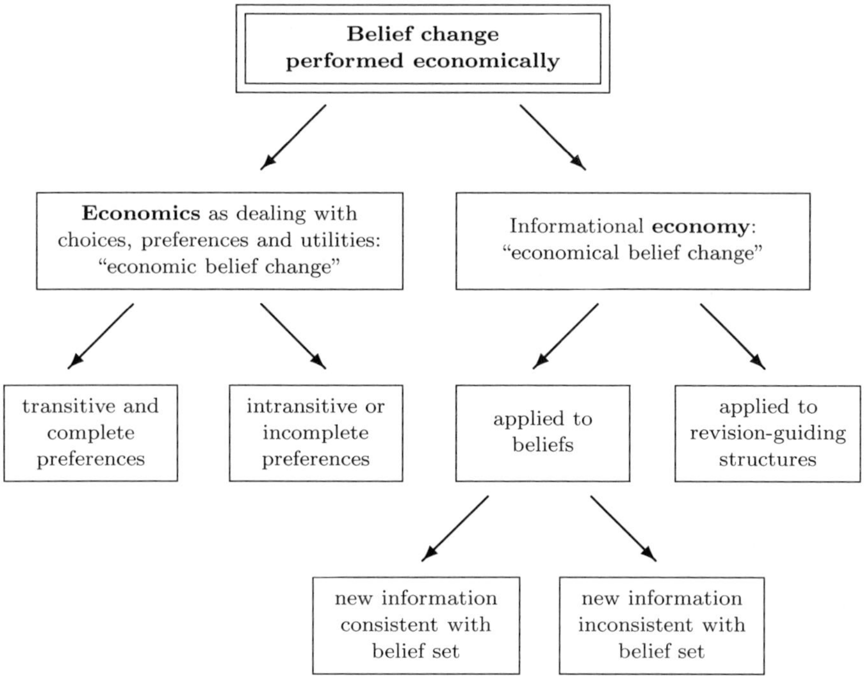

FIGURE 1. Belief change performed economically

downwards adds economic constraints on the rationality of choices. The label *c-conservative* denotes conservativity restricted to the case where the input is consistent with the current belief set, without a similar commitment for the belief-contravening case.

Before entering the systematic discussion, let us add a few historical remarks. As the talk of "dimensions" meant to suggest, it is possible to add to the basic form of belief revision elements of conservatism and elements of rational choice independently from one another. In their seminal work of the 1980s, AGM explored both pure conservatism with respect to sentences (so-called *maxichoice* contraction and revision functions) and completely unconstrained choices (the case where only AGM's six *basic* rationality postulates hold).[20] However, AGM rejected the idea of maxichoice functions as intuitively inadequate, and I think it is fair to say that the main elegance and force of their theories derives precisely from the *supplementary* postulates that go beyond the basic case. So what makes the work of AGM distinctive is, on the one hand, a rather strong concept of rational choice generated by transitive and connected preferences,

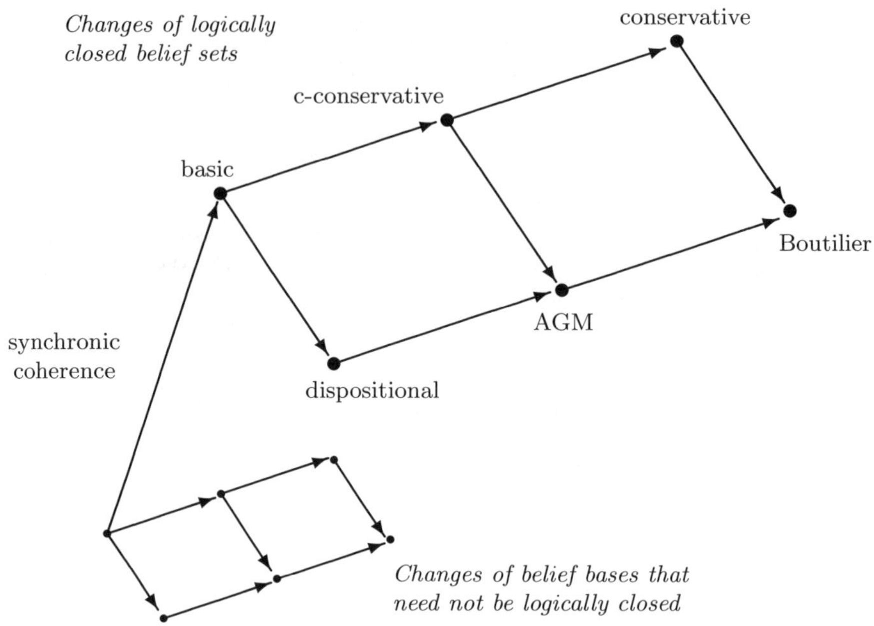

FIGURE 2. Three dimensions of coherence

and on the other hand a rather weak concept of conservatism. They provided for conservatism with respect to beliefs in the consistent case (where revision reduces to set-theoretic addition plus logical closure), but they provided neither for conservatism in the belief-contravening case nor for conservatism with respect to revision-guiding structures (they provided no change mechanisms for revision-guiding structures at all). Contrary to wide-spread folklore, AGM paid a lot more respect to ideas found in economics than to the idea of informational economy.

Systematic variations of the strength of the relevant ideas were investigated only in the 1990s. On the one hand, *weakenings* of AGM's strong presuppositions with respect to the rationalisability of choices are suggested by Lindström (111) and Rott ((126), (129)).[21] On the other hand, *strengthenings* of the very weak concept of conservatism in AGM are investigated by Boutilier ((86), (87)) and Rott (131), thus offering models for economical belief change. Interestingly, it has turned out that the most efficient way – and perhaps the only way – of implementing conservatism with respect to beliefs in the belief-contravening case is at the same time a form of conservatism with respect to revision-guiding structures. This variant of conservative belief revision has actually first been discussed as a particular strategy of extending the classical AGM model in order to equip it with means for performing iterated belief revisions. While Boutilier did that in a context that presupposes the full strength of AGM's requirements for rational choice, Rott lifts this restriction and shows that the conservative method can be brought to bear without any assumptions about the coherence of the choices involved.[22]

This little sketch of some developments in the belief change literature indicates that the concept of *economical* belief change is independent of the concept of *economic* belief change. In the sense specified, AGM belief revision (minus two axioms for revisions by inputs that are consistent with the prior belief set[23]) is not at all economical but, thanks to AGM's "supplementary" postulates, fully economic; the conservative approach investigated in (131) on the other hand is very economical, but not at all economic.

In the following sections, we recapitulate relevant parts of the actual development of belief revision theory, and then discuss the merits and problems of changing beliefs economically. I will first detail my reasons for claiming that conservatism with respect to *beliefs* has hardly been followed in classical AGM-style belief revision models, and that it is doubtful indeed whether it would be a good idea to follow it. Conservatism with respect to belief-revision guiding structures has been studied as a particular strategy for iterable belief change, but it has turned out that it should not be followed either. On the economics side, I briefly survey the (severe) constraints on rational choices which have been endorsed in classical AGM-style belief revision and its iterable extensions. Although the AGM postulates can be liberalised systematically according to one's wishes, I will finally argue that even modest economic postulates for belief change are problematic – just as problematic as even the fundamental constraints on rational choices are. We shall find that doxastic preferences appear to be context-dependent, a fact that gives rise in particular to a formidable problem sometimes labelled "the informational value of the menu".

5. INFORMATIONAL ECONOMY WITH RESPECT TO BELIEFS: WHAT HAS BEEN DONE?

In discussing informational economy with respect to beliefs, we keep on making two important idealisations: We stipulate that the set of sentences accepted by an agent be logically consistent and closed. This condition is, of course, wrong as a description of the set of sentences that a real agent would assent to when queried in an interview. However, if we consider a belief set to be the set of sentences that we *ascribe* to an agent from a third person perspective, or the set of sentences that the agent is *committed to*, then the ideas of consistency and closure lose their implausible appearance. Another simplification we make is that when a belief set is revised in response to some new piece of information, the revision process successfully incorporates the new information, so that it is in fact an element of the revised belief set. This is not always sound strategy in realistic belief change situations, but I think we can safely disregard the complications for the discussion to follow. So let us call a consistent and logically closed belief set that includes a new piece of information φ a *candidate revision* of a belief set B by φ. A (candidate) revision of B by φ is called *belief-contravening*, if φ is inconsistent with B.

Let us discuss two attempts at capturing the idea of informational economy on the level of beliefs:

(1) When accepting a new piece of information, an agent should aim at a minimal change of his old belief set.
(2) If there are different ways of effecting the belief revision, the agent should give up those sentences that are least entrenched.

These two maxims have frequently been appealed to as the principal motivation for logical models of belief change. However, in their most straightforward readings, they are a caricature of what has really been done in the development of the standard models of belief revision. I have argued for this in (128), and briefly recall the results presented in that paper.

As regards maxim (1), one can show that no two distinct belief-contravening candidate revisions of a consistent and logically closed belief set by a sentence φ can be set-theoretically compared in terms of the sets of sentences on which they differ with the prior belief set.

For the discussion of maxim (2), we need a little bit of terminological preparation. A sentence φ is *more entrenched* in a belief set than another sentence ψ if and only if the agent holds on to φ and gives up ψ upon learning that (it may be the case that) not both φ and ψ are true.[24] A new piece of information φ is called *moderately surprising* if $\neg\varphi$ is a non-minimal element of the prior belief set with respect to epistemic entrenchment. Let us call a revision by φ *amnesic* if the revised belief set consists of nothing else but $Cn(\varphi)$ (where Cn is some ordinary well-behaved Tarskian logic); otherwise we call the revision *anamnestic*. Now suppose we want to revise a belief set by a sentence φ and identify two elements of the initial belief set that non-redundantly entail $\neg\varphi$. Then it may well happen, when performing an ordinary AGM-style revision by φ, that the agent removes the *more* entrenched and retains the *less* entrenched sentence. An instance of such a situation can indeed *always* be identified when φ is moderately surprising and the revision by φ is anamnestic. Thus neither of the two maxims that have always belonged to the core rhetoric about AGM-style belief change models is actually obeyed in these very models. This observation may seem too baffling at first sight, but it has turned out to be rather robust. We briefly present four objections and give rejoinders to each of them. For a more extensive treatment, the reader is referred to (128).

First, one may hold that it is not belief *revision*, but belief *contraction* that is the right kind of operation to be judged in terms of minimal change. As was mentioned above, AGM first thought of focussing on so-called "maxichoice contractions", but these were immediately seen to yield counterintuitive consequences.[25] On a more general level, the postulate of "Recovery" says that inserting back again a belief that had just been withdrawn should recover the whole of the original theory. Recovery was explicitly introduced as a codification of the idea of minimal change. However, it fulfils this function only partially; its effects are destroyed if the contraction is part of a revision using the so-called Levi identity; and, most importantly, the recovery condition has been forcefully and severely criticized on intuitive grounds by many authors (see (103), Section 2.3).

Second, the well-known representation theorems of AGM (and their possible-worlds reinterpretation by Grove) seem to show that "rational" belief contraction and revision operations can be represented as being generated by a minimization process with respect to some underlying preference relation. However, the interpretation of such a preference relation is completely open (it might, for instance, mean remoteness rather than closeness); the minimization process is compromised by overriding principles of preference and indifference;[26] and finally, since the AGM postulates do not encode any notion of minimal change in the belief-contravening case, we should not even expect to find substantial traces of this idea in a semantics that can be proved adequate for the AGM axiomatization.

Third, it may be pointed out that we need not aim at the preservation of all of our old beliefs, but only of those that are true. So even if the idea of informational economy is not effective when applied to the whole of the prior belief set, it may still do good work if we restrict our attention to the beliefs that we really treasure, viz., the true beliefs. Unfortunately, however, that move does not help either, since essentially the same results can be reproduced for the conservation of true beliefs as for the conservation of beliefs *tout court*: No two belief-contravening candidate revisions of a consistent belief set that contain different sets of true beliefs can be set-theoretically compared in terms of the *true* beliefs on which they differ with the prior belief set.

A fourth route to saving the idea of minimal change can be taken by applying the idea of informational economy not to belief sets, but to richer representations of doxastic states: to belief-change dispositions, or equivalently, to structures suitable for guiding (iterated) belief revision. This is a point that we will address presently in some detail. Before doing that, however, we have a look at potential norms for belief change.

6. INFORMATIONAL ECONOMY WITH RESPECT TO BELIEFS: WHAT SHOULD BE DONE?

First of all, we have to be aware of the fact that the demand for informational economy conflicts with other desiderata. For instance, it competes with the *synchronic* or *static coherence* constraints of *logical consistency* and *closure*. If we find ourselves caught in an inconsistency, we should give up *something* and we typically have to give up not only a single culprit sentence, but also many sentences that are deductively related with the latter. This is because we want to maintain the logical closure of our belief sets. But of course, a change that is minimal subject to the constraints of consistency and closure will in general be a bigger change than one that is minimal when no constraints are to be respected. Conservativity may itself be viewed as a criterion of *diachronic* or *dynamic coherence*, (127). There are more concepts of coherence that we will have reason to consider below, viz., *dispositional coherence* and *temporal coherence*. At this juncture it is not at all clear whether the latter two concepts give rise to more requirements that compete with the requirement of informational economy.

Secondly, it is instructive to contrast the ideas that are advocated in the logical literature on belief revision with ideas recommended by philosophers of science who usually think of belief change as arising in the (r)evolution of scientific theories or research programmes. For the latter point of view, it may suffice here to rely on the elementary but thought-provoking little book *The Web of Belief* by Quine and Ullian (122). In Fig. 3, the 'virtues' of hypotheses that these authors mention are contrasted with the criteria advocated in the belief revision literature (the terms in the figure will be explained in due course). What we can immediately see from Fig. 3 is that informational economy is the only criterion that is endorsed both by Quine and Ullian and the logical modellings of belief revision. A moment's thought makes it clear that at least some of the virtues listed here compete with one another. Simplicity often requires deviations from informational economy, modesty conflicts with refutability. We don't have to commit ourselves to one or the other set of criteria here, nor do we need to specify some ranking or weighting of the criteria. It is enough at this juncture to note that an account of how to integrate various criteria of *theory choice* (the perspective dominant in the philosophy of science) and *theory change* (the main perspective of philosophical logic) is badly needed, but has never been offered. There is no obvious reason for according informational economy a privileged status among the many contenders that we have identified. It seems fair to say that informational economy can only claim a very restricted normative force.

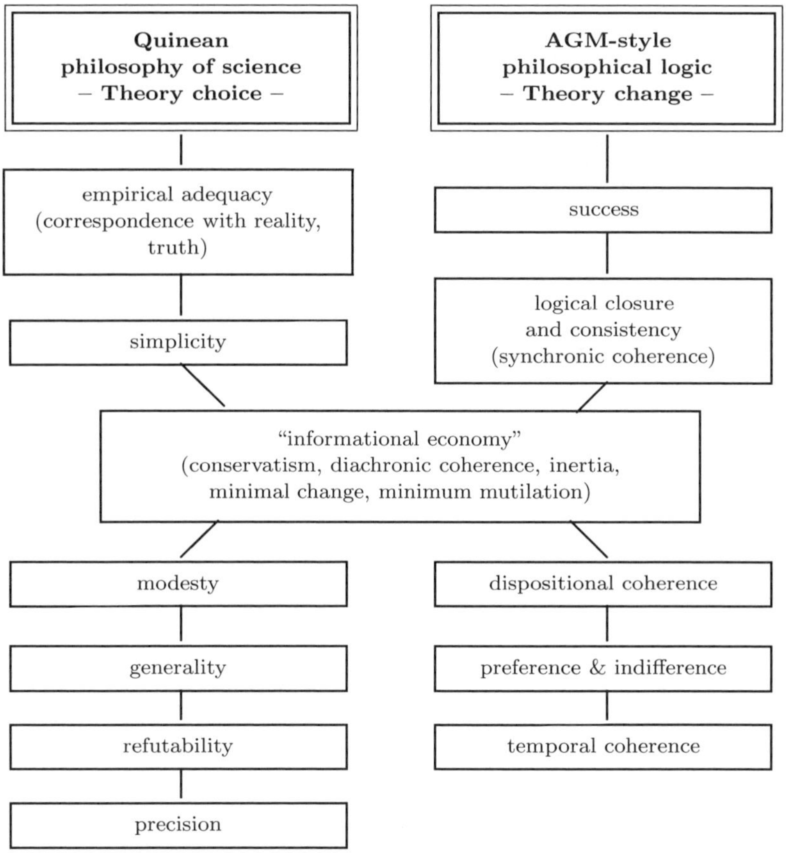

FIGURE 3. Criteria for theory choice and theory change

7. CONSERVATISM WITH RESPECT TO BELIEF-REVISION GUIDING STRUCTURES: WHAT HAS BEEN DONE?

We now turn to a second interpretation of the idea that agents should aim at preserving what they have. The propositional content encoded in sentences of the agent's language is not the only kind of information that may be deemed valuable. One may also be interested in preserving the non-propositional information encoded in belief-revision guiding structures, i.e., in richer representations of belief states. Two such representations that have gained some currency in the literature are two kinds of doxastic *preference relations* to which we shall now turn.

First, we consider *plausibility orderings* $\preceq$ of the set W of possible worlds, with the understanding that $u \preceq v$ means that u is *at least as* *plausible* as v in the belief state represented by $\preceq$.[27] Given such an ordering $\preceq$, the core set $min_{\preceq} W = \{u \in W : \text{there is no } v \in W \text{ such that } v \prec u\}$ of the $\preceq$-minimal worlds contains exactly those worlds that are consistent with the current belief set B, i.e., those that could be the real world given what the agent believes. The ordering of the remaining worlds reflects their relative distance from this core set. Belief revision prompted by a new piece of information φ then proceeds by manipulating the ordering of worlds in such a way that all the minimal worlds in the revised ordering $\preceq^*_\varphi$ satisfy φ. This constraint is mild and leaves a lot of leeway for the exact specification of a coherent revision mechanism. The most *conservative* or *economical* way of changing the plausibility ordering on W that respects the constraint was first defined and investigated in Boutilier ((86), (87)):

$$u \preceq^*_\varphi v \text{ iff } \begin{cases} u \in min_{\preceq}[\varphi] & \text{or} \\ v \notin min_{\preceq}[\varphi] \text{ and } u \preceq v & \end{cases}$$

Here $[\varphi]$ denotes the set of all possible worlds satisfying φ. Given the basic constraint that the set $min_{\preceq^*_\varphi} W$ of worlds defining the revised belief set $B{*}\varphi$ should be identical with the set $min_{\preceq}[\varphi]$,[28] the posterior ordering $\preceq^*_\varphi$ preserves as much of the prior ordering $\preceq$ as possible.[29]

Another way of richly representing belief states consists in *entrenchment orderings* $\leq$ of the set L of sentences (phrased in a given language), with the understanding that $\varphi \leq \psi$ means that sentence ψ is *at least as entrenched as* sentence φ in the belief state represented by $\leq$ (as already indicated in Section 5). Given an entrenchment ordering $\leq$, the set $min_{\leq} L = \{\varphi \in L : \text{there is no } \psi \in L \text{ such that } \psi < \varphi\}$ of sentences that are minimally entrenched contain exactly the agent's non-beliefs, i.e., the complement of his belief set B. The ordering of the sentences within B reflects how firmly they are endorsed by the agent, the relative tenacity with which he is determined to cling to his beliefs. In this model, belief revision prompted by a new piece of information φ proceeds by manipulating the ordering of sentences in such a way that φ is not minimally entrenched under the revised ordering $\leq^*_\varphi$. A constraint that follows from basic AGM-theory is that the revised belief set $B{*}\varphi = L - min_{\leq^*_\varphi} L$ should equal the set $\{\psi \in L : \neg\varphi < \varphi \rightarrow \psi\}$.[30] Again, this constraint is mild and leaves a lot of leeway for the exact specification of the appropriate revision mechanism. The most *conservative* or *economical* way of changing the entrenchment ordering on L that respects the constraint is investigated in Rott (131):

$$\psi \leq^*_\varphi \chi \text{ iff } \begin{cases} \psi \notin B * \varphi & \text{or} \\ \chi \in B * \varphi \text{ and } \psi \leq \chi & \end{cases}$$

$$\text{iff } \begin{cases} \varphi \rightarrow \psi \leq \neg\varphi & \text{or} \\ \neg\varphi < \varphi \rightarrow \chi \text{ and } \psi \leq \chi & \end{cases}$$

Given the above-mentioned constraint, this ordering $\leq^*_\varphi$ preserves as much of the prior entrenchment ordering $\leq$ as possible. To see this, we look at the pairs for which $\leq^*_\varphi$ reverses the ordering of $\leq$. When do we have $\psi \leq \chi$ but not $\psi \leq^*_\varphi \chi$? Inspection of the definition shows that this can only happen if ψ is in, but χ is not in $B * \varphi$, and this deviation is well motivated by the fact that non-beliefs can never be as entrenched as beliefs. Conversely, when do we have $\psi \leq^*_\varphi \chi$ but not $\psi \leq \chi$? Inspecting the definition once more, we find that this can only happen if ψ is not in $B{*}\varphi$, and the same motivation applies: non-beliefs are the least entrenched sentences. We see that there is no unforced deviation of $\leq^*_\varphi$ from $\leq$. This is why this recipe defines the most *conservative* or *economical* way of changing an entrenchment ordering (cf. (131)).[31]

It has turned out (130) that the account based on entrenchment orderings is essentially a generalisation of the possible worlds account proposed by Boutilier. In the specific context of the full comparability assumption made by Boutilier, the methods are equivalent. Both methods satisfy an axiom for iterated belief revision that characterises conservative revisions of richer representations of belief states. It is sufficient to deal with the case of two subsequent revisions. Any finite number of further revisions can easily be constructed from this case by induction. As is shown in (86) and (87) and in a more general setting in (131), a repeated conservative change of B first by a sentence φ and then by a second sentence ψ leads to the same result as a single conservative revision of B by ψ, if ψ is inconsistent with the result of the revision of B by φ. Taken together with basic AGM theory, this amounts to the following recipe for iterated belief revision:

$$(B * \varphi) * \psi \;=\; \begin{cases} (B * \varphi) + \psi & \text{if } \neg\psi \notin B * \varphi \\ B * \psi & \text{if } \neg\psi \in B * \varphi \end{cases}$$

Why would we want to call this recipe "conservative"? Because the upper case is just AGM's c-conservativity generalised to the iterated case, and the lower line suggests that if ψ cannot be accommodated consistently, the way of handling it in the revised belief set $B * \varphi$ is just the same as it was in the original belief set B. Loosely speaking, the structure of the old belief set is stronger than the new piece of evidence φ, making it seem as if the agent had never learnt about φ.[32]

8. CONSERVATISM WITH RESPECT TO BELIEF-REVISION GUIDING STRUCTURES: WHAT SHOULD BE DONE?

Almost immediately after Boutilier had suggested conservative belief revision as a natural extension of the AGM model, Darwiche and Pearl ((89), (90)) discovered that the behaviour defined by this model is queer. They gave the following example. A person who we may for the sake of argument take to be in a state of complete ignorance observes an animal that she takes to be a bird (b). As the animal comes closer, the person perceives that the animal is red (r). A few moments later, she realises (perhaps informed by an ornithologist) that the animal is not a bird after all ($\neg b$). If we use Boutilier's method of conservative belief revision, the result of these three subsequent revisions is $Cn(\emptyset) * b * r * \neg b = Cn(\neg b)$.

Darwiche and Pearl rightly argue that this is counterintuitive. Why "forget" the colour of the animal just because it turns out that it has misclassified as a bird? In more general terms, it can be shown that this model is *temporally incoherent*. The AGM-postulate of "success" for revisions says that the most recent piece of information should always be included in the revised belief set. Thus, at the moment of receipt a piece of information is being treated as the most important one. But this privilege is immediately lost when another, new piece of information happens to come in. To see this, let φ, ψ and χ stand for sentences that are pairwise consistent, but jointly inconsistent. Then iterated conservative change of the trivial belief set $Cn(\emptyset)$ first by φ, then by ψ and finally by χ results in the belief set

$$Cn(\emptyset) * \varphi * \psi * \chi = Cn(\varphi, \chi)$$

The first and the last piece of information are stronger than the one that comes in between. Conservatism with respect to revision-guiding structures thus has unacceptable consequences when applied as a method for iterated belief revision. It violates the requirement that a good method of belief revision be *temporally coherent*, i.e., coherent in its attitude towards the value of the recency of information.

Both AGM's and Boutilier's models assume that the orderings of worlds or sentences involved are complete pre-orderings, i.e., that all worlds and all sentences are comparable as regards their plausibility or entrenchment, respectively. It might be suspected that the problem of conservative revision is (at least in part) due to the strong requirements of "dispositional coherence" inherent in the AGM model upon which Boutilier's model is built. However, the unwelcome effects of temporal incoherence remain present in exactly the same way even if *all* of the dispositional requirements of the AGM model are dropped, (131).

As long as one decides invariably to accept new information (i.e., to regard the last piece of information as the most important one), the only coherent attitude towards the recency of information is to regard the second-last piece of information as the second-most important one, and so on. Instead of $Cn(\varphi, \chi)$ as above, the desired result would thus be

$$Cn(\emptyset) * \varphi * \psi * \chi = Cn(\psi, \chi)$$

There is an alternative model of iterated belief revision that yields precisely this result. This less conservative, more *moderate* model has been mentioned and used quite a number of times in the literature, without there being a canonical paper where the model was first endorsed.[33] I take the opportunity to give definitions paralleling those that characterise conservative belief change. Like the latter definitions, the definitions of moderate belief change make good sense also for the case when dispositional coherence is not presupposed.

Using the representation of belief states by means of orderings between models, the moderate way of changing such states is this:

$$u \preceq^*_\varphi v \text{ iff } \begin{cases} u \in [\varphi] \text{ and } v \notin [\varphi] & \text{or} \\ (u \in [\varphi] \text{ or } v \notin [\varphi]) \text{ and } u \preceq v \end{cases}$$

Since here the whole $[\varphi]$-area (not just the set $\min_\preceq[\varphi]$) is shifted, this definition is intuitively less conservative than Boutilier's model. However, it can be shown that if Boutilier's method is stripped of dispositional coherence (of its *economical* features), it ceases to be conservative (or *economic*) in a sense that can be given a precise mathematical definition.[34]

Using the representation of belief states by means of entrenchment orderings, the moderate way of revising one's belief state can be represented thus:

$$\psi \leq^*_\varphi \chi \text{ iff } \begin{cases} \psi \wedge \chi \notin Cn(\varphi) \text{ and } \varphi \rightarrow \psi \leq \varphi \rightarrow \chi & \text{or} \\ \psi \wedge \chi \in Cn(\varphi) \text{ and } \psi \leq \chi \end{cases}$$

Let us finally have a look at the properties of the iterated revision functions that result from this approach. The moderate idea can be shown to amount to the following recipe:

$$(B * \varphi) * \psi = \begin{cases} B * (\varphi \wedge \psi) & \text{if } \neg\psi \notin Cn(\varphi) \\ B * \psi & \text{if } \neg\psi \in Cn(\varphi) \end{cases}$$

In marked contrast to conservative belief change, the case distinction for moderate belief change tests the consistency of ψ with respect to the previous input sentence φ, and not with respect to the intermediate belief set $B*\varphi$ (which includes φ). That the most recent piece of information still is the preferred one is evident from the lower line of this definition. Otherwise, however, the method of moderate revision goes some way towards treating φ and ψ symmetrically. Philosophically, this seems to be on the right track, since here the two pieces of evidence are grouped together and distinguished from the initial theory B (which may now be regarded as playing the role of a general "background theory"). In conservative belief change the first piece of evidence, φ, is merged with B, and only after the merging is done, the second piece of evidence, ψ, gets processed. At this second stage, there is no reliable way of knowing that φ had been the same kind of thing as ψ.

Having gone thus far, it is natural to argue in favour of a *perfectly* symmetrical treatment of the pieces of evidence and thus call in question the primacy of the most recent piece of information as expressed by AGM's success postulate and respected by all the methods we have been discussing so far. Being altogether indifferent towards the time at which a certain piece of information is received is certainly a form of temporal coherence, too. This is an interesting topic for further research, but it cannot be dealt with here.

We now leave the field of "economical reasoning" and turn to "economic reasoning", i.e., to the left branch of Fig. 1 which refers us to the realm of choices, preferences and utilities.

9. RATIONAL CHOICES AND LOGICAL PROPERTIES: WHAT HAS BEEN DONE?

As pointed out above, the classical AGM model of belief revision embodies a strong idea of dispositional coherence. More precisely, the agent's dispositions to change his belief set in potential revisions are reflected in choice functions that can be rationalised by a complete pre-ordering. That is, the agent acts *as if* he was a maximiser with respect to such an ordering. That the ordering is complete means that all possible worlds are presumed to be comparable with each other in terms of plausibility (AGM (82), Grove (101)), and all sentences are presumed to be comparable with each other in terms of entrenchment (Gärdenfors and Makinson (98)). These facts find expression in the seventh and eighth postulates of AGM which constrain the agent's disposition to change his belief set: ($*7$) which is sometimes called *Disjunction in the premises* and ($*8$) which is sometimes called *Rational monotonicity*.

So far we have been discussing preference relations between worlds and sentences. We will now adopt a related, but more general approach using choice functions. Preferences are used in the selection of elements from a given 'menu' of options open to the agent, and the economic man will usually select those that are 'best' according to his preferences. In the converse direction, suppose that we have given a certain choice function that selects, for each potential menu, the elements that are 'best' in some unspecified sense. It is a sensible question to ask whether there exists a preference relation $\leq$ such that the choices as determined by the choice function can be rationalised as picking the best elements according to $\leq$. It is an important fact that not just any choice function can be rationalised in this way, and in it is in this sense that the approach using choice functions is more general than the approach based on preference maximisation. The question is how to characterise, in purely choice-theoretic terms those choice functions that are rationalizable by some preference relation.

Rott ((129), Chapter 7) describes how exactly one can use semantic choice functions (for the selection of most plausible worlds) and syntactic choice functions (for the selection of least entrenched sentences) in the construction of belief revisions, and also how postulates for belief revision correspond to rationality requirements for semantic and syntactic choice functions.[35]

Table 1 shows how a number of postulates for belief revision correspond to requirements for the choice functions that govern the selection of most plausible models or the selection of least entrenched sentences. In the table, σ refers to a choice functions which selects for any menu S the (typically non-empty) choice set $\sigma(S)$ of 'best' elements of S.

POSTULATES FOR REVISIONS		POSTULATES FOR CHOICES	
(∗7c)	If $\psi \in B * \varphi$, then $B * (\varphi \wedge \psi) \subseteq B * \varphi$		If $S \subseteq S'$ and $\sigma(S') \subseteq S$, then $\sigma(S') \subseteq \sigma(S)$
(∗7) (∗7′)	$(B*\varphi) \cap (B*\psi) \subseteq B*(\varphi \vee \psi)$ $B * (\varphi \wedge \psi) \subseteq (B * \varphi) + \psi$	(α)	If $S \subseteq S'$, then $S \cap \sigma(S') \subseteq \sigma(S)$
(∗8c)	If $\psi \in B * \varphi$, then $B * \varphi \subseteq B* (\varphi \wedge \psi)$	(Aiz)	If $S \subseteq S'$ and $\sigma(S') \subseteq S$, then $\sigma(S) \subseteq \sigma(S')$
(∗8)	If $\neg\psi \notin B * \varphi$, then $(B * \varphi) + \psi \subseteq B * (\varphi \wedge \psi)$	(β^+)	If $S \subseteq S'$ and $\gamma(S') \cap S \neq \emptyset$, then $\sigma(S) \subseteq \sigma(S')$
(∗8d)	$B*(\varphi \vee \psi) \subseteq (B*\varphi) \cup (B*\psi)$		If $x \in \sigma(S)$ and $y \in \sigma(S')$, then $x \in \sigma(S \cup S')$ or $y \in \sigma(S \cup S')$
(∗8wd)	$B * (\varphi \vee \psi) \subseteq (B * \varphi) + \psi \cup (B * \psi) + \varphi$	(γ)	$\sigma(S) \cap \sigma(S') \subseteq \sigma(S \cup S')$ for syntactic choices
(∗8vwd)	$B * (\varphi \vee \psi) \subseteq Cn((B * \varphi) \cup (B * \psi))$	(γ)	$\sigma(S) \cap \sigma(S') \subseteq \sigma(S \cup S')$ for semantic choices
(∗8n)	$B * \varphi \subseteq B * (\varphi \wedge \psi) \cup B * (\varphi \wedge \neg\psi)$		If $S \cap S' = \emptyset$, then $\sigma(S) \subseteq \sigma(S \cup S')$ or $\sigma(S') \subseteq \sigma(S \cup S')$ for semantic choices If $S \cap S' \subseteq Cn(\emptyset)$, then $\sigma(S) \subseteq \sigma(S \cup S')$ or $\sigma(S') \subseteq \sigma(S \cup S')$ for syntactic choices
(∗8m)	$B * \varphi \subseteq B * (\varphi \wedge \psi)$		If $S \subseteq S'$, then $\sigma(S) \subseteq \sigma(S')$

TABLE 1. Correspondences between revisions and choices

(∗7) and (∗8) have turned out to correspond to conditions on semantic or syntactic choice functions known as *Sen's Properties* α and β^+, which in effect require that the revision function be rationalizable by a complete and transitive preference relation.

In order to illustrate how central the conditions α and β^+ are, we have a look at a number of equivalent conditions:

Observation. The following conditions are all equivalent.

(i) Sen's properties α and β^+ taken together.

(ii) If $S \subseteq S'$ and $\sigma(S') \cap S \neq \emptyset$, then $\sigma(S') \cap S = \sigma(S)$.
('*Arrow's axiom*'; see (114), p. 153, and (136), p. 25; used for the semantics of counterfactuals in (109), p. 58)

(iii) Either $\sigma(S \cup S') = \sigma(S)$ or $\sigma(S \cup S') = \sigma(S')$ or $\sigma(S \cup S') = \sigma(S) \cup \sigma(S')$.
(*'Ventilation'*; used for deontic logic in (81), p. 71, and for a logical reconstruction of linguistic optimality theory in (85), pp. 159–160)

(iv) If $S \cap S' \neq \emptyset$, then either $\sigma(S \cup S') = \sigma(S)$ or $\sigma(S \cup S') = \sigma(S')$ or $\sigma(S \cup S') = \sigma(S) \cup \sigma(S')$.
(*'Restricted Ventilation'*)

Assuming that the domain of σ is closed under finite unions and differences, the proof of this observation is straightforward. I take it that the multiplicity of conditions that have been used by researchers in different context testifies to the importance of these conditions, or to the representability in terms of a complete and transitive relation.

Many concrete systems of belief revision, however, do not satisfy ($*7$) and ($*8$) – a fact that shows that these AGM axioms are very strong. Knowing this, it is reassuring to find that one can draw on the rich resources of the theory of rational choice in order to introduce appropriate weakenings of the belief revision postulates. Both Property α and Property β^+ can be weakened in various interesting and reasonable ways, some of which are represented in the table. Postulate ($*7$c) is a weakening of ($*7$) that corresponds to the condition *Cut* in non-monotonic reasoning; the parallel weakening of Property α does not seem to play any significant role in the theory of rational choice. The weakening ($*8$c) of ($*8$) corresponds to the condition of *cumulative monotonicity* in non-monotonic reasoning; the parallel weakening of Property β^+ is known as *Aizerman's axiom* in the theory of rational choice (see (114)). Postulates ($*8$d), ($*8$wd) and ($*8$vwd) are known as variants of *Disjunctive rationality*. The latter two conditions have a well-established counterpart in the theory of choice, viz., Sen's *Property* γ. Postulate ($*8$n) is known as *negation rationality* in non-monotonic reasoning.

The theory of rational choice has turned out to be a powerful instrument suitable for analysing and constructing revision operations that are much more flexible than the original AGM ones. Seen from this perspective, belief revision theory can indeed be interpreted as being based on economical principles. We are now going, however, to cast a shadow over this neat picture.

10. RATIONAL CHOICES AND LOGICAL PROPERTIES: WHAT SHOULD BE DONE?

Almost from its beginning the classical theory of rational choice has been subjected to serious criticism. In this section I will present an argument to the effect that a fundamental problem for the theory of rational choice transfers directly to belief revision theories.

Consider the following example. A well-known philosophy department has announced a position in metaphysics. Among the applicants for the job there are a few persons we happen to know. First, there is Amanda Anderson, a young but already distinguished, excellent metaphysician. Second, we have Bernice Becker, who is also definitely very good, though not quite as accomplished in metaphysics as Anderson. Becker has also done some substantial research in logic. A third applicant is Carlos Cortez. He has a comparatively slim record in metaphysics, but he is widely recognised as one of the most brilliant logicians of his generation.

Suppose that our initial set of beliefs and expectations about the case includes that neither Anderson nor Becker nor Cortez will get the job (say, because we think that Derek Davidson, an outstanding metaphysician, is the obvious candidate who everyone expects to be appointed anyway). Let us also be clear about the fact that there is only one job available.

Consider now three hypothetical scenarios, each of which describes a *potential* development of the selection procedure (the scenarios do *not* describe a sequence of stages of the procedure). In each of these alternative scenarios we are genuinely taken by surprise, because we learn that one of the candidates we had believed to be losing will be offered the position. To make things shorter, we introduce some abbreviations. Let the letters a, b and c stand for the statements that Anderson, Becker and Cortez, respectively, will be offered the position.

Scenario 1. The dean tells us in confidence that it has been decided that either Anderson or Becker will be appointed.[36] This message comes down to supplying us with the premise $a \vee b$. Given this premise, we conclude that Anderson, being the better metaphysician, will get the job. We also infer that the other candidates will return empty-handed.

Scenario 2. This is a very unexpected scenario in which we are told by the dean that Cortez is actually the only serious candidate left in the competition. Fortunately, there is no need to invest a lot of thinking here. We accept c in this case.

Scenario 3. In this scenario the dean tells us that it has been decided that either Anderson or Becker or Cortez will get the job, thus supplying us with the premise $a \vee b \vee c$. This piece of information triggers off a rather subtle line of reasoning. Knowing that Cortez is a splendid logician, but that he can hardly be regarded as a metaphysician, we realise that competence in logic is considered to be a non-negligible asset by the selection committee. Still we keep on believing that Cortez will not make it, because his credentials in metaphysics are just too weak. Since, however, logic appears to contribute positively to a candidate's profile, we conclude that Becker, and not Anderson, will get the job.

This qualitative description should do for our purposes, but for readers who prefer more precision, the following story may help. The selection committee has decided to assign points to evaluate the candidates' work.

Anderson scores 97 out of 100 in metaphysics, but as she has done no logic whatsoever, she scores 0 here. Becker scores 92 in metaphysics and a respectable 50 in logic. Cortez scores only 40 in metaphysics, but boasts of 99 in logic. In scenario 1, we take it that metaphysics is the only desideratum, so clearly Anderson must be the winner. Scenario 2 is trivial. In scenario 3, we gather that, rather unexpectedly, logic matters. As can easily be verified, any weight we attach to logic between $^1/_{10}$ and $^1/_2$ (with metaphysics taking the rest) will see Becker end up in front of both Anderson and Cortez.

Let us now summarise our conclusions from the various premises that the dean supplies us with. Our initial belief set B contains $\neg a$, $\neg b$ and $\neg c$ among other things. In scenario 1, the new piece of information $a \vee b$ leads us to accept a and $\neg b$ (along with $\neg c$). In scenario 2, accepting c simply makes us retain $\neg a$ and $\neg b$. In scenario 3, the new piece of information $a \vee b \vee c$ leads us to accept that $\neg a$ and b. We can now show that this situation refutes some of the basic logical principles of "economic" belief revision.

First, the example shows that Disjunction in the premises, $(*7)$, does not hold. Take $(*7)$ and substitute $a \vee b$ for φ and c for ψ. Then notice that $\neg b$ is believed if the input is $a \vee b$, and also if the input is c. But $\neg b$ is not believed if the input is $a \vee b \vee c$. Thus the revised belief set $B * (a \vee b \vee c)$ does not include what is common to $B * (a \vee b)$ and $B * c$, and $(*7)$ is violated.

Secondly, we find that the situation does not conform to the weakened monotonicity postulate $(*8c)$. Take $(*8c)$ and substitute $a \vee b \vee c$ for φ and $a \vee b$ for ψ. Even though we believe that $a \vee b$ is true if we are given the information $a \vee b \vee c$, it is not the case that everything believed on the basis of the latter is also believed on the basis of $(a \vee b \vee c) \wedge (a \vee b)$ which is equivalent with $a \vee b$. Sentences $\neg a$ and b are counterexamples. Thus the revised belief set $B * (a \vee b \vee c)$ is not a subset of the belief set $B * ((a \vee b \vee c) \wedge (a \vee b)) = B * (a \vee b)$, and $(*8c)$ is violated. *A fortiori*, $(*8)$ is violated as well.

What do these problems derive from? We said that principles of belief revision can be systematically interpreted in terms of rational choice. On this interpretation, Disjunction in the premises, $(*7)$, turns out to be an instantiation of one of the most fundamental conditions – perhaps *the* most fundamental condition – of the theory of rational choice: Sen's Property α. This condition, also called *Independence of Irrelevant Alternatives* or *Chernoff property*, says that any element which is optimal in a certain menu remains an optimal element after some other elements have been cancelled from the menu. The three scenarios in our example are modelled after well-known choice situations in which Property α is violated – cases that also happen to infringe Aizerman's axiom. Both properties may fail to be satisfied if the very 'menu' from which the agent is invited to choose carries important information. This phenomenon which Sen calls the 'epistemic value' or the 'epistemic relevance of the menu'[37] suggests that the context of choice has a decisive influence upon the shape of the preference relation of the agent – an idea strongly opposed to the idea of context-independent preferences that underlies the classical theory of rational choice. The *locus classicus* for the problem is a passage in Luce and Raiffa ((112), p. 288) who chose to avoid the problem of the epistemic value of the menu by *fiat*:

> This illustrates the important assumption implicit in axiom 6 [essentially Property α, H.R.], namely, that adding new acts to a decision problem under uncertainty *does not alter one's a priori information as to which is the true state of nature*. In what follows, we shall suppose that this proviso is satisfied. In practice this means that, if a problem is first formulated so that the availability of certain acts influences the plausibility of certain states of nature, then it must be reformulated by redefining the states of nature so that the interaction is eliminated.

This may make good sense as a rejoinder in the context of the general theory of choice and decision. An explanation of how information is surreptitiously conveyed through the particular contents of the menu and how it affects the chooser's preferences is simply not this theory's business. Unfortunately, the same defence is not available for the problem highlighted by our example above. It *is* the task of the theory of belief formation to model how one's prior belief set is affected by information received from external sources. This is precisely what this theory has been devised to explain, and therefore the anomaly cannot be pushed to a neighbouring research field. We cannot find fault with the dean's message for the very fact that it conveys information!

The question raised by our example is a general one. It is hard to get rid of the feeling that the dean's remark about the final candidates tells us more than meets the ear. The fact that a logician gets *mentioned* as a top-ranking contender or that logic becomes a *topic* seems to carry surplus information, over and above the propositional content of the corresponding statement. Does the very fact that a sentence is offered in a menu for acceptance have a special relevance for processes of belief revision that has been overlooked so far? Or are there other ways out of the predicament?

11. CONCLUSION

We have reviewed work in the tradition of the AGM approach to belief revision, arguably the most prominent logical paradigm for the purification of belief sets from contradictions. Our overarching questions were to what extent economic(al) principles have played a role in the *actual* development of this paradigm, and to what extent such considerations *should* have been followed. Our conclusions are mostly negative. Informational economy (conservatism) with respect to beliefs, although widely advertised as *the* central motivation of belief revision models, turns out not to have played anything like a dominant role in the development of such models, and we have found no reason why it should. Conservatism with respect to revision-guiding preferences has in fact been suggested as a strategy for iterated belief revision, but it soon turned out to have unwelcome consequences. So belief revision theory has as a matter of fact not focused on *economy*, and the idea of *economical* belief revisions has very limited normative force, too. Regarding *economic* belief revision, our findings are more encouraging. It is possible to reconstruct large portions of belief revision in terms of rational choice theory. As a matter of fact, ideas coming from *economics* have prevailed in the AGM paradigm and related approaches. However, at the end of the paper we have found that a fundamental problem of the general theory of choice seriously infects the specific application area of belief revision. Thus the use of rational choice theory has helped us to spot a new puzzle rather than to solve old problems. There is a lot of work that waits to be done in cognitive economics.[38]

Department of Philosophy
University of Regensburg
Germany

NOTES

[1]There are philosophers who deny that knowledge entails belief. In another famous little paper of the 1960s, Colin Radford (123) presented the case of an agent who reliably answers questions without being conscious of the truth of his answers. This, Radford argued, is a case of knowledge without belief.

[2]The maintenance of consistency may also be regarded as a problem not for belief as consciously experienced or expressed by the agent, but for belief as *ascribed* to the agent by a third person. Such a view can indeed take inspiration from Aristotle: "For it is impossible for any one to believe the same thing to be and not to be, as some think Heraclitus says. For what a man says, he does not necessarily believe; and if it is impossible that contrary attributes should belong at the same time to the same subject ..., and if an opinion which contradicts another is contrary to it, obviously it is impossible for the same man at the same time to believe the same thing to be and not to be; for if a man were mistaken on this point he would have contrary opinions at the same time." (*Met.* 1005b, transl. W.D. Ross)

[3]The quotation is taken from (113), p. 73. Simon himself famously advocated an alternative model of rationality, viz., that of *satisficing* instead of maximising. In this model, economic agents set out for achieving a certain level of aspiration, without investing any extra efforts to find out whether they could obtain something even more valuable.

[4]According to Rosenberg (124), economics is not an empirical science, but a branch of applied mathematics – but Rosenberg does not say applied to *what*. My picture below is more in line with the view that economics is a normative discipline, a theory of rationality.

[5]Bernard Walliser (personal communication) has told me that the widespread insistence on transitive and complete preference relations was due to the fact that for a long time, economists simply did not know how to handle intransitive and/or incomplete relations. Now that they know how to treat them, the insistence has gone. For some state-of-the-art work in this area, see (93) and (118).

[6]It takes more than transitivity and completeness for a preference relation to be representable by a utility function. An additional technical continuity property is needed ((91), pp. 54–59). A concise presentation of ordinal and expected utility theory is given in (105), Chapter 3 on 'Rationality'.

[7]This is economics in a narrow sense. Economics in a wider sense has a social component and presumes interpersonal comparability or aggregability of preferences. Blending with social science, political philosophy and ethics, it includes considerations of justice, fairness, solidarity, liberty and equity in the distribution of scarce goods. All this supplements, or rather corrects, the rather restricted focus on maximization in economics in the narrow sense. The present paper does not address any social component of rationality, nor any social phenomena in doxastic matters (like common or distributed belief, information exchange, or multi-agent belief revision).

[8]"Egocentric" is not meant to imply "selfish" here. Egocentric agents only look at their personal preference, but the preferences themselves may embody all kinds of (possibly altruistic) thoughts and feelings.

[9]The landmark paper is Alchourrón, Gärdenfors and Makinson (82), for book-length treatments see Gärdenfors (97), Hansson (103) and Rott (129).

[10]See the papers on "non-prioritised belief revision" collected in (102).

[11] Throughout this paper, it is presupposed that *revisions* have to be *successful* in the sense that they efficiently incorporate the specified new piece of information into the current belief set. *Contractions* are called *successful* if they efficiently remove some specified sentence from the belief set (unless that sentence happens to be a logical truth).

[12]Compare for instance (87), pp. 264–265, and (90), p. 2.

[13]However, it abstracts from the case that one may be *forced* to give away what is valuable, or that one may *invest* something at a given time in order to make profit later on.

[14]I am ready to grant that this train of thought is not very compelling. Alternatively, the second premise might be replaced by another one which, however, is at least as dubious: "It is always better to have something than to have nothing."

[15]In the following, a *belief set* is meant to be a set of sentences that contains its own logical consequences. Thus we endorse the idealisation or stipulation that the beliefs of an agent be deductively closed.

[16]Sometimes, as in approaches working with belief *bases*, use is made of a partitioning or lumping together of the informational contents of the beliefs .

[17]Belief-revision guiding structures typically encode *more* information than the set of current beliefs. Since such structures in general allow to retrieve the set of current beliefs, there is no need for a second component specifying the belief set. Therefore, it is possible to formally identify the agent's *belief state* with a belief-revision guiding structure.

[18]As pointed out in (119), there is a link with the theory of choice in the early history of belief revision theory in Gärdenfors's (95) article on Ramsey test conditionals. Here Gärdenfors tried to simulate Lewis's (109) logic for counterfactuals that is based on a possible worlds semantics with choice functions. Philosophically, however, Gärdenfors set out to *avoid* possible worlds semantics and *replace* it by a belief revision semantics for conditionals (for some serious formal problems of this undertaking, see (96), (94) and (84)). With hindsight, it is somewhat ironic that 10 years after Gärdenfors's early article, Grove (101) showed how closely AGM's belief change model in terms of partial meet operations relates to the systems-of-spheres modelling of Lewis after all.

[19]For a thorough treatment of this topic, see (103).

[20]See (82).

[21]For similar projects in the related field of non-monotonic reasoning, see (132) and (108).

[22]But see footnote 34 below.

[23]In the common AGM numbering of axioms, these are the third and fourth postulates; taken together they state that if $\neg\varphi$ is not in B, then $B * \varphi$ equals $Cn(B \cup \{\varphi\})$.

[24]See (98) and (129).

[25]Alchourrón and Makinson (83) proved a result that may be viewed as a strong argument against maxichoice revisions as applied to belief sets.

[26]Principles of Preference and Indifference are discussed in (120).

[27]This reading is perhaps that reverse of what the reader has expected. An explanation for having more plausible theories smaller under $\preceq$ is that they are less distant from the agent's beliefs and expectations.

[28]More formally, the constraint says that the revised belief set $B * \varphi$ should be identified with the set of all sentences that are satisfied by every world in $min_{\preceq}[\varphi]$.

[29]This claim is true if $\preceq$ is connected (i.e., "fully economical" in our sense) which is what Boutilier presupposes. The claim becomes problematic if the restriction to connected preference relations is lifted. See footnote 34 below.

[30]See for instance (130).

[31]Notice that this procedure tends to introduce new comparabilities: Any new non-belief is comparable to every other sentence, even if it was an 'isolated' belief before.

[32]The appearance is deceptive, though, since in general $(\preceq^*_\varphi)^*_\psi \neq \preceq^*_\psi$ and $(\leq^*_\varphi)^*_\psi \neq \leq^*_\psi$.

[33]To my knowledge, the model was first studied systematically by Abhaya Nayak (115) (also see (116), (117)), but many people have had the idea independently of Nayak. See (100), (106), (107), (110) and (121). I discuss the merits of this model and explain my label "moderate belief revision" for it in (131).

[34]If a preference relation is not connected, i.e. not fully *economic*, its conservative revision cannot strictly speaking be called fully *economical*. For any two relations R_1 and R_2 over a given domain, we can define the *difference* between R_1 and R_2 to be the set of pairs in the domain that are related by R_1 but not by R_2, or vice versa. The difference between an ordering of possible worlds $\preceq$ and its revision $\preceq^*_\varphi$ is not strictly smaller for conservative revision as it is for, say, moderate revision. Consider three φ-worlds w_1, w_2 and w_3. Let $w_1 \prec w_2$, let w_3 be unrelated by $\preceq$ to both w_1 and w_2, and suppose that both w_1 and w_3 are minimal in $[\varphi]$. Then conservative revision with respect to φ introduces the new comparison $w_3 \preceq^*_\varphi w_2$ which moderate revision does not. Thus the difference between $\preceq$ and its conservative revision by φ is not strictly smaller (in terms of set inclusion) than between $\preceq$ and its moderate revision by φ. So for the concept of informational *economy* to make perfectly well-defined sense, it seems that fully *economical* behaviour is presupposed. This suggests that the ideas of economy and economics in belief change cannot be fully separated from each other – *pace* (131).

[35]Important earlier work was done by Lindström (111).

[36]We take it for granted in this example that the dean is not playing games with us, that she is not lying, that she has the relevant knowledge etc.

[37]Sen ((133), pp. 500–503; (134), pp. 24–26) has brought the problem to wide attention.

[38]Thanks go to Vincent F. Hendricks, Eckehart Köhler, Carsten Köllmann, Maria Kronfeldner, Hannes Leitgeb, Nils-Eric Sahlin, Gerhard Schurz, Krister Segerberg, Wolfgang Spohn and Bernard Walliser for helpful comments and discussions.

REFERENCES

[81] Carlos Alchourrón. Philosophical Foundations of Deontic Logic and the Logic of Defeasible Conditionals. in J.-J. Ch. Meyer and R.J. Wieringa (eds.): *Deontic Logic in Computer Science: Normative Systems Specifications*, Wiley, pp. 43–84, 1993.

[82] Carlos Alchourrón, Peter Gärdenfors, and David Makinson. On the Logic of Theory Change: Partial Meet Contraction Functions and Their Associated Revision Functions. *Journal of Symbolic Logic*, 50:510–530, 1985.

[83] Carlos Alchourrón and David Makinson. On the Logic of Theory Change: Contraction Functions and Their Associated Revision Functions. *Theoria*, 48:14–37, 1982.

[84] Horacio Arló-Costa and Isaac Levi. Two Notions of Epistemic Validity: Epistemic Models for Ramsey's Conditionals. *Synthese*, 109:217–262, 1996.

[85] Philippe Besnard, Gisbert Fanselow, and Torsten Schaub. Optimality Theory as a Family of Cumulative Logics. *Journal of Logic, Language and Information*, 12:153–182, 2003.

[86] Craig Boutilier. Revision Sequences and Nested Conditionals. in R. Bajcsy (ed.), *IJCAI-93 – Proceedings of the Thirteenth International Joint Conference on Artificial Intelligence*, pp. 519–525, 1993.

[87] Craig Boutilier. Iterated Revision and Minimal Change of Conditional Beliefs. *Journal of Philosophical Logic*, 25:263–305, 1996.

[88] John Broome. *Ethics Out of Economics.* Cambridge University Press, Cambridge, 1999.

[89] Adnan Darwiche and Judea Pearl. On the Logic of Iterated Belief Revision. in Ronald Fagin, ed., *TARK '94 – Proceedings of the Fifth Conference on Theoretical Aspects of Reasoning About Knowledge*, Pacific Grove, Cal.: Morgan Kaufmann, 5–23, 1994.

[90] Adnan Darwiche and Judea Pearl. On the Logic of Iterated Belief Revision. *Artificial Intelligence*, 89:1–29, 1997.

[91] Gerard Debreu. *Theory of Value.* Wiley, New York, 1959.

[92] Francis Ysidro Edgeworth. *Mathematical Psychics.* Kegan Paul, London, 1881.

[93] Kfir Eliaz and Efe A. Ok. Indifference or Indecisiveness? Choice-Theoretic Foundations of Incomplete Preferences. manuscript, Department of Economics, New York University, April, 2003.

[94] André Fuhrmann. Observations on Validity and Conditionals in Belief Revision Systems. *Journal of Applied Non-Classical Logics*, 3:225–238, 1993.

[95] Peter Gärdenfors. Conditionals and Changes of Belief. in Illkka Niiniluoto and Raimo Tuomela (eds.), 'The Logic and Epistemology of Scientific Change', *Acta Philosophica Fennica* 30 (1978), nos. 2–4, 381–404, 1979.

[96] Peter Gärdenfors. Belief Revisions and the Ramsey Test for Conditionals. *Philosophical Review*, 95:81–93, 1986.

[97] Peter Gärdenfors. *Knowledge in Flux. Modeling the Dynamics of Epistemic States.* Bradford Books, MIT Press, Cambridge, Mass, 1988.

[98] Peter Gärdenfors and David Makinson. Revisions of Knowledge Systems Using Epistemic Entrenchment. in Moshe Vardi (ed.), *TARK'88 – Proceedings of the Second Conference on Theoretical Aspects of Reasoning About Knowledge*, Los Altos: Morgan Kaufmann, 83–95, 1988.

[99] Edmund Gettier. Is Justified True Belief Knowledge. *Analysis*, 23:121–123, 1963.

[100] Stephen Glaister. Symmetry and Belief Revision. *Erkenntnis*, 49:21–56, 1998.

[101] Adam Grove. Two Modellings for Theory Change. *Journal of Philosophical Logic*, 17:157–170, 1988.

[102] Sven Ove Hansson. Special Issue on 'Non-Prioritized Belief Revision'. *Theoria*, 63:1–134, 1997.

[103] Sven Ove Hansson. *A Textbook of Belief Dynamics: Theory Change and Database Updating.* Kluwer, Dordrecht, 1999.

[104] Daniel Hausman. Economics, Philosophy of. *Routledge Encyclopedia of Philosophy*, electronic edition, 1998.

[105] Daniel M. Hausman and Michael S. McPherson. *Economic Analysis and Moral Philosophy.* Cambridge University Press, Cambridge, 1996.

[106] Kevin Kelly. Iterated Belief Revision, Reliability, and Inductive Amnesia. *Erkenntnis*, 50:11–58, 1999.

[107] Sébastien Konieczny and Ramón Pino Pérez. A Framework for Iterated Revision. *Journal of Applied Non-Classical Logics*, 10:339–367, 2000.

[108] Daniel Lehmann. Nonmonotonic Logics and Semantics. *Journal of Logic and Computation*, 11:229–256, 2001.

[109] David Lewis. *Counterfactuals.* Blackwell, Oxford, 1973.

[110] Paolo Liberatore. The Complexity of Iterated Belief Revision. in *Proceedings of the Sixth International Conference on Database Theory (ICDT'97)*, Lecture Notes in Computer Science 1186, Berlin: Springer, 276–290, 1997.

[111] Sten Lindström. A Semantic Approach to Nonmonotonic Reasoning: Inference Operations and Choice. Uppsala Prints and Preprints in Philosophy, Department of Philosophy, University of Uppsala, 1991:6, 1991.

[112] R. Duncan Luce and Howard Raiffa. *Games and Decisions.* Wiley, New York, 1957.

[113] Daniel McFadden. Rationality for Economists? *Journal of Risk and Uncertainty*, 19:73–105, 1999.

[114] Hervé Moulin. Choice Functions over a Finite Set: A Summary. *Social Choice and Welfare*, 2:147–160, 1985.

[115] Abhaya Nayak. Iterated Belief Change Based on Epistemic Entrenchment. *Erkenntnis*, 41:353–390, 1994.

[116] Abhaya Nayak, Norman Foo, Maurice Pagnucco, and Abdul Sattar. Changing Conditional Beliefs Unconditionally. in Yoav Shoham (ed.), *TARK'96 – Proceedings of the Sixth Conference on Theoretical Aspects of Rationality and Knowledge*, pp. 119–135, 1996.

[117] Abhaya Nayak, Maurice Pagnucco, and Pavlos Peppas. Dynamic Belief Revision Operations. *Artificial Intelligence*, 146:193–228, 2003.

[118] Efe A. Ok. Utility Representation of an Incomplete Preference Relation. *Journal of Economic Theory*, 104:429–449, 2002.

[119] Erik Olsson. Belief Revision, Rational Choice and the Unity of Reason. *Studia Logica*, 73:219–240, 2003.

[120] Maurice Pagnucco and Hans Rott. Severe Withdrawal (and Recovery). *Journal of Philosophical Logic*, 28:501–547, 1999. Corrected reprint in the *JPL* issue of February 2000.

[121] Odile Papini. Iterated Revision Operations Stemming from the History of an Agent's Observations. in Mary-Anne Williams and Hans Rott (eds.), *Frontiers in Belief Revision*, Dordrecht: Kluwer, 279–301, 2001.

[122] Willard V.O. Quine and Joseph S. Ullian. *The Web of Belief.* Random House, New York, second edition, 1978.

[123] Colin Radford. Knowledge – By Examples. *Analysis*, 27:1–11, 1966.

[124] Alexander Rosenberg. If Economics Isn't Science, What Is It? *Philosophical Forum*, 14:296–314, 1983. Reprinted in E.D. Klemke et al. (eds.), *Introductory Readings in the Philosophy of Science*, 3rd edition, Prometheus Books, Amherst 1998, 154–170.

[125] Alexander Rosenberg. Philosophy of Economics. in Robert Audi (ed.), *Cambridge Dictionary of Philosophy*, Cambridge University Press, Cambridge, pp. 582–583, 1995.

[126] Hans Rott. Belief Contraction in the Context of the General Theory of Rational Choice. *Journal of Symbolic Logic*, 58:1426–1450, 1993.

[127] Hans Rott. Coherence and Conservatism in the Dynamics of Belief. Part I: Finding the Right Framework. *Erkenntnis*, 50:387–412, 1999.

[128] Hans Rott. Two Dogmas of Belief Revision. *Journal of Philosophy*, 97:503–522, 2000.

[129] Hans Rott. *Change, Choice and Inference.* Oxford University Press, 2001.

[130] Hans Rott. Basic Entrenchment. *Studia Logica*, 73:257–280, 2003.

[131] Hans Rott. Coherence and Conservatism in the Dynamics of Belief. Part II: Iterated Belief Change Without Dispositional Coherence. *Journal of Logic and Computation*, 13:111–145, 2003.

[132] Karl Schlechta. Some Completeness Results for Stoppered and Ranked Classical Preferential Models. *Journal of Logic and Computation*, 6:599–622, 1996.

[133] Amartya K. Sen. Internal Consistency of Choice. *Econometrica*, 61:495–521, 1993.

[134] Amartya K. Sen. Is the Idea of Purely Internal Consistency of Choice Bizarre? in J. E. J. Altham and R. Harrison (eds.), *World, Mind, and Ethics. Essays on the Ethical Philosophy of Bernard Williams*, Cambridge University Press, Cambridge, 19–31, 1995.

[135] Wolfgang Spohn. Die Logik und das Induktionsproblem. in Peter Schroeder-Heister und Wolfgang Spohn (eds.), *Logik in der Philosophie*, Synchron-Verlag, Heidelberg, forthcoming, 2003.

[136] Kotaro Suzumura. *Rational Choice, Collective Decisions, and Social Welfare.* Cambridge University Press, Cambridge, 1983.

R. FAGIN, J.Y. HALPERN, Y. MOSES AND M.Y. VARDI

COMMON KNOWLEDGE REVISITED[0]

ABSTRACT

We consider the common-knowledge paradox raised by Halpern and Moses: common knowledge is necessary for agreement and coordination, but common knowledge is unattainable in the real world because of temporal imprecision. We discuss two solutions to this paradox: (1) modeling the world with a coarser granularity, and (2) relaxing the requirements for coordination.

1. INTRODUCTION

The notion of *common knowledge*, where everyone knows, everyone knows that everyone knows, etc., has proven to be fundamental in various disciplines, including Philosophy (158), Artificial Intelligence (159), Game Theory (137; 148; 149), Psychology (142), and Distributed Systems (153). This key notion was first studied by the philosopher David Lewis (158) in the context of conventions. Lewis pointed out that in order for something to be a convention, it must in fact be common knowledge among the members of a group. (For example, the convention that green means 'go' and red means 'stop' is presumably common knowledge among the drivers in our society.)

Common knowledge also arises in discourse understanding (142). Suppose Ann asks Bob 'What did you think of the movie?' referring to a showing of *Monkey Business* they have just seen. Not only must Ann and Bob both know that 'the movie' refers to *Monkey Business*, but Ann must know that Bob knows (so that she can be sure that Bob will give a reasonable answer to her question), Bob must know that Ann knows that Bob knows (so that Bob knows that Ann will respond appropriately to his answer), and so on. In fact, by a closer analysis of this situation, it can be shown that there must be common knowledge of what movie is meant in order for Bob to answer the question appropriately.

Finally, as shown in (153), common knowledge also turns out to be a prerequisite for agreement and coordinated action. This is precisely what makes it such a crucial notion in the analysis of interacting groups of agents. On the other hand, in practical settings common knowledge is impossible to achieve. This puts us in a somewhat paradoxical situation, in that we claim both that common knowledge is a prerequisite for agreement and coordinated action and that it cannot be attained. We discuss two answers to this paradox: (1) modeling the world with a coarser granularity, and (2) relaxing the requirements for *coordination*.

V.F. Hendricks, K.F. Jørgensen and S.A. Pedersen (eds.), Knowledge Contributors, 87–104.

2. TWO PUZZLES

We start by discussing two well-known puzzles that involve attaining common knowledge. The first is the 'muddy children' puzzle (which goes back at least to (147), although the version we consider here is taken from (139)).

The story goes as follows: Imagine n children playing together. Some, say k of them, get mud on their foreheads. Each can see the mud on others but not on his own forehead. Along comes the father, who says, 'At least one of you has mud on your forehead,' thus expressing a fact known to each of them before he spoke (if $k > 1$). The father then asks the following question, over and over: 'Does any of you know whether you have mud on your own forehead?' Assuming that all the children are perceptive, intelligent, truthful, and that they answer simultaneously, what will happen?

There is a straightforward proof by induction that the first $k-1$ times he asks the question, they will all say 'No,' but then the kth time the children with muddy foreheads will all answer 'Yes.' Let us denote the fact 'at least one child has a muddy forehead' by p. Notice that if $k > 1$, i.e., more than one child has a muddy forehead, then every child can see at least one muddy forehead, and the children initially all know p. Thus, it would seem that the father does not provide the children with any new information, and so he should not need to tell them that p holds when $k > 1$. But this is false! What the father provides is common knowledge. If exactly k children have muddy foreheads, then it is straightforward to see that $E^{k-1}p$ holds before the father speaks, but $E^k p$ does not (here $E^k \varphi$ means φ, if $k = 0$, and everyone knows $E^{k-1}\varphi$, if $k \geq 1$). The father's statement actually converts the children's state of knowledge from $E^{k-1}p$ to Cp (here Cp means that there is common knowledge of p). With this extra knowledge, they can deduce whether their foreheads are muddy.

In the muddy children puzzle, the children do not actually need common knowledge; $E^k p$ suffices for them to figure out whether they have mud on their foreheads. On the other hand, the *coordinated attack* problem introduced by Gray (150) provides an example where common knowledge is truly necessary. In this problem, two generals, each commanding a division of an army, want to attack a common enemy. They will win the battle only if they attack the enemy simultaneously; if only one division attacks, it will be defeated. Thus, the generals want to coordinate their attack. Unfortunately, the only way they have of communicating is by means of messengers, who might get lost or captured by the enemy.

Suppose a messenger sent by General A reaches General B with a message saying '*attack at dawn*.' Should General B attack? Although the message was in fact delivered, General A has no way of knowing that it was delivered. A must therefore consider it possible that B did not receive the message (in which case B would definitely not attack). Hence A will not attack given his current state of knowledge. Knowing this, and not willing to risk attacking alone, B cannot attack based solely on receiving A's message. Of course, B can try to improve matters by sending the messenger back to A with an acknowledgment. Even if the messenger reaches A, similar reasoning shows that neither A nor B will attack at this point either. In fact, Yemini and Cohen (172) proved, by induction on the number of messages, that no number of successful deliveries of acknowledgments to acknowledgments can allow the generals to attack. Halpern and Moses (153) showed the relationship between coordinated attack and common knowledge, and used this to give a 'knowledge-based' proof of Yemini and Cohen's result. Specifically, assume that the generals behave according to some predetermined deterministic protocol; that is, a general's actions (what messages he sends and whether he attacks) are a deterministic function of his history and the time on his clock. Assume further that in the absence of any successful communication, neither general will attack. Halpern and Moses then prove the following theorem:

THEOREM 1. (153) A correct protocol for the coordinated attack problem must have the property that whenever the generals attack, it is common knowledge that they are attacking.

Halpern and Moses then define the notion of a system where *communication is not guaranteed.* Roughly speaking, this means (1) it is always possible that from some point on, no messages will be received, and (2) if a processor (or general) i does not get any information to the contrary (by receiving some message), then i considers it possible that none of its messages were received. In particular, in the coordinated attack problem as stated, communication is not guaranteed. Halpern and Moses then prove that in such a system, nothing can become common knowledge unless it is also common knowledge in the absence of communication. This implies the impossibility of coordinated attack:

THEOREM 2. (153) Any correct protocol for the coordinated attack problem guarantees that neither general ever attacks.

Common knowledge of φ is defined to be the infinite conjunction of the formulas $E^k\varphi$. This definition seems to suggest that common knowledge has an 'inherently infinite' nature. Indeed, for a fact that is not common knowledge to become common knowledge, each participating agent must come to know an infinite collection of new facts. Could this be one of the reasons that common knowledge is impossible to attain in this case? As we shall see, it is not.

In practice, there is always a finite bound on the number of possible local states of an agent in a real-world system. A *finite-state system* is one where each agent's set of possible local states is finite. Fischer and Immerman (146) showed that in a finite-state system, common knowledge is equivalent to E^k for a sufficiently large k. Nevertheless, the result that common knowledge is not attainable if communication is not guaranteed applies equally well to finite-state systems (as do our later results on the unattainability of common knowledge). Thus, in such cases, $E^k\varphi$ is unattainable for some sufficiently large k. (Intuitively, k is large enough so that the agents cannot count up to k; that is, k is tantamount to infinity for these agents.) So the unattainability of common knowledge in this case is not due to the fact that common knowledge is defined in terms of an infinite conjunction.

3. COMMON KNOWLEDGE AND UNCERTAINTY

As we have seen, common knowledge cannot be attained when communication is not guaranteed. That is, common knowledge is not attainable when communication errors are possible, regardless of how unlikely these errors are and how long and detailed the communication is. Halpern and Moses show further that common knowledge cannot be attained in a system in which communication *is* guaranteed, but where there is no bound on the time it takes for messages to be delivered. It would seem that when all messages are guaranteed to be delivered within a fixed amount of time, say one second, attaining common knowledge should be a simple matter. But things are not always as simple as they seem; even in this case, uncertainty causes major difficulties.

Consider the following example: Assume that two agents, Alice and Bob, communicate over a channel in which (it is common knowledge that) message delivery is guaranteed. Moreover, suppose that there is only slight uncertainty concerning message delivery times. It is commonly known that any message sent from Alice to Bob reaches Bob within ε time units. Now suppose that at some point Alice sends Bob a message μ that does not specify the sending time in any way. Bob does not know initially that Alice sent him a message. We assume that when Bob receives Alice's message, he knows that it is from her. How do Alice and Bob's state of knowledge change with time?

Let $sent(\mu)$ be the statement that Alice sent the message μ. After ε time units, we have $K_A K_B sent(\mu)$, that is, Alice knows that Bob knows that she sent the message μ. And clearly, this state of knowledge does not occur before ε time units. Define $(K_A K_B)^k sent(\mu)$ by letting it be $sent(\mu)$ for $k = 0$, and $K_A K_B (K_A K_B)^{k-1} sent(\mu)$ for $k \geq 1$. It is not hard to verify that $(K_A K_B)^k sent(\mu)$ holds after $k\varepsilon$ time units, and does not hold before then. In particular, common knowledge of $sent(\mu)$ is never attained. This may not seem too striking when we think of ε that is relatively large, say a day, or an hour. The argument, however, is independent of the magnitude of ε, and remains true even for small values of ε. Even if Alice and Bob are guaranteed that Alice's message arrives within one nanosecond, they still never attain common knowledge that her message was sent!

Now let us consider what happens if both Alice and Bob use the *same* clock, and suppose that, instead of sending μ, Alice sends at time m a message μ' that specifies the sending time, such as

'This message is being sent at time m; μ.'

Recall that it is common knowledge that every message sent by Alice is received by Bob within ε time units. When Bob receives μ', he knows that μ' was sent at time m. Moreover, Bob's receipt of μ' is guaranteed to happen no later than time $m + \varepsilon$. Since Alice and Bob use the same clock, it is common knowledge at time $m + \varepsilon$ that it is $m + \varepsilon$. It is also common knowledge that any message sent at time m is received by time $m + \varepsilon$. Thus, at time $m + \varepsilon$, the fact that Alice sent μ' to Bob is common knowledge.

Note that in the first example common knowledge will never hold regardless of whether ε is a day, an hour, or a nanosecond. The slight uncertainty about the sending time and the message transmission time prevents common knowledge of μ from ever being attained in this scenario. What makes the second example so dramatically different? When a fact φ is common knowledge, everybody must know that it is. It is impossible for agent i to know that φ is common knowledge without agent j knowing it as well. This means that the transition from φ not being common knowledge to its being common knowledge must involve a *simultaneous* change in all relevant agents' knowledge. In the first example, the uncertainty makes such a simultaneous transition impossible, while in the second, having the same clock makes a simultaneous transition possible and this transition occurs at time $m + \varepsilon$. These two examples help illustrate the connection between simultaneity and common knowledge and the effect this can have on the attainability of common knowledge. We now formalize and further explore this connection.

4. SIMULTANEOUS EVENTS

The Alice and Bob examples illustrate how the transition from a situation in which a fact is not common knowledge to one where it is common knowledge requires simultaneous events to take place at all sites of the system. The relationship between simultaneity and common knowledge, is in fact even more fundamental than that. We saw by example earlier that actions that must be performed simultaneously by all parties, such as attacking in the coordinated attack problem, become common knowledge as soon as they are performed: common knowledge is a prerequisite for simultaneous actions. In this section, we give a result that says that a fact's becoming common knowledge requires the occurrence of simultaneous events at different sites of the system. Moreover, the results say that in a certain technical sense, the occurrence of simultaneous events is necessarily common knowledge. This demonstrates the strong link between common knowledge and simultaneous events.

To make this claim precise, we need to formalize the notion of simultaneous events. We begin by briefly reviewing the framework of (145) for modeling multi-agent systems.[1] We assume that at each point in time, each agent is in some *local state*. Informally, this local state encodes the information available to the agent at this point. In addition, there is an *environment* state, that keeps track of everything relevant to the system not recorded in the agents' states.

A *global state* is an $(n+1)$-tuple $(s_e, s_1, \ldots, s_n)$ consisting of the environment state s_e and the local state s_i of each agent i. A *run* of the system is a function from time (which, for ease of exposition, we assume ranges over the natural numbers) to global states. Thus, if r is a run, then $r(0), r(1), \ldots$ is a sequence of global states that, roughly speaking, is a complete description of how the system evolves over time in one possible execution of the system. We take a *system* to consist of a set of runs. Intuitively, these runs describe all the possible sequences of events that could occur in a system.

Given a system $\mathcal{R}$, we refer to a pair (r, m) consisting of a run $r \in \mathcal{R}$ and a time m as a *point*. If $r(m) = (s_e, s_1, \ldots, s_n)$, we define $r_i(m) = s_i$, for $i = 1, \ldots, n$; thus, $r_i(m)$ is process i's local state at the point (r, m). We say two points (r, m) and (r', m') are *indistinguishable* to agent i, and write $(r, m) \sim_i (r', m')$, if $r_i(m) = r'_i(m')$, i.e., if agent i has the same local state at both points. Finally, we define an *interpreted system* to be a pair $(\mathcal{R}, \pi)$ consisting of a system $\mathcal{R}$ together with a mapping π that associates a truth assignment to the primitive propositions with each global state.

An interpreted system can be viewed as a Kripke structure: the points are the possible worlds, and $\sim_i$ plays the role of the accessibility relation. We give semantics to knowledge formulas in interpreted systems just as in Kripke structures: Given a point (r, m) in an interpreted system $\mathcal{I} = (\mathcal{R}, \pi)$, we have $(\mathcal{I}, r, m) \models K_i\varphi$ if $(\mathcal{I}, r', m') \models \varphi$ for all points (r', m') such that $(r', m') \sim_i (r, m)$. Notice that under this interpretation, an agent knows φ if φ is true at all the situations the system could be in, given the agent's current information (as encoded by his local state). Since $\sim_i$ is an equivalence relation, knowledge in this framework satisfies the axioms of the modal system S5. If G is a set of agents, we define E_G ('everyone in the group G knows') by saying $(\mathcal{I}, r, m) \models E_G\varphi$ if $(\mathcal{I}, r, m) \models K_i\varphi$ for every $i \in G$. We define C_G ('it is common knowledge among the agents in G') by saying $(\mathcal{I}, r, m) \models C_G\varphi$ if $(\mathcal{I}, r, m) \models (E_G)^k\varphi$ for every k. When G is the set of all agents, we may write E for E_G, and C for C_G. We write $\mathcal{I} \models \varphi$ if $(\mathcal{I}, r, m) \models \varphi$ for every point (r, m) of the system $\mathcal{I}$.

We now give a few more definitions, all relative to a fixed interpreted system $\mathcal{I} = (\mathcal{R}, \pi)$. Let S denote the set of points of the system $\mathcal{R}$. Define an *event* in $\mathcal{R}$ to be a subset of S; intuitively, these are the points where the event e holds. An event e is said to *hold* at a point (r, m) if $(r, m) \in e$. Of special interest are events whose occurrence is reflected in an agent's local state. More formally, an event e is *local to* i (in interpreted system $\mathcal{I}$) if there is a set L_i^e of i's local states such that for all points (r, m) we have $(r, m) \in e$ iff $r_i(m) \in L_i^e$. The events of sending a message, receiving a message, and performing an internal action are examples of local events for agent i. We remark that the definition of a local event does not imply that an event that is local to i cannot also be local to j. In order to be local to both agents, it only needs to be reflected in the local states of both agents.

Certain events depend only on the global state. An event e is a *state event* if there is a set $\mathcal{G}^e$ of global states such that for all points (r, m) we have $(r, m) \in e$ iff $r(m) \in \mathcal{G}^e$. It is easy to see that local events are state events. More generally, a state event is one that depends only on what is recorded in the local states of the agents and the state of the environment. We associate with every state event e a primitive proposition ψ_e that is true at the global state $r(m)$ if and only if $(r, m) \in e$. This is well-defined, because it follows easily from the definition of state events that if e is a state event and (r, m) and (r', m') are points such that $r(m) = r'(m')$, then $(r, m) \in e$ if and only if $(r', m') \in e$.

We can similarly associate with every formula φ an event $\mathtt{ev}_{\mathcal{I}}(\varphi) = \{(r, m) : (\mathcal{I}, r, m) \models \varphi\}$. The event $\mathtt{ev}_{\mathcal{I}}(\varphi)$ thus holds exactly when φ holds. We call $\mathtt{ev}_{\mathcal{I}}(\varphi)$ *the event of* φ *holding (in* $\mathcal{I}$*)*. It is easy to check that an event e is local to i if and only if $K_i\psi_e$ holds, that is, if and only if i knows that e is holding. Moreover, the event of $K_i\varphi$ holding is always a local event for i.

We are now ready to address the issue of simultaneous events. Intuitively, two events are simultaneous if they occur at the same points. Our interest in simultaneity is primarily in the context of coordination. Namely, we are interested in events that are local to different agents and are coordinated in time. Thus, we concentrate on events whose occurrence is simultaneously reflected in the local state of the agents. More formally, we define an *event ensemble for* G(or just *ensemble* for short) to be a mapping e assigning to every agent $i \in G$ an event $\mathrm{e}(i)$ local to i. An ensemble e for G is said to be *perfectly coordinated* if the local events in e hold simultaneously; formally, if $(r, m) \in \mathrm{e}(i)$ for some $i \in G$, then $(r, m) \in \mathrm{e}(j)$ for all $j \in G$. Thus, the ensemble e for G is perfectly coordinated precisely if $\mathrm{e}(i) = \mathrm{e}(j)$ for all $i, j \in G$. Since an event e that is local to agent i is defined in terms of a set L_i^e of states local to agent i, the ensemble e for G is perfectly coordinated if all the agents in G enter their respective sets $L_i^{\mathrm{e}(i)}$ simultaneously. Thus, the events in a perfectly coordinated ensemble are simultaneous.

An example of a perfectly coordinated ensemble is the set of local events that correspond to the ticking of a global clock, if the ticking is guaranteed to be reflected simultaneously at all sites of a system. Another example is the event of shaking hands: being a mutual action, the handshakes of the parties are perfectly coordinated.

Given an ensemble e for G, the proposition $\psi_{\mathrm{e}(i)}$ corresponds to the state event e(i) holding. We also define $\psi_{\mathrm{e}} = \bigvee_{i \in G} \psi_{\mathrm{e}(i)}$. Thus, ψ_{e} is true whenever one of the state events e(i) holds.

PROPOSITION 1. Let $\mathcal{I}$ be an interpreted system and G a set of agents.

(a) For every formula φ, the ensemble e for G defined by e$(i) = \mathtt{ev}_{\mathcal{I}}(K_i C_G \varphi)$ is perfectly coordinated.

(b) If e is a perfectly coordinated ensemble for G, then $\mathcal{I} \models \psi_{\mathrm{e}} \Rightarrow C_G \psi_{\mathrm{e}}$.

(In fact, $K_i C_G \varphi$ in part (a) of Proposition 1 is logically equivalent to $C_G \varphi$, but we write $K_i C_G \varphi$ to bring out the similarities between this result and Proposition 3 below.) Proposition 1 precisely captures the close correspondence between common knowledge and simultaneous events. It asserts that the local events that correspond to common knowledge are perfectly coordinated, and the local events in a perfectly coordinated ensemble are common knowledge when they hold. Notice that part (a) implies in particular that the transitions from $\neg K_i C_G \varphi$ to $K_i C_G \varphi$, for $i \in G$, must be simultaneous. Among other things, this helps clarify the difference between the two examples considered in Section 3: In the first example, Alice and Bob cannot attain common knowledge of $sent(\mu)$ because they are unable to make such a simultaneous transition, while in the second example they can (and do).

The close relationship between common knowledge and simultaneous actions is what makes common knowledge such a useful tool for analyzing tasks involving coordination and agreement. It also gives us some insight into how common knowledge arises. For example, the fact that a public announcement has been made is common knowledge, since the announcement is heard simultaneously by everyone. (Strictly speaking, of course, this is not quite true; we return to this issue in Section 6.) More generally, simultaneity is inherent in the notion of *copresence.* As a consequence, when people sit around a table, the existence of the table, as well as the nature of the objects on the table, are common knowledge.

Proposition 1 formally captures the role of simultaneous actions in making agreements and conventions common knowledge. As we discussed earlier, common knowledge is inherent in agreements and conventions. Hand shaking, face-to-face or telephone conversation, and a simultaneous signing of a contract are standard ways of reaching agreements. They all involve simultaneous actions and have the effect of making the agreement common knowledge.

5. TEMPORAL IMPRECISION

As we illustrated previously and formalized in Proposition 1, simultaneity is inherent in the notion of common knowledge (and vice versa). It follows that simultaneity is a prerequisite for attaining common knowledge. Alice and Bob's failure to reach common knowledge in the first example above can therefore be blamed on their inability to perform a simultaneous state transition. As might be expected, the fact that simultaneity is a prerequisite for attaining common knowledge has additional consequences. For example, in many distributed systems each process possesses a clock. In practice, in any distributed system there is always some uncertainty regarding the relative synchrony of the clocks and regarding the precise message transmission times. This results in what is called the *temporal imprecision* of the system. The amount of temporal imprecision in different systems varies, but it can be argued that every practical system will have some (possibly very small) degree of imprecision. Formally, a given system $\mathcal{R}$ is said to have *temporal imprecision* if for all pairs i, j such that $i \neq j$ and all points (r, m) with $m > 0$, there exists a point (r', m') such that $r'_i(m') = r_i(m)$ and either $r'_j(m') = r_j(m+1)$ or $r'_j(m') = r_j(m-1)$. Intuitively, in a system with temporal imprecision, i is uncertain about j's clock reading; at the point (r, m), process i cannot tell whether j's clock is characterized by j's local state at (r, m), by j's local state at $(r, m+1)$ or by j's local state at $(r, m-1)$. Techniques from the distributed-systems literature (143; 152) can be used to show that any system in which, roughly speaking, there is some initial uncertainty regarding relative clock readings and uncertainty regarding exact message transmission times must have temporal imprecision.

Systems with temporal imprecision turn out to have the property that no protocol can be guaranteed to synchronize the processes' clocks perfectly. As we now show, events cannot be perfectly coordinated in systems with temporal imprecision either. These two facts are closely related.

We define an ensemble e for G in $\mathcal{I}$ to be *nontrivial* if there exist a run r in $\mathcal{I}$ and times m, m' such that $(r, m) \in \cup_{i \in G} \mathrm{e}(i)$ while $(r, m') \notin \cup_{i \in G} \mathrm{e}(i)$. Thus, if e is a perfectly coordinated ensemble for G, it is *trivial* if for each run r of the system and for each agent $i \in G$, the events in $\mathrm{e}(i)$ hold either at all points of r or at no point of r. The definition of systems with temporal imprecision implies the following:

PROPOSITION 2. In a system with temporal imprecision there are no nontrivial perfectly coordinated ensembles for G, if $|G| \geq 2$.

We thus have the following corollary.

COROLLARY 1. (153) Let $\mathcal{I}$ be a system with temporal imprecision, let φ be a formula, and let $|G| \geq 2$. Then for all runs r and times m we have $(\mathcal{I}, r, m) \models C_G\varphi$ iff $(\mathcal{I}, r, 0) \models C_G\varphi$.

In simple terms, Corollary 1 states that no fact can become common knowledge during a run of a system with temporal imprecision. If the units by which time is measured in our model are sufficiently small, then all practical distributed systems have temporal imprecision. For example, if we work at the nanosecond level, then there is bound to be some uncertainty regarding exact message transmission times. As a result, Corollary 1 implies that no fact can ever become common knowledge in practical distributed systems. Carrying this argument even further, we can view essentially all real-world scenarios as ones in which true simultaneity cannot be guaranteed. For example, the children in the muddy children puzzle neither hear nor comprehend the father simultaneously. There is bound to be some uncertainty about how long it takes each of them to process the information. Thus, according to our earlier discussion, the children in fact do not attain common knowledge of the father's statement.

We now seem to have a paradox. On the one hand, we have argued that common knowledge is unattainable in practical contexts. On the other hand, given our claim that common knowledge is a prerequisite for agreements and conventions and the observation that we do reach agreements and that conventions are maintained, it seems that common knowledge *is* attained in practice. Note that this paradox applies not only to situations that explicitly require coordination, such as the coordinated attack problem, but even to situations that do not require coordination, such as conventions and discourse understanding. If a convention requires common knowledge, then this common knowledge must arise somehow. (After all, we do not have innate knowledge about red traffic lights meaning stop.) This cannot happen in any real-world system, since common knowledge must arise simultaneously for all participants.

What is the catch? How can we explain this discrepancy between our practical experience and our technical results? In the next two sections, we consider two resolutions to this paradox. The first rests on the observation that if we model time at a sufficiently coarse level, we can and do attain common knowledge. The question then becomes when and whether it is appropriate to model time in this way. The second says that, although we indeed cannot attain common knowledge, we can attain close approximations of it, and this suffices for our purposes.

6. THE GRANULARITY OF TIME

Given the complexity of the real world, any mathematical model of a situation must abstract away many details. A useful model is typically one that abstracts away as much of the irrelevant detail as possible, leaving all and only the relevant aspects of a situation. When modeling a particular situation, it can often be quite difficult to decide the level of granularity at which to model time. The notion of time in a run rarely corresponds to real time. Rather, our choice of the granularity of time is motivated by convenience of modeling. Thus, in a distributed application, it may be perfectly appropriate to take a round to be sufficiently long for a process to send a message to all other processes, and perhaps do some local computation as well.

As we have observed, the argument that every practical system has some degree of temporal imprecision holds only relative to a sufficiently fine-grained model of time. For Proposition 2 and Corollary 1 to apply, time must be represented in sufficiently fine detail for temporal imprecision to be reflected in the model. If a model has a coarse notion of time, then simultaneity, and hence common knowledge, are often attainable. For example, in synchronous systems (those where the agents have access to a shared clock, so that, intuitively, the time is common knowledge) there is no temporal imprecision. As an example, consider a simplified model of the muddy children problem. The initial states of the children and the father describe what they see; later states describe everything they have heard. All communication proceeds in rounds. In round 1, if there is at least one muddy child, a message to this effect is sent to all children. In the odd-numbered rounds 1, 3, 5, ..., the father sends to all children the message 'Does any of you know whether you have mud on your own forehead?' The children respond 'Yes' or 'No' in the even-numbered rounds. In this simplified model, the children do attain common knowledge of the father's statement (after the first round). If, however, we 'enhance' the model to take into consideration the minute details of the neural activity in the children's brains, and considered time on, say, a millisecond scale, the children would not be modeled as hearing the father simultaneously. Moreover, the children would not attain common knowledge of the father's statement. We conclude that whether a given fact becomes common knowledge at a certain point, or in fact whether it *ever* becomes common knowledge, depends in a crucial way on the model being used. While common knowledge may be attainable in a certain model of a given real world situation, it becomes unattainable once we consider a more detailed model of *the same situation*.

When are we justified in reasoning and acting as if common knowledge is attainable? This reduces to the question of when we can argue that one model—in our case a coarser or less detailed model—is 'as good' as another, finer, model. The answer, of course, is 'it depends on the intended application.' Our approach for deciding whether a less detailed model is as good as another, finer, model, is to assume that there is some 'specification' of interest, and to consider whether the finer model satisfies the same specification as the coarser model. For example, in the muddy children puzzle, our earlier model implicitly assumed that the children all hear the father's initial statement and his later questions simultaneously. We can think of this as a coarse model where, indeed, the children attain common knowledge. For the fine model, suppose instead that every time the father speaks, it takes somewhere between 8 and 10 milliseconds for each child to hear and process what the father says, but the exact time may be different for each child, and may even be different for a given child every time the father speaks. Similarly, after a given child speaks, it takes between 8 and 10 milliseconds for the other children and the father to hear and process what he says. (While there is nothing particularly significant in our choice of 8 and 10 milliseconds, it is important that a child does not hear any other child's response to the father's question before he utters his own response.) The father does not ask his k^{th} question until he has received the responses from all children to his $(k-1)^{\text{st}}$ question.

The specification of interest for the muddy children puzzle is the following: A child says 'Yes' if he knows whether he is muddy and says 'No' otherwise. This specification is satisfied in particular when each child follows the protocol that if he sees k muddy children, then he responds 'No' to the father's first k questions and 'Yes' to all the questions after that. This specification is true in both the coarse model and the fine model. Therefore, we consider the coarse model adequate. If part of the specification had been that the children answer simultaneously, then the coarse model would not have been adequate. For a more formal presentation of our approach, see (145).

The observation that whether or not common knowledge is attainable depends in part on how we model time was made in a number of earlier papers (138; 146; 153; 157; 165; 166). Our approach formalizes this observation and offers a rigorous way to determine when the coarse model is adequate.

7. APPROXIMATIONS OF COMMON KNOWLEDGE

Section 4 shows that common knowledge captures the state of knowledge resulting from simultaneous events. It also shows, however, that in the absence of events that are guaranteed to hold simultaneously, common knowledge is not attained. In Section 6, we tried to answer the question of when we can reason and act as if certain events were simultaneous. But there is another point of view we can take. There are situations where events holding at different sites need not happen simultaneously; the level of coordination required is weaker than absolute simultaneity. For example, we may want the events to hold at most a certain amount of time apart. It turns out that just as common knowledge is the state of knowledge corresponding to perfect coordination, there are states of shared knowledge corresponding to other forms of coordination. We can view these states of knowledge as approximations of true common knowledge. It is well known that common knowledge can be defined in terms of a fixed point, as well as an infinite conjunction. As shown in (153), $C_G\varphi$ is equivalent to $\nu x[E_G(\varphi \wedge x)]$, where νx is the *greatest fixed-point operator.*[2] As we shall see, the approximations of common knowledge have similar fixed-point definitions. Fortunately, while perfect coordination is hard to attain in practice, weaker forms of coordination are often attainable. This is one explanation as to why the unattainability of common knowledge might not spell as great a disaster as we might have originally expected. This section considers two of these weaker forms of coordination, and their corresponding states of knowledge.

Let us return to the first Alice and Bob example. Notice that if $\varepsilon = 0$, then Alice and Bob attain common knowledge of *sent*(μ) immediately after the message is sent. In this case, it is guaranteed that once the message is sent, both agents immediately know the contents of the message, as well as the fact that it has been sent. Intuitively, it seems that the closer ε is to 0, the closer Alice and Bob's state of knowledge should be to common knowledge. Compare the situation when $\varepsilon > 0$ with $\varepsilon = 0$. As we saw, if $\varepsilon > 0$ then Alice does not know that Bob received her message immediately after she sends the message. She does, however, know that *within* ε *time units* Bob will receive the message and know both the contents of the message and that the message has been sent. The sending of the message results in a situation where, within ε time units, everyone knows that the situation holds. This is analogous to the fact that common knowledge corresponds to a situation where everyone knows that the situation holds. This suggests that the state of knowledge resulting in the Alice and Bob scenario should involve a fixed point of some sort. We now formalize a notion of coordination related to the Alice and Bob example, and define an approximation of common knowledge corresponding to this type of coordination.

An ensemble e for G is said to be ε*-coordinated* (in a given system $\mathcal{I}$) if the local events in e never hold more than ε time units apart; formally, if $(r, m) \in \mathrm{e}(i)$ for some $i \in G$, then there exists an interval $I = [m', m' + \varepsilon]$ such that $m \in I$ and for all $j \in G$ there exists $m_j \in I$ for which $(r, m_j) \in \mathrm{e}(j)$. Note that ε-coordination with $\varepsilon = 0$ is perfect coordination. While it is essentially infeasible in practice to coordinate events so that they hold simultaneously at different sites of a distributed system, ε-coordination is often attainable in practice, even in systems where there is uncertainty in message delivery time. Moreover, when ε is sufficiently small, there are many applications for which ε-coordination is practically as good as perfect coordination. For example, instead of requiring a simultaneous attack in the coordinated attack problem, it may be sufficient to require only that the two divisions attack within a certain ε-time bound of each other. This is called an ε*-coordinated attack*.

More generally, ε-coordination may be practically as good as perfect coordination for many instances of agreements and conventions. One example of ε-coordination results from a message being broadcast to all members of a group G, with the guarantee that it will reach all of the members within ε time units of one another. In this case it is easy to see that when an agent receives the message, she knows the message has been broadcast, and knows that within ε time units each of the members of G will have received the message and will know that within ε ...

Let ε be arbitrary. We say that *within an ε interval everyone in G knows φ*, denoted $E_G^\varepsilon\varphi$, if there is an interval of ε time units containing the current time such that each process comes to know φ at some point in this interval. Formally, $(\mathcal{I}, r, m) \models E_G^\varepsilon\varphi$ if there exists an interval $I = [m', m' + \varepsilon]$ such that $m \in I$ and for all $i \in G$ there exists $m_i \in I$ for which $(\mathcal{I}, r, m_i) \models K_i\varphi$. Thus, in the case of Alice and Bob, we have $\mathcal{I} \models \mathit{sent}(\mu) \Rightarrow E_{\{A,B\}}^\varepsilon \mathit{sent}(\mu)$. We define ε-common knowledge, denoted by C_G^ε, using a greatest fixed-point operator: $C_G^\varepsilon\varphi =_{\mathrm{def}} \nu x[E_G^\varepsilon(\varphi \wedge x)]$. Notice how similar this definition is to the fixed-point definition of common knowledge. The only change is in replacing E_G by E_G^ε.

Just as common knowledge is closely related to perfect coordination, ε-common knowledge is closely related to ε-coordination. We now make this claim precise. The next proposition is analogous to Proposition 1.

PROPOSITION 3. Let $\mathcal{I}$ be an interpreted system and G a set of agents.

(a) For every formula φ, the ensemble e for G defined by $\mathrm{e}(i) = \mathtt{ev}_{\mathcal{I}}(K_i C_G^\varepsilon\varphi)$ is ε-coordinated.

(b) If e is an ε-coordinated ensemble for G, then $\mathcal{I} \models \psi_{\mathrm{e}} \Rightarrow C_G^\varepsilon\psi_{\mathrm{e}}$.

Note that in part (a), we write $K_i C_G^\varepsilon\varphi$; we cannot write $C_G^\varepsilon\varphi$, since $\mathtt{ev}_{\mathcal{I}}(C_G^\varepsilon\varphi)$ is not an event local to agent i.

Since in the coordinated attack problem message delivery is not guaranteed, it can be shown that the generals cannot achieve even ε-coordinated attack. On the other hand, if messages are guaranteed to be delivered within ε units of time, then ε-coordinated attack can be accomplished. General A simply sends General B a message saying '*attack*' and attacks immediately; General B attacks upon receipt of the message.

The notion of ε-coordination enables us to quantify how closely (temporally) we want to approximate perfect coordination. Although ε-coordination is useful for the analysis of systems where the uncertainty in message communication time is small, it is not quite as useful in the analysis of systems where message delivery may be delayed for a long period of time. In such systems, rather than perfect or ε-coordination, what can often be achieved is *eventual* coordination. An ensemble e for G is *eventually coordinated* (in a given system $\mathcal{I}$) if, for every run of the system, if some event in e holds during the run, then all events in e do. More formally, if $(r, m) \in \mathrm{e}(i)$ for some $i \in G$, then for all $j \in G$ there exists some m_j for which $(r, m_j) \in \mathrm{e}(j)$. An example of an eventual coordination of G consists of the delivery of (copies of) a message broadcast to every member of G in a system with message delays. An agent receiving this message knows the contents of the message, as well as the fact that each other member of G must receive the message at some point in time, either past, present, or future.

Eventual coordination gives rise to *eventual* common knowledge, denoted by $C_G^\diamond$, and defined by $C_G^\diamond \varphi =_{\mathrm{def}} \nu x[E_G^\diamond(\varphi \wedge x)]$. Here we define $E_G^\diamond \varphi$ to hold at $(\mathcal{I}, r, m)$ if for each $i \in G$ there is some time m_i such that $(\mathcal{I}, r, m_i) \models K_i\varphi$. Thus, $E_G^\diamond$ can be viewed as the limit of E_G^ε as ε approaches infinity. It is straightforward to show that $C_G^\diamond$ is related to eventual coordination just as C_G is related to perfect coordination, and C_G^ε to ε-coordination. Interestingly, although C_G^ε is definable as an infinite conjunction, it can be shown that $C_G^\diamond$ is not (145). We really need to use fixed points here; cf. (140).

Just as ε-coordinated attack is a weakening of the simultaneity requirement of coordinated attack, a further weakening of the simultaneity requirement is given by *eventually coordinated attack*. This requirement says that if one of the two divisions attacks, then the other division eventually attacks. If messages are guaranteed to be delivered eventually, then even if there is no bound on message delivery time, an eventually coordinated attack can be carried out.

The notions of ε-common knowledge and of eventual common knowledge are from (153). Our contribution here is in introducing ensembles as a formalization of the concept of coordination and in showing that approximations of common knowledge correspond to approximations of coordination. Other similar variants of common knowledge, also defined by means of fixed points, have been considered in the literature, including *timestamped common knowledge* (153), *continual common knowledge* (154), and *concurrent common knowledge* (167). Another way to approximate common knowledge requires the introduction of probability. *Probabilistic common knowledge* (141; 144; 155; 156; 160; 161; 162; 163; 164; 171), corresponds to probabilistic coordination. In probabilistic coordination we can quantify how closely (probabilistically) we want to approximate perfect coordination. Thus, in both ε-coordination and probabilistic coordination we can control the risk of deviating from perfect coordination. For a game-theoretical analysis of this perspective see, for example, (161; 163; 164; 171).

8. SUMMARY

The central theme of this paper is an attempt to resolve the paradox of common knowledge raised in (153): Although common knowledge can be shown to be a prerequisite for day-to-day activities of coordination and agreement, it can also be shown to be unattainable in practice. The resolution of this paradox leads to a deeper understanding of the nature of common knowledge and simultaneity, and shows once again the importance of the modeling process. In particular, it brings out the importance of the granularity at which we model time, and stresses the need to consider the applications for which these notions are being used. Moreover, by using the notion of event ensembles, we are able to clarify the tight relationship between common knowledge and coordination.

R. Fagin
IBM Almaden Research Center
650 Harry Road
San Jose, CA 95120–6099
USA

J. Halpern
Department of Computer Science
Cornell University
Ithaca, NY 14853
USA

Y. Moses
Department of Electrical Engineering
Technion
Haifa, 32 000
Israel

M.Y. Vardi
Department of Computer Science
Rice University
Houston, TX 77005-1892
USA

NOTES

[0]Reprinted from *Annals of Pure and Applied Logic*, Vol 96, Fagin et al., 'Common knowledge revisited', pages 89–105, Copyright (1999), with permission from Elsevier Science.

[1]The general framework presented here for ascribing knowledge in multi-agent systems originated with Halpern and Moses (153; 162) and Rosenschein (169). Variants were also introduced by Fischer and Immerman (146), Halpern and Fagin (151), Parikh and Ramanujam (168), and Rosenschein and Kaelbling (170).

[2]Formal definitions of this operator can be found in (145; 153).

REFERENCES

[137] R. J. Aumann. Agreeing to disagree. *Annals of Statistics*, 4(6):1236–1239, 1976.

[138] R. J. Aumann. Formal common knowledge: an approach to the Halpern-Moses problem. Manuscript, 1989.

[139] J. Barwise. Scenes and other situations. *Journal of Philosophy*, 78(7):369–397, 1981.

[140] J. Barwise. Three views of common knowledge. In M. Y. Vardi, editor, *Proc. Second Conference on Theoretical Aspects of Reasoning about Knowledge*, pages 365–379. Morgan Kaufmann, San Francisco, Calif., 1988.

[141] A. Brandenburger and E. Dekel. Common knowledge with probability 1. *Journal of Mathematical Economics*, 16:237–245, 1987.

[142] H. H. Clark and C. R. Marshall. Definite reference and mutual knowledge. In A. K. Joshi, B. L. Webber, and I. A. Sag, editors, *Elements of discourse understanding.* Cambridge University Press, Cambridge, U.K., 1981.

[143] D. Dolev, J. Y. Halpern, and H. R. Strong. On the possibility and impossibility of achieving clock synchronization. *Journal of Computer and System Sciences*, 32(2):230–250, 1986.

[144] R. Fagin and J. Y. Halpern. Reasoning about knowledge and probability. *Journal of the ACM*, 41(2):340–367, 1994.

[145] R. Fagin, J. Y. Halpern, Y. Moses, and M. Y. Vardi. *Reasoning about Knowledge.* MIT Press, Cambridge, Mass., 1995.

[146] M. J. Fischer and N. Immerman. Foundations of knowledge for distributed systems. In J. Y. Halpern, editor, *Theoretical Aspects of Reasoning about Knowledge: Proc. 1986 Conference*, pages 171–186. Morgan Kaufmann, San Francisco, Calif., 1986.

[147] G. Gamow and M. Stern. *Puzzle Math.* Viking Press, New York, 1958.

[148] J. Geanakoplos. Common knowledge. In Y. Moses, editor, *Theoretical Aspects of Reasoning about Knowledge: Proc. Fourth Conference*, pages 255–315. Morgan Kaufmann, San Francisco, Calif., 1992.

[149] J. Geanakoplos. Common knowledge. In R. Aumann and S. Hart, editors, *Handbook of Game Theory, Vol. 2.* Elsevier Science, 1994.

[150] J. Gray. Notes on database operating systems. In R. Bayer, R. M. Graham, and G. Seegmuller, editors, *Operating Systems: An Advanced Course*, Lecture Notes in Computer Science, Vol. 66. Springer-Verlag, Berlin/New York, 1978. Also appears as IBM Research Report RJ 2188, 1978.

[151] J. Y. Halpern and R. Fagin. Modelling knowledge and action in distributed systems. *Distributed Computing*, 3(4):159–179, 1989. A preliminary version appeared in *Proc. 4th ACM Symposium on Principles of Distributed Computing*, 1985, with the title "A formal model of knowledge, action, and communication in distributed systems: preliminary report".

[152] J. Y. Halpern, N. Megiddo, and A. Munshi. Optimal precision in the presence of uncertainty. *Journal of Complexity*, 1:170–196, 1985.

[153] J. Y. Halpern and Y. Moses. Knowledge and common knowledge in a distributed environment. *Journal of the ACM*, 37(3):549–587, 1990. A preliminary version appeared in *Proc. 3rd ACM Symposium on Principles of Distributed Computing*, 1984.

[154] J. Y. Halpern, Y. Moses, and O. Waarts. A characterization of eventual Byzantine agreement. In *Proc. 9th ACM Symp. on Principles of Distributed Computing*, pages 333–346, 1990.

[155] J. Y. Halpern and M. R. Tuttle. Knowledge, probability, and adversaries. *Journal of the ACM*, 40(4):917–962, 1993.

[156] P. Krasucki, R. Parikh, and G. Ndjatou. Probabilistic knowledge and probabilistic common knowledge (preliminary report). In Z. W. Ras, M. Zemankova, and M. L. Emrich, editors, *Methodologies for Intelligent Systems*, volume 5, pages 1–8. Elsevier Science Publishing Co., Inc., The Hague, 1990.

[157] R. Kurki-Suonio. Towards programming with knowledge expressions. In *Proc. 13th ACM Symp. on Principles of Programming Languages*, pages 140–149, 1986.

[158] D. Lewis. *Convention, A Philosophical Study.* Harvard University Press, Cambridge, Mass, 1969.

[159] J. McCarthy, M. Sato, T. Hayashi, and S. Igarishi. On the model theory of knowledge. Technical Report STAN-CS-78-657, Stanford University, 1979.

[160] D. Monderer and D. Samet. Approximating common knowledge with common beliefs. *Games and Economic Behavior*, 1:170–190, 1989.

[161] S. Morris and H.S. Shin. Approximate common knowledge and co-ordination: Recent lessons from game theory. *Journal of Logic, Language and Information*, 6:171–190, 1997.

[162] Y. Moses. *Knowledge in a distributed environment.* PhD thesis, Stanford University, 1986.

[163] Z. Neeman. Approximating agreeing to disagree results with common p-beliefs. *Games and Economic Behavior*, 12:162–164, 1996.

[164] Z. Neeman. Common beliefs and the existence of speculative trade. *Games and Economic Behavior*, 16:77–96, 1996.

[165] G. Neiger. Knowledge consistency: a useful suspension of disbelief. In M. Y. Vardi, editor, *Proc. Second Conference on Theoretical Aspects of Reasoning about Knowledge*, pages 295–308. Morgan Kaufmann, San Francisco, Calif., 1988.

[166] G. Neiger and S. Toueg. Simulating real-time clocks and common knowledge in distributed systems. *Journal of the ACM*, 40(2):334–367, 1993.

[167] P. Panangaden and S. Taylor. Concurrent common knowledge: defining agreement for asynchronous systems. *Distributed Computing*, 6(2):73–93, 1992.

[168] R. Parikh and R. Ramanujam. Distributed processing and the logic of knowledge. In R. Parikh, editor, *Proc. Workshop on Logics of Programs*, pages 256–268, 1985.

[169] S. J. Rosenschein. Formal theories of AI in knowledge and robotics. *New Generation Computing*, 3:345–357, 1985.

[170] S. J. Rosenschein and L. P. Kaelbling. The synthesis of digital machines with provable epistemic properties. In J. Y. Halpern, editor, *Theoretical Aspects of Reasoning about Knowledge: Proc. 1986 Conference*, pages 83–97. Morgan Kaufmann, San Francisco, Calif., 1986.

[171] A. Rubinstein. The electronic mail game: strategic behavior under "almost common knowledge". *American Economic Review*, 79:385–391, 1989.

[172] Y. Yemini and D. Cohen. Some issues in distributed processes communication. In *Proc. of the 1st International Conf. on Distributed Computing Systems*, pages 199–203, 1979.

H.P. VAN DITMARSCH, W. VAN DER HOEK AND B.P. KOOI

CONCURRENT DYNAMIC EPISTEMIC LOGIC

ABSTRACT

When giving an analysis of knowledge in multiagent systems, one needs a framework in which higher-order information and its dynamics can both be represented. A recent tradition starting in original work by Plaza treats all of knowledge, higher-order knowledge, and its dynamics on the same foot. Our work is in that tradition. It also fits in approaches that not only dynamize the epistemics, but also epistemize the dynamics: the actions that (groups of) agents perform are epistemic actions. Different agents may have different information about which action is taking place, including higher-order information. We demonstrate that such information changes require subtle descriptions. Our contribution is to provide a complete axiomatization for an action language of van Ditmarsch, where an action is interpreted as a relation between epistemic states (pointed models) and sets of epistemic states. The applicability of the framework is found in every context where multiagent strategic decision making is at stake, and already demonstrated in game-like scenarios such as Cluedo and card games.

1. INTRODUCTION

Since Hintikka's (186) epistemic logic, the logic of knowledge, has been a subject of research in philosophy (187), computer science (181), artificial intelligence (190) and game theory (176). The latter three application areas made it more and more apparent that in multiagent systems *higher-order information*, knowledge about other agents' knowledge, is crucial.

The famous paper (174) by Alchourrón *et al.* put the *change of information*, or belief revision, as a topic on the philosophical and logical agenda: it was followed by a large stream of publications and much research in belief revision, fine-tuning the notion of epistemic entrenchement (191), revising (finite) belief bases (179), highlighting differences between belief revision and belief updates (188), and addressing the problem of iterated belief change (180). However, in all these approaches the dynamics is studied on a level above the informational level, making it impossible to reason about change of agents' knowledge and ignorance within the framework, let alone about the change of other agents' information.

Our work takes these observations on higher-order knowledge and change of information as a starting point: when giving an analysis of knowledge in multiagent systems, one needs a framework in which higher-order information and its dynamics can be represented.

Although the notion of a run in an interpreted system as described in (181) makes it in principle possible to reason about the dynamics of an

V.F. Hendricks, K.F. Jørgensen and S.A. Pedersen (eds.), Knowledge Contributors, 105–143.

agent's knowledge, the interpretation of a run is typically that of a standard program. Further, the pioneering work of Moore (190) also studies the relation between actions and knowledge: there the emphasis is on epistemic preconditions that are needed to perform certain actions in the world, such as knowing a key-combination in order to open a safe.

From the point of view of expressivity, one can say that the work on interpreted systems enables one to reason about the (change of) knowledge over time, and adding actions to the language, one can also reason about the change of knowledge brought about by performing certain plans. This enables one to express properties like *perfect recall* and *no learning*. Recently, based on work by Alur et al (175), van der Hoek and Wooldridge (199) added a *social* or *coalitional aspect* to an epistemic framework, giving them the possibility to express that for instance a group can establish that some knowledge is eventually obtained, or that two agents can enforce that they exchange a secret, without a third agent getting to know this.

Our work fits in approaches that not only dynamize the epistemics, but also epistemize the dynamics: the actions that (groups of) agents perform are epistemic actions. Different agents may have different information about which action is taking place, including higher-order information. This rather recent tradition treats all of knowledge, higher-order knowledge, and its dynamics on the same foot. Following an original contribution by Plaza in 1989 (196), a stream of publications appeared around the year 2000 (183; 182; 189; 177; 200; 198; 173; 203; 202; 197).

The following, possibly simplest example in the setting of multiagent systems (two agents, one atom) attempts to demonstrate that the notions of higher-order information and epistemic actions are indeed important and may be subtle.

> *Anne and Bert are in a bar, sitting at a table. A messenger comes in and delivers a letter that is addressed to Anne. The letter contains either an invitation for a night out in Amsterdam, or an obligation to give a lecture instead. Anne and Bert commonly know that these are the only alternatives.*

This situation can be modelled as follows: There is one atom p, describing 'the letter invites Anne for a night out in Amsterdam', so that $\neg p$ stands for her lecture obligation. There are two agents 1 (Anne) and 2 (Bert). Whatever happens in each of the following action scenarios, is publicly known (to Anne and Bert). Also, assume that in fact p is true.

ACTION SCENARIO 1. (TELL) Anne reads the letter aloud.

ACTION SCENARIO 2. (READ) Bert is seeing that Anne reads the letter.

ACTION SCENARIO 3. (MAYREAD) Bert orders a drink at the bar so that Anne may have read the letter.

ACTION SCENARIO 4. (BOTHMAYREAD) Bert orders a drink at the bar while Anne goes to the bathroom. Both may have read the letter.

After execution of the first scenario it is common knowledge that p: in the resulting epistemic state $C_{12}p$ (i.e. $C_{\{1,2\}}p$) holds. This is not the case in the second scenario, but still, some common knowledge is obtained there: $C_{12}(K_1 p \vee K_1 \neg p)$: it is commonly known that Anne knows the contents of the letter, irrespective of it being p or $\neg p$. Does this higher-order information change in Scenario 3? Yes, in this case Bert does not even know if Anne knows p or knows $\neg p$: $\neg K_2(K_1 p \vee K_1 \neg p)$. In Scenario 4 something similar is happening, that may best be described by saying that the agents concurrently learn that the other may have learnt p or $\neg p$. Note that in this case both agents may have learnt p, so that p is generally known: $E_{12}p$, but they are in that case unaware of each other's knowledge – $\neg C_{12}p$ –, and *that* is commonly known.

Van Ditmarsch has described such actions as *knowledge actions* (with corresponding dynamic modal operators) in a multiagent dynamic epistemic language (200; 203). Knowledge actions are interpreted as a relation between epistemic states. The contribution of our paper is that it provides a complete axiomatization for the extension of this language with concurrency as found in (201; 202). This builds on work on concurrency in dynamic logic (PDL) (195; 185; 184) and is partially related to game theoretical semantics for (extensions of) dynamic logic (193; 194).

The applicability of the framework is found in every context where multiagent strategic decision making is at stake, and already demonstrated in game-like scenarios such as Cluedo and card games (200).

Section 2 introduces the language and its semantics. Section 3 defines the axioms and derivation rules, and prerequisites for their formulation, such as syntactic equivalence of actions, and shows the soundness of this proof system. Section 4 shows its completeness. Section 5 gives some applications of the language in specifying multiagent system dynamics, and is followed by the conclusions (Section 6).

2. LANGUAGE AND SEMANTICS

2.1. *Structures*

Given a finite set of *agents* N and a set of *atoms* P, a (Kripke) *model* $M = \langle W, R, V \rangle$ consists of a domain W of *worlds* or *factual states*, for each agent $n \in N$ a binary *accessibility relation* R_n on W, and a *valuation* $V : P \to \mathcal{P}(W)$, or in other words: for each atom $p \in P$, a subset V_p of W. In an *epistemic model* (commonly known as an $S5$ model) all accessibility relations are equivalence relations. We then write $\sim_n$ for the equivalence relation for agent n. If $w \sim_n w'$ we say that *w is the same as w'* for n, or

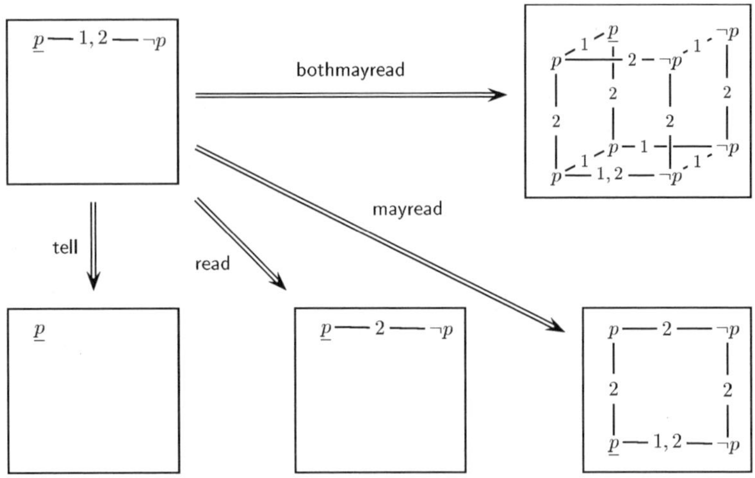

FIGURE 1. Epistemic states resulting from the execution of actions described in the four Action Scenarios. The top left figure represents (Arc, u). Points of epistemic states are underlined. Assume transitivity of access. For mayread and bothmayread only one of more executions is shown.

that w *is equivalent to* w' for n. Write $\sim_B$ for $(\bigcup_{n\in B} \sim_n)^*$ (where R^* is the transitive closure of a binary relation R).

Given a epistemic model M and a world $w \in M$, (M, w) is called an *epistemic state*, w the *point* of that epistemic state, and M the model *underlying* that epistemic state.

For a given model M, $\mathcal{D}(M)$ returns its domain. Instead of $w \in \mathcal{D}(M)$ we also write $w \in M$. If $s = (M, w)$ and $v \in M$ we also write $v \in s$ (and $\mathcal{D}(s)$ for $\mathcal{D}(M)$). Write $\mathcal{S}5_N(P)$ for the class of epistemic models for agents N and atoms P, and $\mathcal{S}5_{\subseteq N}(P)$ for $\bigcup_{B\subseteq N} \mathcal{S}5_B(P)$. Write $\bullet\mathcal{S}5_N(P)$ for the class of epistemic states for agents N and atoms P (i.e., 'pointed' – $\bullet$ – models). We drop the 'P' if it is clear from the context.

Given an epistemic model M or epistemic state s for a set of agents N, the operator gr returns that set: $gr(M) = gr(s) = N$. This is called the *group* of that epistemic model / state. The group of a set is the union of the groups of its members.

EXAMPLE 1. The background setting for 'Lecture or Amsterdam' can be represented by an epistemic state. *Arc* is the model $\langle\{u, v\}, \sim, V\rangle$ such that both $\sim_1$ and $\sim_2$ are the universal relation on $\{u, v\}$, and $V_p = \{u\}$. The epistemic state (Arc, u) corresponds to p being actually the case. After

Anne has read the letter, an epistemic state is reached that is like (Arc, u) but with $\sim_1 = \{(u,u),(v,v)\}$ instead. See Figure 1.

2.2. *Syntax*

To a standard multiagent epistemic language with common knowledge for a set N of agents and a set P of atoms (190; 181), we add dynamic modal operators for programs that are called knowledge actions or just actions. Actions may change the knowledge of the agents involved. The formulas $\mathcal{L}_N(P)$, the actions $\mathcal{L}_N^{\mathsf{act}}(P)$, and the group gr of an action are defined by simultaneous induction:

DEFINITION 1. (FORMULAS AND ACTIONS)
The *formulas* $\mathcal{L}_N(P)$ are defined by

$$\varphi ::= p \mid \neg\varphi \mid (\varphi \wedge \varphi) \mid K_n\varphi \mid C_B\varphi \mid [\alpha]\psi$$

where $p \in P$, $n \in N$, $B \subseteq N$, $\alpha \in \mathcal{L}_N^{\mathsf{act}}(P)$, and $\psi \in \mathcal{L}_{gr(\alpha)}(P)$. The *actions* $\mathcal{L}_N^{\mathsf{act}}(P)$ are defined by

$$\alpha ::= ?\varphi \mid L_B\beta \mid (\alpha \mathbin{!} \alpha) \mid (\alpha \mathbin{¡} \alpha) \mid (\alpha \mathbin{;} \beta') \mid (\alpha \cup \alpha) \mid (\alpha \cap \alpha)$$

where $\varphi \in \mathcal{L}_N(P)$, $B \subseteq N$, $\beta \in \mathcal{L}_B^{\mathsf{act}}(P)$, and $\beta' \in \mathcal{L}_{gr(\alpha)}^{\mathsf{act}}(P)$, and where the *group* $gr(\alpha)$ of an action $\alpha \in \mathcal{L}_N^{\mathsf{act}}(P)$ is defined as: $gr(?\varphi) := \emptyset$, $gr(L_B\alpha) := B$, and $gr(\alpha \bullet \alpha') := gr(\alpha) \cap gr(\alpha')$ for $\bullet = \,!\,, \cap, \cup, \,;\,$.

Other propositional connectives and modal operators are defined by standard abbreviations, in particular $E_B\varphi := \bigwedge_{n \in B} K_n\varphi$. Outermost parentheses of formulas and actions are deleted whenever convenient. As we may generally assume an arbitrary P, write $\mathcal{L}_N$ instead of $\mathcal{L}_N(P)$, and $\mathcal{L}_N^{\mathsf{act}}$ instead of $\mathcal{L}_N^{\mathsf{act}}(P)$. Instead of, e.g., $C_{\{a,b,c\}}$ we always write C_{abc}. For an arbitrary epistemic ('box'-like) operator K, write $\hat{K}$ for its dual ('diamond'). The dual of $[\alpha]$ is $\langle\alpha\rangle$.

The program constructor L_B is called *learning.* Action $?\varphi$ is a *test*, $(\alpha \,;\, \alpha')$ is *sequential execution*, $(\alpha \cup \alpha')$ is *nondeterministic choice*, $(\alpha \,!\, \alpha')$ is called *(left) local choice* and $(\alpha \,¡\, \alpha')$ is called *(right) local choice*, and $(\alpha \cap \alpha')$ is *concurrent execution.* The construct $L_B?\varphi$ is pronounced as 'B learn *that* φ'. Local choice $\alpha \,!\, \alpha'$ may, somewhat inaccurately, be seen as 'from α and α', choose the first.' Local choice $\alpha \,¡\, \alpha'$ may be seen as 'from α and α', choose the second.' We will see that the interpretation of local choice '!' and '¡' depends on the context of learning that binds it: in $L_B(\alpha \,!\, \alpha')$, everybody in B but not in learning operators occurring in α, α', is unaware of the choice for α. That choice is therefore 'local'. Typically, we show properties of local choice for '!' only.

The group gr was already used for the agents 'occurring' in epistemic states and models. It serves a similar function on actions, whence the overloading. The constructs $[\alpha]\psi$, $L_B\beta$, and $[\alpha \,;\, \beta]$, wherein gr is used (implicitly in $L_B\beta$), guarantee that in an epistemic state for agents N that is the result of action execution, formulas containing modal operators for agents *not* in N are not considered for interpretation.

EXAMPLE 2. The description in $\mathcal{L}^{\mathsf{act}}_{12}(\{p\})$ of the actions in the introduction are:

$$
\begin{array}{rl}
\mathsf{tell} & L_{12}?p \cup L_{12}?\neg p \\
\mathsf{read} & L_{12}(L_1?p \cup L_1?\neg p) \\
\mathsf{mayread} & L_{12}(L_1?p \cup L_1?\neg p \cup\ ?\top) \\
\mathsf{bothmayread} & L_{12}(\ (L_1?p \cap L_2?p) \cup (L_1?\neg p \cap L_2?\neg p) \\
 & \cup L_1?p \cup L_1?\neg p \cup L_2?p \cup L_2?\neg p \cup\ ?\top)
\end{array}
$$

For example, the description of read (Anne reads the letter) reads as follows: 'Anne and Bert learn that either Anne learns that she is invited for a night out in Amsterdam or that Anne learns that she has to give a lecture instead.' In the last two actions, instead of $?\top$ (for 'nothing happens') we may as well write $?p \cup ?\neg p$. (Associativity of $\cup$ is for now assumed, and proved later.)

A nondeterministic action can have more than one execution in a given epistemic state. The only way to get such an action is to use nondeterministic choice operators $\cup$ in its description. If we use ! operators instead, typically, only some but not all of the agents are aware of the choices made. Constructs $\cup$ and ! are related as follows:

DEFINITION 2. (TYPE AND INSTANCE OF AN ACTION) By replacing all occurrences of '!' and '¡' in an action α by '$\cup$', except when under the scope of ?, we get the *type* $t(\alpha)$ of that action. Slightly informally we can write:

$$t(\alpha) := \alpha[!/\cup, ¡/\cup]$$

By replacing all occurrences of '$\cup$' in an action α for either '!' or '¡', except when under the scope of ?, we get the set of *instances* $T(\alpha)$ of that action. Informally we can write:

$$T(\alpha) := \{\alpha[\cup/!, ¡]\}$$

If $t(\alpha) = t(\beta)$ we say that α and β are the same type of action. Further, if α and β are identical modulo swapping of occurrences of '!' for '¡' or vice versa, write

$$\alpha =_T \beta$$

Obviously, $=_T$ is an equivalence. We say that α, β are *comparable* actions.

Instead of $\alpha\ !\ \alpha'$ we generally write $!\alpha \cup \alpha'$. This expresses more clearly that given choice between α and α', the agents involved in those actions choose α, whereas that choice remains invisible to the agents that learn about these alternatives but are not involved. Similarly, instead of α ¡ α' we generally write $\alpha \cup\ !\alpha'$.

Comparable actions $\alpha =_T \beta$ are 'on the same level of abstraction in the type hierarchy'. This means that they can be 'compared': it can be determined if they are (syntactically) the same for a given agent or not, a notion needed in the proof system to be introduced in Section 3.

EXAMPLE 3. The action read where Bert is seeing that Anne reads the letter is different from the instance of that action where *Anne is actually invited for a night out* and Bert is seeing that Anne reads the letter. The last is described as $L_{12}(L_1?p \,!\, L_1?\neg p)$: of the two alternatives $L_1?p$ and $L_1?\neg p$, the first is chosen, but agent 2 is unaware of that choice. A different way of writing that action is $L_{12}(!L_1?p \cup L_1?\neg p)$. The action read is its *type*. The other instance of action read is $L_{12}(L_1?p \text{ ¡ } L_1?\neg p)$ $(L_{12}(L_1?p\cup !L_1?\neg p))$. Actions $L_{12}(!L_1?p\cup L_1?\neg p)$ and $L_{12}(L_1?p\cup !L_1?\neg p)$ are *comparable* to each other.

Somewhat similarly, the action bothmayread has four different executions if p is true and another four if p is false: there are eight actions instances (state transformers) of that type.

2.3. Semantics

The semantics of $\mathcal{L}_N(P)$ (on epistemic models) is defined as usual (190), plus an additional clause for the meaning of dynamic operators. The interpretation of a dynamic operator is a relation between an epistemic state and a set of epistemic states. The *composition* $(R \circ R')$ of two relations $R, R' : W \to \mathcal{P}(W)$ (such as $[\![\cdot]\!]$) is defined as follows: let $v \in W, V \subseteq W$, then: $(R \circ R')(v, V) :\Leftrightarrow \exists X : R(v, X)$ and $\forall x \in X : \exists V_x : R'(x, V_x)$ and $V = \bigcup_{x \in X} V_x$. Further, $R \sqcup R' := \{(v, V) \mid \exists V', V'' : R(v, V'), R'(v, V'')$, and $V = V' \cup V''\}$.

In the semantics, we need a notion of equivalence between sets of epistemic states. We lift equivalence of worlds in an epistemic state to equivalence of epistemic states and to equivalence of sets of epistemic states. Sets of epistemic states will occur as worlds in Definition 4 of action interpretation, and equivalence of such worlds for an agent will be defined as equivalence of those sets.

DEFINITION 3. (EQUIVALENCE OF SETS OF EPISTEMIC STATES)

Let $M, M' \in \mathcal{S}5_N$, $v, w \in M$, and $w' \in M'$. Let $S, S' \subseteq \bullet\mathcal{S}5_{\subseteq N}$. Let $n \in N$. Then:

$(M, w) \sim_n (M, v)$	iff	$w \sim_n v$
$(M, w) \sim_n (M', w')$	iff	$\exists v \in M : (M, v) \leftrightarroweq (M', w')$ and $(M, w) \sim_n (M, v)$
$S \sim_n S'$	iff	$[\, \forall s \in S : n \in gr(s) \Rightarrow \exists s' \in S' : s \sim_n s' \,]$ and $[\, \forall s' \in S' : n \in gr(s') \Rightarrow \exists s \in S : s \sim_n s' \,]$

In the second clause of the definition, $\underline{\leftrightarrow}$ stands for 'is bisimilar to' (192). Bisimilarity is a notion of sameness between epistemic states that implies equivalence of their logical descriptions (theories), though not vice versa. The implicit symmetric closure in the third clause of the definition is needed to keep $\sim_n$ an equivalence relation.

We now continue with the semantics. The interpretation of formulas and actions is defined simultaneously.

DEFINITION 4. (INTERPRETATION OF FORMULAS AND ACTIONS)

Let $s = (M, w) \in \bullet\mathcal{S}5_N(P)$, where $M = \langle W, \sim, V\rangle$; let $\varphi \in \mathcal{L}_N(P)$, and let $\alpha \in \mathcal{L}_N^{\mathsf{act}}(P)$. The interpretation $\models$ of φ in (M, w) and the interpretation $[\![\cdot]\!]$ of α in (M, w) are both defined by inductive cases.

$$
\begin{array}{lll}
M, w \models p & \text{: iff} & w \in V(p) \\
M, w \models \neg\varphi & \text{: iff} & M, w \not\models \varphi \\
M, w \models \varphi \wedge \psi & \text{: iff} & M, w \models \varphi \text{ and } M, w \models \psi \\
M, w \models K_n\varphi & \text{: iff} & \forall w' : w' \sim_n w \Rightarrow M, w' \models \varphi \\
M, w \models C_B\varphi & \text{: iff} & \forall w' : w' \sim_B w \Rightarrow M, w' \models \varphi \\
M, w \models [\alpha]\varphi & \text{: iff} & \forall S \subseteq \bullet\mathcal{S}5_{\subseteq N} : (M, w)[\![\alpha]\!]S \Rightarrow \exists s' \in S : s' \models \varphi
\end{array}
$$

$$
\begin{array}{rlll}
s[\![?\varphi]\!]S & \text{: iff} & s \models \varphi \text{ and } S = \{(\langle W_\varphi, \emptyset, V|W_\varphi\rangle, w)\} & \text{(see below)} \\
s[\![L_B\alpha]\!]S & \text{: iff} & \exists S' : s[\![\alpha]\!]S' \text{ and } S = \{(\langle W', \sim', V'\rangle, S')\} & \text{(see below)} \\
[\![\alpha\ ;\ \alpha']\!] & := & [\![\alpha]\!] \circ [\![\alpha']\!] & \\
[\![\alpha \cup \alpha']\!] & := & [\![\alpha]\!] \cup [\![\alpha']\!] & \\
[\![\alpha\ !\ \alpha']\!] & := & [\![\alpha]\!] & \\
[\![\alpha \cap \alpha']\!] & := & [\![\alpha]\!] \sqcup [\![\alpha']\!] &
\end{array}
$$

For arbitrary S: $S \models \varphi$ iff for all $s \in S$: $s \models \varphi$. In the clause of action interpretation for 'test': $W_\varphi = \{v \in \mathcal{D}(M) \mid M, v \models \varphi\}$. In the clause for 'learning': $W' := \{S'' \mid \exists v \in M : (M, v)[\![t(\alpha)]\!]S''\}$; for an arbitrary agent n: if $(M, v)[\![t(\alpha)]\!]S$ and $(M, v')[\![t(\alpha)]\!]S'$ then: $S \sim_n' S'$ iff $v \sim_n v'$ and $S \sim_n S'$, where the last $\sim_n$ is equivalence of sets of epistemic states; and for an arbitrary atom p: $S'' \in V_p'$ iff [for all $(\langle W'', \sim'', V''\rangle, w'') = s'' \in S'' : w'' \in V_p''$].

The notion $\langle\alpha\rangle$ is dual to $[\alpha]$ and can be conveniently defined as

$$s \models \langle\alpha\rangle\varphi \text{ iff } \exists S : s[\![\alpha]\!]S \text{ and } S \models \varphi$$

This may be intuitively more appealing: from the given epistemic state s, we can reach a set of of epistemic states S where φ holds everywhere ('concurrently'). Our treatment of the dynamic operators is similar to that in dynamic logic (195; 184).

A test results in an epistemic state without access for any agent. This is appropriate: how knowledge changes is only expressed in 'learning', so before we encounter a learn operator we cannot say anything at all about the knowledge of the agents in the epistemic state resulting from action execution: no access. One might as well say that, while compositionally interpreting an action, the computation of agents' knowledge is *deferred* until L operators are encountered.

Learning $L_B\alpha$ is defined in terms of $t(\alpha)$, and *this* is how local choice constructions $\alpha \,!\, \alpha'$ get their meaning from being bound by a learning operator: specifically, $[\![L_B(\beta \,!\, \beta')]\!]$ is computed from $[\![\beta \cup \beta']\!]$, and therefore from $[\![\beta]\!]$ *and* $[\![\beta']\!]$. To execute an action $L_B\alpha$ in an epistemic state s, we do not just have to execute the *actual* action α in the *actual* epistemic state s, but also any *other* action of the same type $t(\alpha)$ as α in any *other* epistemic state s' with the same underlying model as s. The results are the *worlds* in the epistemic state that results from executing $L_B\alpha'$ in s. Such worlds (that are sets of epistemic states) cannot be distinguished from each other by an agent $n \in B$ if they are indistinguishable as sets. This induces a notion of n-equivalence among action interpretations:

DEFINITION 5. (SEMANTIC ACCESSIBILITY OF ACTIONS)
Let $\alpha, \alpha' \in \mathcal{L}_N^{\mathsf{act}}$, and $n \in N$. Let $M \in \mathcal{S}5_N$, $w, w' \in M$, and $S \subseteq \bullet\mathcal{S}5_N$. Then:

$$[\![\alpha]\!] \sim_n [\![\alpha']\!] \quad \text{iff} \quad \begin{array}{l} [\; w \sim_n w' \text{ and } (M,w)[\![\alpha]\!]S \;] \Rightarrow \\ [\; \exists S' : (M,w')[\![\alpha']\!]S' \text{ and } S \sim_n S' \;] \end{array}$$

In other words, modulo nondeterminism and concurrency: two actions are the same for an agent, if always when two worlds are the same for an agent, executing those actions doesn't make them different. An infinite number of actions is similar in this sense. For example, $?p$ is the same for any agent as $?(p \vee p)$. However, given an action, it can be determined which actions that are comparable to it (which is the finite set $[\cdot]_{=_T}$), are the same for a given agent or not. This will be addressed in Section 3.

The semantics may *appear* complex, because worlds in the model resulting from learning are actually sets of epistemic states. It is therefore important to realize that this is *merely a complex naming device* for worlds, but that the semantics is simple where it matters: the accessibility between worlds (simple: use $\sim_n$), and the value of atoms (simple: keep current value).

If the interpretation of α in s is not empty, we say that α is *executable* in s. For all actions except concurrent knowledge actions it is more intuitive to think of their interpretation as a relation between epistemic states than as a relation between an epistemic state and a set of epistemic states: if $s[\![\alpha]\!]\{s'\}$, we like to think of s' as the result of executing α in s. The notational abbreviation $s[\![\alpha]\!]s' :\Leftrightarrow s[\![\alpha]\!]\{s'\}$ allows us to keep using this helpful intuition. Further, if the interpretation is functional as well, write

$s[\![\alpha]\!]$ for the unique s' such that $s[\![\alpha]\!]s'$. If this is the case for arbitrary s, we call α a *state transformer*. Note that tests are state transformers.

EXAMPLE 4. The interpretation of $\mathsf{read} = L_{12}(L_1?p \cup L_1?\neg p)$ (see Action scenario 2) on (Arc, u) (see Example 1) is defined in terms of the interpretation of $L_1?p \cup L_1?\neg p$ on (Arc, u) and (Arc, v). To interpret $L_1?p \cup L_1?\neg p$ on (Arc, u) we may either interpret $L_1?p$ or $L_1?\neg p$. Only the first can be executed. The interpretation of $L_1?p$ on (Arc, u) is defined in terms of the interpretation of $?p$ on any epistemic state (Arc, x) where $?p$ can be executed, i.e. where p holds, that is on (Arc, u); $(Arc, u)[\![?p]\!]$ is the singleton epistemic state consisting of world u without access. This epistemic state is therefore the single world in the domain of $(Arc, u)[\![L_1?p]\!]$. That world has reflexive access for 1, because the epistemic state it stands for lacks access for 1, so that:

$$(Arc, u)[\![?p]\!] \sim_1 (Arc, u)[\![?p]\!]$$

In the next and final stage of the interpretation, note that (as worlds)

$$(Arc, u)[\![L_1?p]\!] \sim_2 (Arc, u)[\![L_1?\neg p]\!]$$

because agent 2 does not occur in those epistemic states, but that

$$(Arc, u)[\![L_1?p]\!] \not\sim_1 (Arc, u)[\![L_1?\neg p]\!]$$

because $(Arc, u)[\![L_1?p]\!]$ is not bisimilar to $(Arc, u)[\![L_1?\neg p]\!]$. Further details have been omitted. See Figure 2.

EXAMPLE 5. The interpretation of $\mathsf{tell} = L_{12}?p$ (see Action scenario 1) on (Arc, u) can be computed along the same lines as that of read but is much simpler. The interpretation of $\mathsf{bothmayread} = L_{12}((L_1?p \cap L_2?p) \cup (L_1?\neg p \cap L_2?\neg p) \cup L_1?p \cup L_1?\neg p \cup L_2?p \cup L_2?\neg p \cup\ ?p \cup\ ?\neg p)$ (see Action scenario 4) is more complex. The choice action bound by L_{12} can be executed in four ways in (Arc, u), and similarly in four ways in (Arc, v). These result in the eight worlds of the cube-shaped model of Figure 1. We give a detail of the computation that involves concurrency.

The world in the left-front-top corner of the cube in Figure 1 is the set of epistemic states S such that $(Arc, u)[\![L_1?p]\!]S$, i.e., as the interpretation is clearly functional: $S = \{(Arc, u)[\![L_1?p]\!]\}$. The world in the left-back-top corner is the set of epistemic states S' such that $(Arc, u)[\![L_1?p \cap L_2?p]\!]S'$, i.e. $S' = S \cup S''$, with S'' such that $(Arc, u)[\![L_2?p]\!]S''$. Therefore, $S' = \{(Arc, u)[\![L_1?p]\!], (Arc, u)[\![L_2?p]\!]\}$. We have that $S \sim_1 S'$, because $(Arc, u)[\![L_1?p]\!] \in S$ can be mapped to ditto in S', and because $(Arc, u)[\![L_1?p]\!] \sim_1 (Arc, u)[\![L_1?p]\!]$; and because, vice versa, $(Arc, u)[\![L_1?p]\!] \in S'$ can be mapped to ditto in S, and agent 1 does not occur at all in $(Arc, u)[\![L_2?p]\!] \in S'$.

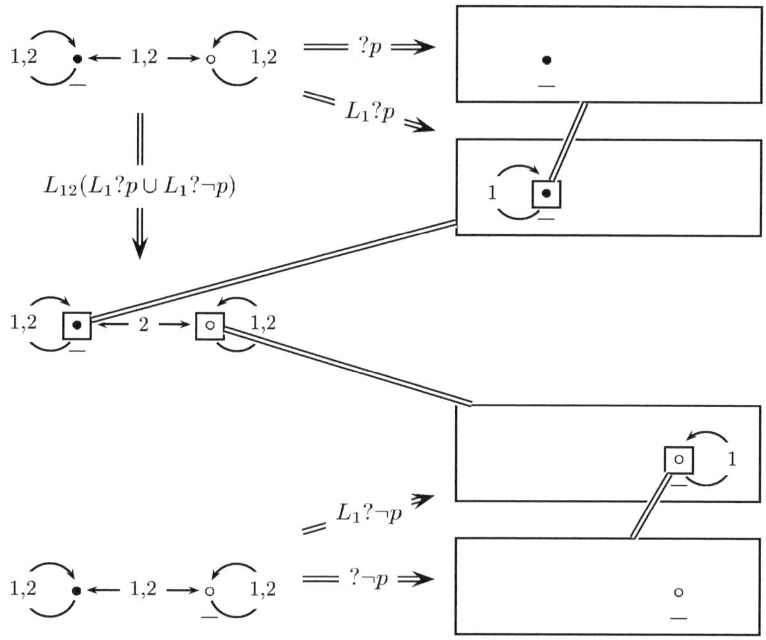

FIGURE 2. Details of the interpretation of action read in (Arc, u). All access is visualized. Atom p holds in • worlds, and does not hold in ∘ worlds. Linked boxes are identical. See also Figure 1.

EXAMPLE 6. The second clause in Definition 3, where bisimilarity to an n-equal epistemic state is a sufficient condition for n-equivality of epistemic states, can*not* be removed from the definition of equivalence between epistemic states.

E.g., with the stronger condition of identity (or isomorphism, even), agent 1 is unable to distinguish action

$$L_{12}(!L_1L_1?p \cup (L_1?p \cap L_2?p) \cup L_1?\neg p \cup ?\top)$$

from action

$$L_{12}(L_1L_1?p \cup\ !(L_1?p \cap L_2?p) \cup L_1?\neg p \cup ?\top)$$

after execution in epistemic state (Arc, u). Unlike before, we cannot now establish that $(Arc, u)[\![L_1L_1?p]\!] \sim_1 (Arc, u)[\![L_1?p \cap L_2?p]\!]$. This 1-equivalence fails, because $(Arc, u)[\![L_1L_1?p]\!] \not\sim_1 (Arc, u)[\![L_1?p]\!]$, because their underlying models are *different*: the domain of the first consists of an epistemic state $(Arc, u)[\![L_1?p]\!]$ (consisting of one world, accessible to 1, p holds), the domain of the second of an epistemic state $(Arc, u)[\![?p]\!]$ (consisting of one world, no access, p holds). However, obviously

$$(Arc, u)[\![L_1 L_1?p]\!] \leftrightarrows (Arc, u)[\![L_1?p]\!]$$

(both have a domain consisting of one world, that is accessible to 1, and where p holds).

Without the bisimilarity clause, in the resulting epistemic state agent 1 would know that agent 2 has not learnt p after execution of the first action. So, also from a conceptual point of view, we can easily realise that this cannot be correct.

We close this section with some elementary properties of the semantics. Two actions α, α' are (semantically) *equivalent*, notation $[\![\alpha]\!] = [\![\alpha']\!]$, if they induce the same relation between epistemic states and sets of epistemic states, modulo names of worlds.

PROPOSITION 1. (ACTION ALGEBRA) Let $\alpha, \alpha', \alpha'' \in \mathcal{L}_N^{\mathsf{act}}$. Then:

$$\begin{array}{rcl} [\![(\alpha \cup \alpha') \cup \alpha'']\!] & = & [\![\alpha \cup (\alpha' \cup \alpha'')]\!] \\ [\![(\alpha \ ; \ \alpha') \ ; \ \alpha'']\!] & = & [\![\alpha \ ; \ (\alpha' \ ; \ \alpha'')]\!] \\ [\![(\alpha \cup \alpha') \ ; \ \alpha'']\!] & = & [\![(\alpha \ ; \ \alpha'') \cup (\alpha' \ ; \ \alpha'')]\!] \\ [\![(\alpha \ ; \ \alpha') \cup \alpha'']\!] & = & [\![(\alpha \cup \alpha'') \ ; \ (\alpha' \cup \alpha'')]\!] \end{array}$$

PROOF. By using simple relational algebra. We show the third, the rest is similar: $[\![(\alpha \cup \alpha') \ ; \ \alpha'']\!] = [\![\alpha \cup \alpha']\!] \circ [\![\alpha'']\!] = ([\![\alpha]\!] \cup [\![\alpha']\!]) \circ [\![\alpha'']\!] = ([\![\alpha]\!] \circ [\![\alpha']\!]) \cup ([\![\alpha]\!] \circ [\![\alpha'']\!]) = [\![\alpha \ ; \ \alpha']\!] \cup [\![\alpha \ ; \ \alpha'']\!] = [\![(\alpha \ ; \ \alpha') \cup (\alpha \ ; \ \alpha'')]\!]$. □

Associativity of $\cup$ was already assumed in the text before. There are various other algebraic properties of action interpretations, such as $[\![L_B L_B \alpha]\!] = [\![L_B \alpha]\!]$. The next proposition relates action instances and action types to other actions.

PROPOSITION 2. (ACTION TYPES AND INSTANCES)
Let $\alpha \in \mathcal{L}_N^{\mathsf{act}}$. Then:

- (a) $[\![\alpha]\!] \subseteq [\![t(\alpha)]\!]$
- (b) Action instances have a functional interpretation.
- (c) if $\beta \in T(\alpha)$ then $[\![\beta]\!] \subseteq [\![\alpha]\!]$
- (d) $[\![\alpha]\!] = [\![\bigcup_{\beta \in T(\alpha)} \beta]\!]$

PROOF.

(a) Induction on α. The only nontrivial case is $\alpha' \ ! \ \alpha''$. We have that: $[\![\alpha' \ ! \ \alpha'']\!] = [\![\alpha']\!] \subseteq [\![\alpha' \cup \alpha'']\!] = [\![\alpha']\!] \cup [\![\alpha'']\!] \subseteq_{IH} [\![t(\alpha')]\!] \cup [\![t(\alpha'')]\!] = [\![t(\alpha') \cup t(\alpha'')]\!] = [\![t(\alpha' \ ! \ \alpha'')]\!]$.

(b) Induction on α. The only nontrivial case is nondeterministic choice. Let $\beta \in T(\alpha' \cup \alpha'')$. Then either $\beta = \beta' \ ! \ \beta''$ or $\beta = \beta' \ ¡ \ \beta''$, with $\beta' \in T(\alpha')$ and $\beta'' \in T(\alpha'')$. In the first case, by induction $[\![\beta']\!]$ is functional, and therefore also $\llbracket \beta' \; ! \; \beta'' \rrbracket = \llbracket \beta' \rrbracket$. In the second case, this follows from the functionality of $\llbracket \beta'' \rrbracket$.

(c) Induction on α. A typical case: Let $s \in \bullet\mathcal{S}5_N$, $S \subseteq \bullet\mathcal{S}5_{\subseteq N}$, and suppose that $s\llbracket \alpha' \cup \alpha'' \rrbracket S$. Then either $s\llbracket \alpha' \rrbracket S$ or $s\llbracket \alpha'' \rrbracket S$. If $s\llbracket \alpha' \rrbracket S$ then, by induction, there is a $\beta' \in T(\alpha')$ such that $s\llbracket \beta' \rrbracket S$. Let $\beta'' \in T(\alpha'')$ be arbitrary. Then $\beta' \; ! \; \beta'' \in T(\alpha' \cup \alpha'')$ and $s\llbracket \beta' \rrbracket S = s\llbracket \beta' \; ! \; \beta'' \rrbracket S$.

(d) Induction on α. Some cases. Case $\alpha' \; ; \; \alpha''$: use Proposition 1. Case

$$\begin{aligned} \alpha' \cup \alpha'' \colon \llbracket \alpha' \cup \alpha'' \rrbracket &=_{IH} \llbracket \textstyle\bigcup_{\beta' \in T(\alpha')} \beta' \cup \bigcup_{\beta'' \in T(\alpha'')} \beta'' \rrbracket \\ &= \llbracket \textstyle\bigcup_{\beta' \in T(\alpha'), \beta'' \in T(\alpha'')} (\beta' \; ! \; \beta'') \cup \\ &\quad \textstyle\bigcup_{\beta' \in T(\alpha'), \beta'' \in T(\alpha'')} (\beta' \; ¡ \; \beta'') \rrbracket \\ &= \llbracket \textstyle\bigcup_{\beta \in T(\alpha)} \beta \rrbracket. \end{aligned}$$

Case $L_B\alpha'$: use that $s\llbracket L_B\alpha' \rrbracket \{(M', S)\}$ presupposes $s\llbracket \alpha' \rrbracket S$. □

Proposition 2.a expresses that the interpretation of an action is contained in the interpretation of its type. Proposition 2.b entails that the interpretation of state transformers is indeed functional. Proposition 2.c expresses that the interpretation of an instance of an action is contained in the interpretation of that action. Proposition 2.d expresses that an action is somehow the same (induces the same interpretation) as nondeterministic choice between all its instances.

The two main theorems of interest are the following. The proofs are adapted from (203). They are by simultaneous induction (referring to each other). For convenience in the proof, we lift the notion of bisimilarity from one between epistemic states to one between sets of epistemic states: $S \underline{\leftrightarrow} S'$ iff for all $s \in S$ there is an $s' \in S'$ such that $s \underline{\leftrightarrow} s'$, and for all $s' \in S'$ there is an $s \in S$ such that $s \underline{\leftrightarrow} s'$.

THEOREM 1. (BISIMILARITY IMPLIES MODAL EQUIVALENCE) Let $\varphi \in \mathcal{L}_N$. Let $s, s' \in \bullet\mathcal{S}5_N$. If $s \underline{\leftrightarrow} s'$, then $s \models \varphi \Leftrightarrow s' \models \varphi$.

PROOF. By induction on the structure of φ. The proof is standard, except for the clause $\varphi = [\alpha]\psi$ that we therefore present in detail. Assume $s \models [\alpha]\psi$. We have to prove $s' \models [\alpha]\psi$. Let S' be arbitrary such that $s'\llbracket \alpha \rrbracket S'$. By the simultaneous induction hypothesis (Theorem 2) it follows from $s'\llbracket \alpha \rrbracket S'$ and $s \underline{\leftrightarrow} s'$ that there is an S such that $S \underline{\leftrightarrow} S'$ and $s\llbracket \alpha \rrbracket S$. From $s\llbracket \alpha \rrbracket S$ and $s \models [\alpha]\psi$ (given) follows that there is an $s'' \in S$ such that $s'' \models \psi$. From $S \underline{\leftrightarrow} S'$, $s'' \in S$, and $s'' \models \psi$, follows that there is an $s''' \in S'$ such that $s''' \models \psi$. From $s''' \models \psi$, $s''' \in S'$, and $s'\llbracket \alpha \rrbracket S'$ follows that $s' \models [\alpha]\psi$. □

THEOREM 2. (ACTION EXECUTION PRESERVES BISIMILARITY) Let $\alpha \in \mathcal{L}_N^{\mathsf{act}}$ and $s, s' \in \bullet\mathcal{S}5_N$. If $s \underline{\leftrightarrow} s'$ and there is an $S \subseteq \bullet\mathcal{S}5_{\subseteq N}$ such that $s\llbracket \alpha \rrbracket S$, then there is an $S' \subseteq \bullet\mathcal{S}5_{\subseteq N}$ such that $s'\llbracket \alpha \rrbracket S'$ and $S \underline{\leftrightarrow} S'$.

PROOF. By induction on the structure of α, or, to be slightly more accurate: induction on the complexity of α, where $L_B\alpha > t(\alpha)$.

We remind the reader of previously introduced notational conventions used in this proof: If α is a state transformer and executable in s, write $s[\![\alpha]\!]$ for the s' such that $s[\![\alpha]\!]\{s'\}$; if $(M, w) = s$ is an epistemic state and $v \in \mathcal{D}(M)$, we also write: $v \in s$, or $v \in M$.

Case $?\varphi$: Suppose $\mathfrak{R} : s \underline{\leftrightarrow} s'$. By simultaneous induction (Theorem 1) it follows from $s \underline{\leftrightarrow} s'$ and $s \models \varphi$ that $s' \models \varphi$. Define, for all $v \in s[\![?\varphi]\!]$, $v' \in s'[\![?\varphi]\!]$: $\mathfrak{R}^{?\varphi}(v, v') :\Leftrightarrow \mathfrak{R}(v, v')$. Then $\mathfrak{R}^{?\varphi} : s[\![?\varphi]\!] \underline{\leftrightarrow} s'[\![?\varphi]\!]$, because (Points:) $\mathfrak{R}^{?\varphi}(w, w)$, (Back and Forth:) both epistemic states have empty access, and (Valuation:) $\mathfrak{R}^{?\varphi}(v, v')$ implies $\mathfrak{R}(v, v')$. In other words: $\{s'[\![?\varphi]\!]\}$ is the required S'.

Case $L_B\alpha'$: Suppose $\mathfrak{R} : s \underline{\leftrightarrow} s'$ and $s[\![L_B\alpha']\!]\{s_+\}$. Let $s = (M, w)$ and $s' = (M', w')$. Let $S_+ \in s_+$ be arbitrary (i.e.: a world S_+ that is a set of epistemic states, occurring in the domain of epistemic state s_+). Then there is a $z \in s$ such that $(M, z)[\![t(\alpha)]\!]S_+$. Because $z \in s$ and $\mathfrak{R} : s \underline{\leftrightarrow} s'$, there is a $z' \in s'$ such that $\mathfrak{R}(z, z')$ and obviously we also have that $\mathfrak{R} : (M, z) \underline{\leftrightarrow} (M', z')$ (the domain of an epistemic state is the domain of its underlying model). By induction, using that the complexity of $t(\alpha)$ is smaller than that of $L_B\alpha$, there is an S'_+ such that $(M', z')[\![t(\alpha)]\!]S'_+$ and $S_+ \underline{\leftrightarrow} S'_+$.

Now define s'_+ as follows: its domain consists of worlds S'_+ constructed according to the procedure just outlined; accessibility between such worlds is accessibility between those worlds as sets of epistemic states, and valuation corresponds to those in the bisimilar worlds of s_+. Finally, the point of s'_+ is a set of epistemic states that is the result of executing α in s' and that is bisimilar to the point of s_+. The accessibility on s'_+ corresponds to that on s_+, because for arbitrary sets of epistemic states (and thus for worlds in s_+, s'_+): if $S_1 \sim_n S_2$, $S_1 \underline{\leftrightarrow} S'_1$, and $S_2 \underline{\leftrightarrow} S'_2$, then $S'_1 \sim_n S'_2$. Therefore $s_+ \underline{\leftrightarrow} s'_+$, $s'[\![L_B\alpha]\!]\{s'_+\}$, and $\{s'_+\}$ is the required S'.

Case $\alpha\ ;\ \beta$: Suppose $s \underline{\leftrightarrow} s'$ and $s[\![\alpha\ ;\ \beta]\!]S$. Note that $[\![\alpha\ ;\ \beta]\!] = [\![\alpha]\!] \circ [\![\beta]\!]$. Let S_1 be such that $s[\![\alpha]\!]S_1$ and for all $s_1 \in S_1$ there is an S_{s_1} such that $s_1[\![\beta]\!]S_{s_1}$, and $S = \cup_{s_1} S_{s_1}$. By induction we have an S'_1 such that $s'[\![\alpha]\!]S'_1$ and $S_1 \underline{\leftrightarrow} S'_1$. Again by induction, for an arbitrary $s_1 \in S_1$ such that $s_1 \underline{\leftrightarrow} s'_1 \in S'_1$ and $s_1[\![\beta]\!]S_{s_1}$, we have an $S'_{s'_1}$ such that $s'_1[\![\beta]\!]S'_{s'_1}$ and $S_{s_1} \underline{\leftrightarrow} S'_{s'_1}$. Let $S' = \cup_{s'_1} S'_{s'_1}$. Then $s'[\![\alpha\ ;\ \beta]\!]S'$ and $S \underline{\leftrightarrow} S'$ (S' may be larger than S, but $S \underline{\leftrightarrow} S'$ then also holds, see case $\cap$.)

Case $\alpha \cup \beta$: Suppose $s \underline{\leftrightarrow} s'$ and $s[\![\alpha \cup \beta]\!]S$. Then either $s[\![\alpha]\!]S$ or $s[\![\beta]\!]S$. If $s[\![\alpha]\!]S$, then by induction there is an S' such that $s'[\![\alpha]\!]S'$ and $S \underline{\leftrightarrow} S'$. Therefore also $s'[\![\alpha \cup \beta]\!]S'$. Similarly, if $s[\![\beta]\!]S$.

Cases $\alpha \, ! \, \beta$ and $\alpha \, ¡ \, \beta$ are similar to $\alpha \cup \beta$.

Case $\alpha \cap \beta$. Suppose $s \underline{\leftrightarrow} s'$ and $s[\![\alpha \cap \beta]\!]S$. Let S_1 and S_2 be such that $s[\![\alpha]\!]S_1$, $s[\![\beta]\!]S_2$, and $S_1 \cup S_2 = S$. By induction, there are S_1' and S_2' such that $s'[\![\alpha]\!]S_1'$, $s'[\![\beta]\!]S_2'$, $S_1 \underline{\leftrightarrow} S_1'$, $S_2 \underline{\leftrightarrow} S_2'$. The required S' such that $S \underline{\leftrightarrow} S'$ is $S' := S_1' \cup S_2'$. (It doesn't matter if $S_1 \cap S_2$ is empty or not. In the last case, S_1' and S_2' may have been chosen so that S' contains more epistemic states than S, but $S \underline{\leftrightarrow} S'$ still holds.) □

A corollary of theorem 2 is the following:

COROLLARY 1. Let $s, s' \in \bullet\mathcal{S}5_N$, and let $\alpha \in \mathcal{L}_N^{\mathsf{act}}$ be a state transformer that is executable in s. If $s \underline{\leftrightarrow} s'$, then $s[\![\alpha]\!] \underline{\leftrightarrow} s'[\![\alpha]\!]$.

3. PROOF SYSTEM

In this section we present the proof system for concurrent dynamic epistemic logic. It is based on the dynamic epistemic logics of (182) and (173), and on Concurrent PDL (195). Before we present the proof system we need a syntactic notion for the executability of an action and a syntactic notion for equivalence of actions, because, among other things, we want to express the following as an axiom (*Action use*): 'after an action α an agent n knows that φ, iff the executability of α implies that n knows that, for each action β that is equivalent to α for n, after β is executed φ holds.' The notion of executibility is captured syntactically by the *precondition*, see Definition 7. The notion of equivalence of actions can also be captured syntactically, and this is done in Definition 6. This is merely a partition, for each agent, on the set of actions that are comparable to a given action ($[\alpha]_{=_T}$).

EXAMPLE 7. Consider the action $L_{123}(?\top \cup L_1?p \cup (L_1?p \cap L_2?p))$, i.e., everybody learns that either nothing happens, or 1 learns p or both 1 and 2 learn p. Or, in a more 'natural' setting: an outsider tells Anne (1), Bill (2) and Cath (3), who are sitting in a bar, at a table, that he may have told Anne, or both Anne and Bill, that Anne is invited for a lecture. Even if Anne now knows that she is invited, she doesn't know whether Bill knows that too. In other words, Anne cannot distinguish action $\mathsf{one} := L_{123}(?\top \cup \, !L_1?p \cup (L_1?p \cap L_2?p))$ from action both $:= L_{123}(?\top \cup L_1?p \cup \, !(L_1?p \cap L_2?p))$. On the other hand, Bill can distinguish those actions: if he has learnt p, he knows that Anne has learnt p as well. However, both Anne and Bill *can* distinguish nothing happening

– none $:= L_{123}(!?\top \cup L_1?p \cup (L_1?p \cap L_2?p))$ – from something happening, whereas Cath cannot do so.

A notion of accessibility among actions will be essential for the formulation of axioms and rules in the proof system. Semantically, we were already able to make that distinction, by the obvious way of 'lifting' the notion of access within a model, to one between epistemic states, to one between sets of epistemic states, and to one between relations between epistemic states and sets of epistemic states, such as between actions by means of their interpretation $[\![\cdot]\!]$ (see Definition 4). We now define a *syntactic* notion of accessibility among actions, such that syntactic access implies semantic access.

DEFINITION 6. (SYNTACTIC ACCESSIBILITY) Let $Gr(\alpha)$ be the set of all agents occurring in learning operators in α, except those under the scope of '?'. Then

$$\alpha \sim_n \beta \text{ iff } \alpha =_T \beta \text{ and } \alpha \approx_n \beta$$

where $\approx_n$ is the symmetric closure of the smallest relation satisfying the following conditions:

$$\begin{array}{lll}
\alpha \approx_n \beta & \text{if} & n \notin Gr(\alpha) \cup Gr(\beta) \\
L_B\alpha \approx_n L_B\beta & \text{if} & \alpha =_T \beta \text{ and } \alpha \approx_n \beta \\
\alpha \bullet \alpha' \approx_n \beta \bullet \beta' & \text{if} & \alpha \approx_n \beta \text{ and } \alpha' \approx_n \beta' \qquad \text{for } \bullet = \cap,\ ;\ , \cup \\
\left.\begin{array}{l}
\alpha \approx_n \beta \,!\, \beta' \\
\alpha \,!\, \alpha' \approx_n \beta \,!\, \beta' \\
\alpha' \,¡\, \alpha \approx_n \beta \,!\, \beta' \\
\alpha' \,¡\, \alpha \approx_n \beta' \,¡\, \beta \\
\alpha \approx_n \beta' \,¡\, \beta
\end{array}\right\} & \text{if} & \alpha \approx_n \beta \\
\left.\begin{array}{l}
\alpha \approx_n \beta \cap \beta' \\
\alpha \approx_n \beta' \cap \beta
\end{array}\right\} & \text{if} & \alpha \approx_n \beta \text{ and } (n \notin Gr(\beta') \text{ or } \alpha \approx_n \beta')
\end{array}$$

The 'large group' Gr of an action is the union of all groups learning anything anywhere, except when under the scope of '?'. Relation $\sim_n$ induces a partition on the set of all actions of the same type (see Definition 2 of $=_T$). In the clause for 'learning' it is essential that the type requirement is made once more: note that otherwise, e.g., $L_1?p \sim_1 L_1?q$, as tests are indistinguishable from each other for any agent.

PROPOSITION 3. $\sim_n$ is an equivalence.

PROOF. We prove that $\approx_n$ is an equivalence, from which follows that $\sim_n$ is an equivalence. Obviously, $\approx_n$ is reflexive and symmetrical. Transitivity is proven by distinguishing many cases, we merely do the crucial ones.

Suppose $\alpha \,!\, \alpha' \approx_n \beta \,¡\, \beta'$ and $\beta \,¡\, \beta' \approx_n \gamma \,!\, \gamma'$. Then, using the definition: $\alpha \approx_n \beta'$ and $\beta' \approx_n \gamma$. Using induction, we have $\alpha \approx_n \gamma$. By again using the definition of $\approx_n$: $\alpha \,!\, \alpha' \approx_n \gamma \,!\, \gamma'$.

Suppose $\alpha \approx_n \beta \cap \beta'$ and $\gamma \approx_n \beta \cap \beta'$, and that the first holds because $\alpha \approx_n \beta$ and $n \notin Gr(\beta')$, and the second because $\gamma \approx_n \beta'$ and $n \notin Gr(\beta)$. There is one non-trivial way for which $\alpha \sim_n \beta$, $n \notin Gr(\beta)$, but $n \in Gr(\alpha)$; namely when $\alpha = \alpha' ! \alpha''$ and $n \in Gr(\alpha'')$ but $n \notin Gr(\alpha')$. Same for $\gamma \sim_n \beta$, $n \notin Gr(\beta)$, but $n \in Gr(\gamma)$. From $n \notin Gr(\alpha)$ and $n \notin Gr(\gamma)$ follows $\alpha \approx_n \gamma$. All other such cases follow by induction. □

LEMMA 1. Given an action α, the set $[\alpha]_{\sim_n}$ is effectively computable.

PROOF. If m is the number of $!$ and $¡$ operators in α, there are at most 2^m actions β that are comparable to α (such that $\beta =_T \alpha$). So $[\alpha]_{=_T}$ can easily be determined. The set $[\alpha]_{\sim_n}$ is determined by computing the partition on $[\alpha]_{=_T}$ given $\approx_n$. This can be determined in linear time with respect to the length of the action. □

EXAMPLE 8. (SYNTACTIC ACCESSIBILITY) Consider Example 7 at the beginning of this subsection. The type of action discussed was $L_{123}(?\top \cup L_1?p \cup (L_1?p \cap L_2?p))$. More precisely, we may choose to read $L_{123}((?\top \cup L_1?p) \cup (L_1?p \cap L_2?p))$ (see Proposition 1). There are four instances of this type. This is a $=_T$ equivalence class. One of those instances is $\mathsf{none} := L_{123}((?\top \,!\, L_1?p) \,!\, (L_1?p \cap L_2?p))$, which we informally write as $L_{123}(!?\top \cup L_1?p \cup (L_1?p \cap L_2?p))$. Note that only three of the four instances are essentially different: once you have chosen 'right', it does not matter whether the subsequent choice on the left is 'right' or 'left'. We now compute the mentioned equivalences on the set of instances. Once again, let $\mathsf{one} := L_{123}((?\top \,¡\, L_1?p) \,!\, (L_1?p \cap L_2?p))$, and let both $:= L_{123}((?\top \,¡\, L_1?p) \,¡\, (L_1?p \cap L_2?p))$

'Even if Anne now knows that she is invited, she doesn't know whether Bill is invited too':

one	$\approx_1$	both
$\Leftrightarrow$		
$(?\top \,¡\, L_1?p) \,!\, (L_1?p \cap L_2?p)$	$\approx_1$	$(?\top \,¡\, L_1?p) \,¡\, (L_1?p \cap L_2?p)$
$\Leftarrow$		
$?\top \,¡\, L_1?p$	$\approx_1$	$L_1?p \cap L_2?p$
$\Leftarrow$		
$L_1?p$	$\approx_1$	$L_1?p \cap L_2?p$
$\Leftarrow$		
$L_1?p$	$\approx_1$	$L_1?p$ and $1 \notin Gr(L_2?p)$

'Bill can distinguish those actions': We have that $L_1?p \not\approx_2 L_1?p \cap L_2?p$, because 2 can distinguish an action where he learns something, namely

$L_2?p$, and that is part of $L_1?p \cap L_2?p$, from one that is invisible to him, namely $L_1?p$ (on the left). This results in $\mathsf{one} \not\approx_2 \mathsf{both}$.

Cath cannot distinguish nothing happening from something happening, e.g.:

$$\begin{array}{lll} \mathsf{none} & \approx_3 & \mathsf{one} \\ \Leftrightarrow (\ldots) & & \\ ?\top \ ! \ L_1?p & \approx_3 & ?\top \ ¡ \ L_1?p \\ \Leftarrow & & \\ ?\top & \approx_3 & L_1?p \\ \Leftarrow & & \\ 3 \notin Gr(?\top) \cup Gr(L_1?p) = \{1\} & & \end{array}$$

PROPOSITION 4. (SYNTACTIC IMPLIES SEMANTIC EQUIVALENCE)

$$\beta \sim_n \beta' \Rightarrow [\![\beta]\!] \sim_n [\![\beta']\!]$$

PROOF. We prove that $\beta \approx_n \beta' \Rightarrow [\![\beta]\!] \sim_n [\![\beta']\!]$, from which the required follows. The proof is by induction on the structure of the actions β and β' (i.e. prove each inductive case of β by induction on β'). We show the non-trivial cases.

If $n \notin Gr(\beta) \cup Gr(\beta')$, then trivially $[\![\beta]\!] \sim_n [\![\beta']\!]$: given arbitrary s and S (resp. s and S') such that $s[\![\beta]\!]S$ (resp. $s'[\![\beta]\!]S'$, the group of S (resp. S') must be $\emptyset$. Therefore $S \sim_n S'$. A fortiori $S \sim_n S'$ when $s \sim_n s'$, so that $[\![\beta]\!] \sim_n [\![\beta']\!]$.

If $L_B\alpha \approx_n L_B\beta$ and $n \in B$, by the definition of $\approx_n$: $\alpha \approx_n \beta$, by induction: $[\![\alpha]\!] \sim_n [\![\beta]\!]$, and by the construction of $\sim_n$ in the case 'learning' of the definition of $[\![\cdot]\!]$, $[\![L_B\alpha]\!] \sim_n [\![L_B\beta]\!]$ immediately follows.

If $\alpha \ ! \ \beta \approx_n \alpha' \ ¡ \ \beta'$, then $\alpha \approx_n \beta'$, so by induction $[\![\alpha]\!] \sim_n [\![\beta']\!]$, so, by definition of $[\![\cdot]\!]$, $[\![\alpha \ ! \ \beta]\!] \sim_n [\![\alpha' \ ¡ \ \beta']\!]$.

Suppose $\alpha \approx_n \beta \cap \beta'$ because $\alpha \approx_n \beta$ and $n \notin Gr(\beta')$. By induction $[\![\alpha]\!] \sim_n [\![\beta]\!]$. As for arbitrary sets of epistemic states S, S', S'' it holds that: if $S \sim_n S'$ and $n \notin gr(S'')$, then $S \sim_n S' \cup S''$, the required $[\![\alpha]\!] \sim_n [\![\beta \cap \beta']\!]$ now follows. □

COROLLARY 2. (PRESERVATION OF ACCESSIBILITY) Given an epistemic model M, $v, v' \in M$, and actions β, β' such that β is executable in (M, v) and β' is executable in (M, v'). If $v \sim_n v'$ and $\beta \sim_n \beta'$, then for S such that $(M, v)[\![\beta]\!]S$ there is an S' such that $(M, v')[\![\beta]\!]S'$ and $S \sim_n S'$.

COROLLARY 3. For action instances and state transformers β, β': if $v \sim_n v'$ and $\beta \sim_n \beta'$ (and executability), then $(M, v)[\![\beta]\!] \sim_n (M, v')[\![\beta']\!]$.

In Proposition 4 we have established that if two actions are syntactically the same for an agent, they are also semantically the same: if $\beta \sim_n \beta'$, then $[\![\beta]\!] \sim_n [\![\beta']\!]$. For trivial reasons this is indeed a proper inclusion, because actions of a different type cannot be syntactically the same. For example, we have that $[\![?p]\!] \sim_1 [\![?\neg\neg p]\!]$ but $?p \not\sim_1 ?\neg\neg p$ (because $?p \neq_T ?\neg\neg p$). Also, $[\![L_1?p]\!] \sim_1 [\![L_1L_1?p]\!]$ but $L_1?p \not\sim_1 L_1L_1?p$, and $[\![L_1?p \cup L_1?q]\!] \not\sim_1 [\![L_1?q \cup L_1?p]\!]$ but $L_1?p \cup L_1?q \not\sim_1 L_1?q \cup L_1?p$.

What about actions of the same type? All of the above, and more, can easily be incorporated as alternatives into actions of the same type. For example, consider the actions $L_{12}(L_1?p\cup!(L_1?\neg\neg p\cap L_2?q))$ and $L_{12}(!L_1?p\cup (L_1?\neg\neg p\cap L_2?q))$. These are different for 1, because $L_1?p$ is different for 1 from $L_1?\neg\neg p$, because the types of the respective tests are different (this requires syntactic identity!). Therefore, also in non-trivial cases, $[\![\beta]\!] \sim_n [\![\beta']\!]$ does not imply $\beta \sim_n \beta'$.

This should not necessarily be a problem, as long as we have 'enough' actions that are the same for an agent to a given action to guarantee soudness of the proof system wherein we use syntactic accessibility. But it turns out that we have not enough. The principle of *Action use*, that will indeed occur in the following proof system, says that, if n knows that [after every action that is for n the same as the actual action, φ holds], then [n knows that φ holds] after that action.

Because $L_{12}(L_1?p\cup!(L_1?\neg\neg p \cap L_2?q))$ is different for agent 1 from $L_{12}(!L_1?p\cup(L_1?\neg\neg p\cap L_2?q))$, it is now derivable that after the first action 1 knows that q! In other words: agent 1 can make some epistemic distinction between p and $\neg\neg p$, which does not make sense.

More in general, suppose we have arbitrarily complex and differently described actions $\alpha, \beta \in \mathcal{L}_N^{\mathsf{act}}(P)$ and $n \in N$ such that $\alpha =_T \beta$ and $[\![\alpha]\!] \sim_n [\![\beta]\!]$ but $\alpha \not\sim_n \beta$, and let $q \notin P$, $B \supseteq Gr(\alpha) \cup Gr(\beta)$, and $m \notin B$. Consider the action where (everybody learns that) group B, which includes n, learn that either α or β takes place, but that in the second case agent m, not in B, learns that q. Obviously, we do not want n to be able to determine whether q after that action. However, $L_{B+m}(L_B\alpha\cup\ !(L_B\beta \cap L_m?q))$ is different for agent n from $L_{B+m}(!L_B\alpha \cup (L_B\beta \cap L_m?q))$, so after the first action, because of *Action use*, n knows that q, even though, of course, only m is supposed to know that.

Therefore we have to coarsen (as the opposite of 'refine') the partition on $=_T$ for agents n in Definition 6, in order to guarantee the soundness of the proof system to be introduced in Definition 8: we need more n-equal actions. In all the counterexamples above, the problem was that equivalent actions – actions such that $[\![\alpha]\!] = [\![\beta]\!]$, so that they are trivially n-equivalent as well: $[\![\alpha]\!] \sim_n [\![\beta]\!]$ – *should* also be syntactically n-equal for any n. We therefore suggest to solve our problem tentatively as follows: introduce a notion of 'general' syntactic equivalence of actions: $\alpha \approx \alpha'$ iff, for arbitrary φ (however, depending on the complexity of α and β): $\vdash [\alpha]\varphi \leftrightarrow [\alpha']\varphi$; now add a clause to the definition of $\approx_n$ as follows:

$$\alpha \approx_n \beta \text{ if } \bigvee_{\gamma =_T \alpha} (\alpha \sim_n \gamma \text{ and } \gamma \approx \beta)$$

This definition is unsatisfactory for two reasons. First, because the auxiliary notion of $\sim_n$ and the proof system yet to come are now defined simultaneously, we must show that determining syntactic action equivalence does not need instances of axioms wherein syntactic action access thus established is used. This appears to be solved by the lower complexity of action occurrences in such axioms. Second, Lemma 1 no longer holds. Given an action α, the computation of $[\alpha]_{\sim_n}$ on (the easily determined set) $[\alpha]_{=_T}$ may be undecidable (even though it remains clearly finite), as the notion of action equivalence used in $\sim_n$ is now defined in terms of derivability.

Other options out of the dilemma include: define $\approx_n$ not between arbitrary actions but between normal forms of actions, or we may 'simply' define $\alpha \sim_n \beta$ iff $\alpha =_T \beta$ and $[\![\alpha]\!] \sim_n [\![\beta]\!]$, but incorporating a semantic feature in a syntactic notion seems to 'give away' the computational advantage an axiomatization pretends to have over the semantics. We hope to improve on the given solution.

In the remainder, assume that if $\alpha =_T \beta$, then $\alpha \sim_n \beta$ iff $[\![\alpha]\!] \sim_n [\![\beta]\!]$.

We continue by saying when an action can be executed. An action can be executed in an epistemic state if its precondition is true. 'Precondition' is defined as follows.

DEFINITION 7. (PRECONDITIONS OF AN ACTION)

1. $\mathsf{pre}(?\varphi) := \varphi$
2. $\mathsf{pre}(\alpha\ ;\ \beta) := \mathsf{pre}(\alpha) \wedge \langle\alpha\rangle\mathsf{pre}(\beta)$
3. $\mathsf{pre}(\alpha \cup \beta) := \mathsf{pre}(\alpha) \vee \mathsf{pre}(\beta)$
4. $\mathsf{pre}(\alpha \cap \beta) := \mathsf{pre}(\alpha) \wedge \mathsf{pre}(\beta)$
5. $\mathsf{pre}(\alpha\ !\ \beta) := \mathsf{pre}(\alpha)$
6. $\mathsf{pre}(L_B\alpha) := \mathsf{pre}(\alpha)$

LEMMA 2.

$$\models \mathsf{pre}(\alpha) \leftrightarrow \langle\alpha\rangle\top$$

PROOF. By induction on α. Note that $s \models \langle\alpha\rangle\top$ iff there is a set of epistemic states S such that $s[\![\alpha]\!]S$ (omitting the trivial part: 'and for all $s' \in S : s' \models \top$'). The crucial case 'learning': Suppose $s \models \langle L_B\alpha\rangle\top$. Let S be such that $s[\![L_B\alpha]\!]S$. For a point (world) $S' \in s' \in S$ we have $s[\![\alpha]\!]S'$ (because of the definition of action interpretation). I.e., $s \models \langle\alpha\rangle\top$. By induction $s \models \mathsf{pre}(\alpha)$ and because $\mathsf{pre}(L_B\alpha) = \mathsf{pre}(\alpha)$: $s \models \mathsf{pre}(L_B\alpha)$. □

Now we are ready to provide the proof system. It is based on the proof systems of (173) and (195).

DEFINITION 8. (PROOF SYSTEM)

Propositional tautologies	
Knowledge distribution	$K_n(\varphi \to \psi) \to (K_n\varphi \to K_n\psi)$
Truth	$K_n\varphi \to \varphi$
Positive introspection	$K_n\varphi \to K_nK_n\varphi$
Negative introspection	$\neg K_n\varphi \to K_n\neg K_n\varphi$
Common knowledge use	$C_B\varphi \to (\varphi \wedge E_BC_B\varphi)$
Test	$[?\varphi]\psi \leftrightarrow (\varphi \to \psi)$
Sequential composition	$[\alpha\ ;\ \alpha']\varphi \leftrightarrow [\alpha][\alpha']\varphi$
Nondeterministic choice	$[\alpha \cup \alpha']\varphi \leftrightarrow ([\alpha]\varphi \wedge [\alpha']\varphi)$
Concurrency	$[\alpha \cap \alpha']\varphi \leftrightarrow ([\alpha]\varphi \vee [\alpha']\varphi)$
Learning	$\langle L_B\alpha\rangle\top \leftrightarrow \mathsf{pre}(L_B\alpha)$
Local choice	$[\alpha\ !\ \alpha']\varphi \leftrightarrow [\alpha]\varphi$
Action instances	$[\alpha]\varphi \leftrightarrow \bigwedge_{\beta\in T(\alpha)}[\beta]\varphi$
Atomic permanence	$[\alpha]p \leftrightarrow (\mathsf{pre}(\alpha) \to p)$
C-knowledge induction	$(\varphi \wedge C_B(\varphi \to E_B\varphi)) \to C_B\varphi$
Action use	$[\alpha]K_n\varphi \leftrightarrow (\mathsf{pre}(\alpha) \to K_n \bigwedge_{\alpha'\sim_n\alpha}[\alpha']\varphi)$
Modus Ponens	if φ and $\varphi \to \psi$, then ψ
Knowledge necessitation	if φ, then $K_n\varphi$
Action facilitation	if $\varphi \to \psi$, then $[\alpha]\varphi \to [\alpha]\psi$
Action induction	if: for all β such that $\alpha \sim_B \beta$, there is a χ_β such that $\chi_\beta \to [\beta]\varphi$ and such that $\beta \sim_n \alpha'$ implies $(\chi_\beta \wedge \mathsf{pre}(\beta)) \to E_B\chi_{\alpha'}$, then : $\chi_\alpha \to [\alpha]C_B\varphi$

A formula φ is deducable, abbreviated as $\vdash \varphi$, iff there exists a finite sequence of formulas such that each formula is either an instantiation of one of the axioms above, or if it is obtained by applying one of the rules above to formulas that appear earlier in the sequence.

Below we will give a few examples of proofs using this system. In these proofs every formula in the sequence is given a number and written on one line. At the end of the line is given the axiom that the formula is an instantiation of, or the rule that was applied to obtain it, including the lines of the formulas that the rule was applied to. If a formula follows by simple propositional reasoning, we write PC, accompanied by the lines of formulas.

EXAMPLE 9. We show that $\vdash [L_1?p]K_1p$. To see that this is the case we first determine the precondition of $L_1?p$. It follows from the definition that it is equal to p. Below we will write $\mathsf{pre}(L_1?p)$ for this to make clear which rules are applied.

1. $\mathsf{pre}(L_1?p) \to p$ PC

2. $[L_1?p]p \leftrightarrow (\mathsf{pre}(L_1?p) \rightarrow p)$ — Atomic permanence
3. $[L_1?p]p$ — PC 1,2
4. $K_1[L_1?p]p$ — Knowledge necessitation 3
5. $\mathsf{pre}(L_1?p) \rightarrow K_1[L_1?p]p$ — PC 4
6. $[L_1?p]K_1p \leftrightarrow (\mathsf{pre}(L_1?p) \rightarrow K_1[L_1?p]p)$ — Action use
7. $[L_1?p]K_1p$ — PC 5,6

EXAMPLE 10. We now show that $\vdash [L_{12}?p]C_{12}p$. This example shows how the action induction rule can be applied. Again $\mathsf{pre}(L_{12}?p) = p$.

1. $\mathsf{pre}(L_{12}?p) \rightarrow p$ — PC
2. $[L_{12}?p]p \leftrightarrow (\mathsf{pre}(L_{12}?p) \rightarrow p)$ — Atomic permanence
3. $[L_{12}?p]p$ — PC 1,2
4. $\top \rightarrow [L_{12}?p]p$ — PC 3
5. $\top$ — PC
6. $K_1\top$ — Knowledge necessitation 5
7. $K_2\top$ — Knowledge necessitation 5
8. $((\top \wedge \mathsf{pre}(L_{12}?p)) \rightarrow K_1\top) \wedge ((\top \wedge \mathsf{pre}(L_{12}?p)) \rightarrow K_2\top)$ — PC 6,7
9. $\top \rightarrow [L_{12}?p]C_{12}p$ — Action induction 4,8
10. $[L_{12}?p]C_{12}p$ — PC 9

One might have expected a distribution axiom for $[\alpha]$, but this is not sound. Such an axiom is also unsound in the logic presented in (195), for the same reason: the interpretation of actions are relations between epistemic states and sets of epistemic states. The modality $[\alpha]$ corresponds to a $\forall\exists$ quantifier and distribution does not hold for that. We do have a weaker form of distribution in the form of the action facilitation rule. This is all we need in the completeness proof.

The local choice axiom *suggests* that in arbitrary actions, subactions $\alpha \,!\, \alpha$ can be substituted for α. However, this is not the case, because such substitutions can*not* be performed within the scope of an L_B operator.

The following are used in the completeness proof for formulas of the form $[\alpha]C_B\varphi$ and in the soundness proof of the action induction rule.

DEFINITION 9. (WITNESS PATH) A witness path from $w \in M$ for $\langle\alpha\rangle\hat{C}_B\psi$ (see (173)) is a path

$$w = w_0 \sim_{n_1} w_1 \sim_{n_2} \cdots \sim_{n_k} w_k = v$$

in M, such that $k \geq 0$, $n_i \in N$ and there are actions α_i such that

$$\alpha = \alpha_0 \sim_{n_1} \alpha_1 \sim_{n_2} \cdots \sim_{n_k} \alpha_k = \beta$$

and such that for $0 \leq i \leq k$, $(M, w_i) \models \langle\alpha_i\rangle\top$, and $(M, w_k) \models \langle\alpha_k\rangle\psi$.

LEMMA 3.
$M, w \models \langle\alpha\rangle\hat{C}_B\psi$ iff [there is a witness path for $\langle\alpha\rangle\hat{C}_B\psi$ from w].

PROOF. Note that the right entails that there is a $\beta \sim_B \alpha$ such that $M, w \models \hat{C}_B \langle\beta\rangle\psi$. We reformulate the lemma as one about an arbitrary natural number k and then prove the lemma by induction on k, first the implication to the right, then the one to the left. Write $\sim_B^k$ for a $\sim_B$-path of length k:

Let $\alpha \in \mathcal{L}_N^{\mathsf{act}}$, $(M, w) \in \bullet\mathcal{S}5_N$, $\psi \in \mathcal{L}_N$. For all k: [there is an S_w such that $(M, w)[\![\alpha]\!]S_w$ and for all $(M', w') \in S_w$ there is a $v' \sim_B^k w'$ with $M', v' \models \psi$] iff [there is a witness path of length k for $\langle\alpha\rangle\hat{C}_B\psi$ from w].

First, note that the part '*there is an* S_w *such that* $(M, w)[\![\alpha]\!]S_w$ *and for all* $(M', w') \in S_w$*:*' might as well read '*there is an* (M', w') *resulting from executing* α *in* (M, w)*:*.' The more complex formulation is in accordance with the semantics of actions.

'$\Rightarrow$'. $(k = 0)$ Let $(M', w') \in S_w$. Given $v' \sim_B^0 w'$ with $M', v' \models \psi$. Choose $\beta = \alpha$ and $v = w$ and $S_v = S_w$. The required holds. $(k = k + 1)$ Let $(M', w') \in S_w$. Given $v' \sim_B^{k+1} w'$ with $M', v' \models \psi$. Let n and x' be such that $v' \sim_B^{k+1} w' = v' \sim_n x' \sim_B^k w'$. Choose $\alpha' \sim_n \alpha$ and $x \sim_n w$ such that $(M, x)[\![\alpha']\!]S_x$ and $(M', x') \in S_x$. Now by induction, there is a witness path of length k for $\langle\alpha'\rangle\hat{C}_B\psi$ from x. Let $x \sim_B^k v$ be that path and $\alpha' \sim_B^k \beta$ be the corresponding chain of actions. Then $w \sim_n x \sim_B^k v$ is the required witness path from w, with $\alpha \sim_n \alpha' \sim_B^k \beta$ the required chain of actions.

'$\Leftarrow$'. $(k = 0)$ Given $v = w$ and $\alpha = \beta$ (path length 0). We then have $M, w \models \langle\alpha\rangle\psi$. Therefore, trivially, $M, w \models \langle\alpha\rangle\hat{C}\psi$. Therefore, there is (by the definition of $\models$) an S_w where ψ holds throughout, as required for 'zero length'. $(k = k + 1)$ Let $(M', w') \in S_w$. Given v and β such that $w \sim_B^{k+1} v$ and $\alpha \sim_B^{k+1} \beta$ as required. Let the first steps in those chains be $w \sim_n x$ and $\alpha \sim_n \alpha'$, respectively. By induction, there is an S_x such that for all $(M', x') \in S_x$, there is a $v' \sim_B^k x'$ with $M', v' \models \psi$. We now complete this to a path of length $k+1$ as follows. As $w \sim_n x$ and $\alpha \sim_n \alpha'$, by Corollary 2 we may choose S_w such that $(M, w)[\![\alpha]\!]S_w$ and $S_w \sim_n S_x$. We can now complete our required path by choosing $(M', w') \in S_w$ such that $w' \sim_n x'$ (and note that - as required - *for each* $s \in S_w$ there must be such a corresponding epistemic state $s' \in S_x$, because of the definition of $\sim_n$ between sets of epistemic states; therefore, (M', w') may be considered arbitrary). From $(M, w)[\![\alpha]\!]S_w$, $(M', w') \in S_w$ arbitrary, $w' \sim_n x' \sim_B^k v'$, and $M', v' \models \psi$, follows: $M, w \models \langle\alpha\rangle\hat{C}_B\psi$. □

We are now ready to establish soundness of the proof system, with which we close the section. The following section established the completeness of the proof system.

THEOREM 3. (SOUNDNESS) For all $\varphi \in \mathcal{L}_N(P)$

$$\vdash \varphi \Rightarrow \models \varphi$$

PROOF. By induction on the length of the proof. We omit the familiar purely epistemic cases, for that see, e.g., (190). Throughout the proof, let $(M, w) \in \mathcal{S}5_N(P)$ be arbitrary. Further, assume all introduced sets of epistemic states to be subsets of some proper $\bullet\mathcal{S}5_B$. We remind the reader that '$S \models \varphi$' means '$\forall s \in S : s \models \varphi$.'

Case 'Test'.
Note that in $[?\varphi]\psi \leftrightarrow (\varphi \rightarrow \psi)$, ψ must be a purely propositional formula ($\psi \in \mathcal{L}_\emptyset(P)$), because $gr((M, w)[\![?\varphi]\!]) = \emptyset$. The truth of propositional formulas is unaffected by action execution.

Suppose $M, w \models [?\varphi]\psi$ and $M, w \models \varphi$. Then $(M, w)[\![?\varphi]\!] \models \psi$. Because $\psi \in \mathcal{L}_\emptyset(P)$, also $M, w \models \psi$. Therefore $M, w \models \varphi \rightarrow \psi$.

Suppose $M, w \models \varphi \rightarrow \psi$. If $M, w \not\models \varphi$, then $(M, w) \models [?\varphi]\psi$ trivially holds. Otherwise, because $M, w \models \varphi$, $(M, w)[\![?\varphi]\!]$ exists; and from $M, w \models \varphi$ and $M, w \models \varphi \rightarrow \psi$ follows $M, w \models \psi$. Because $\psi \in \mathcal{L}_\emptyset(P)$, also $(M, w)[\![?\varphi]\!] \models \psi$. Therefore, as well, $(M, w) \models [?\varphi]\psi$.

The axioms 'Sequential composition', 'Nondeterministic choice', and 'Concurrency' are intuitively more appealing in their dual form: $\langle \alpha ; \alpha' \rangle\varphi \leftrightarrow \langle \alpha \rangle\langle \alpha' \rangle\varphi$, $\langle \alpha \cup \alpha' \rangle\varphi \leftrightarrow (\langle \alpha \rangle\varphi \vee \langle \alpha' \rangle\varphi)$, and $\langle \alpha \cap \alpha' \rangle\varphi \leftrightarrow (\langle \alpha \rangle\varphi \wedge \langle \alpha' \rangle\varphi)$. We therefore show the validity of those.

Case 'Sequential composition'.
$M, w \models \langle \alpha ; \alpha' \rangle\varphi$
$\Leftrightarrow$
$\exists S : (M, w)[\![\alpha ; \alpha']\!]S$ and $\forall s \in S : s \models \varphi$
$\Leftrightarrow$
$\exists S, S' : (M, w)[\![\alpha]\!]S'$ and $\forall s' \in S', \exists S_{s'} : s'[\![\alpha]\!]S_{s'}$ and $S = \bigcup_{s' \in S'} S_{s'}$ and $\forall s \in S : s \models \varphi$
$\Leftrightarrow$
$\exists S, S' : (M, w)[\![\alpha]\!]S'$ and $\forall s' \in S', \exists S_{s'} \subseteq S : s'[\![\alpha]\!]S_{s'}$ and $\forall s'' \in S_{s'} : s'' \models \varphi$ and $S = \bigcup_{s' \in S'} S_{s'}$
$\Leftrightarrow$ take $S = \bigcup_{s' \in S'} S_{s'}$
$\exists S' : (M, w)[\![\alpha]\!]S'$ and $\forall s' \in S' : s' \models \langle \alpha' \rangle\varphi$
$\Leftrightarrow$
$M, w \models \langle \alpha \rangle\langle \alpha' \rangle\varphi$

Case 'Nondeterministic choice'.
$M, w \models \langle \alpha \cup \alpha' \rangle\varphi$
$\Leftrightarrow$
$\exists S : (M, w)[\![\alpha \cup \alpha']\!]S$ and $\forall s \in S : s \models \varphi$
$\Leftrightarrow$
$\exists S : [\ (M, w)[\![\alpha]\!]S$ or $(M, w)[\![\alpha']\!]S\ ]$ and $\forall s \in S : s \models \varphi$
$\Leftrightarrow$

$\exists S : [\ (M,w)[\![\alpha]\!]S$ and $\forall s \in S : s \models \varphi\ ]$ or $[\ (M,w)[\![\alpha']\!]S$ and $\forall s \in S : s \models \varphi\ ]$
$\Leftrightarrow$
$[\ \exists S : (M,w)[\![\alpha]\!]S$ and $\forall s \in S : s \models \varphi\ ]$ or $[\ \exists S : (M,w)[\![\alpha']\!]S$ and $\forall s \in S : s \models \varphi\ ]$
$\Leftrightarrow$
$M,w \models \langle\alpha\rangle\varphi$ or $M,w \models \langle\alpha'\rangle\varphi$
$\Leftrightarrow$
$M,w \models \langle\alpha\rangle\varphi \vee \langle\alpha'\rangle\varphi$

Case 'Concurrency'.
$M,w \models \langle\alpha \cap \alpha'\rangle\varphi$
$\Leftrightarrow$
$\exists S : (M,w)[\![\alpha \cap \alpha']\!]S$ and $\forall s \in S : s \models \varphi$
$\Leftrightarrow$
$\exists S_1, S_2 : (M,w)[\![\alpha]\!]S_1$ and $(M,w)[\![\alpha']\!]S_2$ and $\forall s \in S_1, S_2 : s \models \varphi$
$\Leftrightarrow$
$M,w \models \langle\alpha\rangle\varphi$ and $M,w \models \langle\alpha'\rangle\varphi$
$\Leftrightarrow$
$M,w \models \langle\alpha\rangle\varphi \wedge \langle\alpha'\rangle\varphi$

Case 'Learning'.
This follows immediately from Lemma 2, for case $L_B\alpha$. Incidentally, all other cases of Lemma 2 are derivable and therefore not listed as axioms, see Lemma 10, in the continuation.

Case 'Local choice'.
Trivial, as $[\![\alpha\ !\ \alpha']\!] = [\![\alpha]\!]$.

Case 'Action instances'.
This follows directly from Proposition 2 (an action is equivalent to nondeterministic choice between its instances), and repeated application of axiom 'Nondeterministic choice', that has already been proved sound.

Case 'Atomic permanence'.
Trivial.

Case 'Action use'.
We prove the validity of the dual form of action use which is $\langle\alpha\rangle\hat{K}_n\varphi \leftrightarrow (\mathsf{pre}(\alpha) \wedge \hat{K}_n \bigvee_{\alpha' \sim_n \alpha}\langle\alpha'\rangle\varphi)$. Note that $M,w \models \langle\alpha\rangle\hat{K}_n\varphi$ can be rewritten as

$$\exists S : (M,w)[\![\alpha]\!]S \text{ and } S \models \hat{K}_n\varphi \qquad (i)$$

Next, $M, w \models (\mathsf{pre}(\alpha) \wedge \hat{K}_n \bigvee_{\alpha' \sim_n \alpha} \langle \alpha' \rangle \varphi)$ can be rewritten as

$$M, w \models \mathsf{pre}(\alpha) \ \&\ \exists v \sim_n w, \exists \alpha' \sim_n \alpha, \exists S' : (M, v)[\![\alpha']\!]S' \ \&\ S' \models \varphi \qquad (ii)$$

Using Corollary 2, the executability of α in (ii) guarantees the existence of an S such that: $(M, w)[\![\alpha]\!]S$ and $S \sim_n S'$. From this follows by definition of K_n that $S \models \hat{K}_n\varphi$: i.e., (i). Vice versa, given (i), an assumed S' such that $S' \sim_n S$ and $S' \models \varphi$, can only be established by executing some alternative α' to α in a v with $v \sim_n w$ (an agent cannot 'forget' distinctions). We now have $[\![\alpha']\!] \sim_n [\![\alpha]\!]$ by definition, and choosing α' from $[\alpha]_{=_T}$ we get $\alpha \sim_n \alpha'$ as required: i.e., (ii).

Case 'Action facilitation'.
As in other cases, we prove a dual version, namely: '*from* $\varphi \to \psi$ *follows* $\langle \alpha \rangle \varphi \to \langle \alpha \rangle \psi$'. Assume $\models \varphi \to \psi$. Suppose $M, w \models \langle \alpha \rangle \varphi$. Then there is an S such that $(M, w)[\![\alpha]\!]S$ and $S \models \varphi$. As we may assume $\varphi \to \psi$ to be valid, we have $S \models \varphi \to \psi$. From $S \models \varphi$ and $S \models \varphi \to \psi$ follows $S \models \psi$. From $(M, w)[\![\alpha]\!]S$ and $S \models \psi$ follows $M, w \models \langle \alpha \rangle \psi$. Winding up: $M, w \models \langle \alpha \rangle \varphi \to \langle \alpha \rangle \psi$.

Case 'Action induction'.
The soundness of this rule is proved along the lines of (173), using Lemma 3. □

4. COMPLETENESS

The completeness proof is based on (173), (181), and (195). We quite closely follow the structure of the proof in (173). The main difficulty in the proof is the truth lemma, which is proven by induction on formulas. We show that every formula is provably equivalent to a formula in a sublanguage of the full language. The induction follows the structure of the formulas in the sublanguage. We first define the translation to the sublanguage.

DEFINITION 10. (TRANSLATION)
Define the following function $f : \mathcal{L}_N(P) \cup \mathcal{L}_N^{\mathsf{act}}(P) \to \mathcal{L}_N(P) \cup \mathcal{L}_N^{\mathsf{act}}(P)$:

$$\begin{array}{lcl} f(p) & = & p \\ f(\neg\varphi) & = & \neg f(\varphi) \\ f(\varphi \wedge \psi) & = & f(\varphi) \wedge f(\psi) \\ f(K_n\varphi) & = & K_n f(\varphi) \\ f(C_B\varphi) & = & C_B f(\varphi) \end{array}$$

$$\begin{array}{lcl}
f([?\varphi]\psi) & = & f(\varphi) \to f(\psi) \\
f([L_B\alpha]p) & = & f(\mathsf{pre}(\alpha)) \to p \\
f([L_B\alpha]\neg\varphi) & = & \bigvee_{\beta\in T(L_B\alpha)} \neg f([\beta]\varphi) \\
f([L_B\alpha](\varphi\wedge\psi)) & = & f([L_B\alpha]\varphi) \wedge f([L_B\alpha]\psi) \\
f([L_B\alpha]K_n\varphi) & = & f(\mathsf{pre}(\alpha)) \to K_n \bigwedge_{\beta\sim_n L_B\alpha} f([\beta]\varphi) \\
f([L_B\alpha]C_B\varphi) & = & [L_B f(\alpha)]C_B f(\varphi) \\
f([L_B\alpha][\beta]\varphi) & = & f([L_B\alpha]f([\beta]\varphi)) \\
f([\alpha \mathbin{!} \beta]\psi) & = & f([\alpha]\psi) \\
f([\alpha \mathbin{;} \beta]\psi) & = & f([\alpha]f([\beta]\psi)) \\
f([\alpha\cup\beta]\psi) & = & f([\alpha]\psi) \wedge f([\beta]\psi) \\
f([\alpha\cap\beta]\psi) & = & f([\alpha]\psi) \vee f([\beta]\psi) \\
f(?\varphi) & = & ?f(\varphi) \\
f(\alpha \mathbin{;} \beta) & = & f(\alpha) \mathbin{;} f(\beta) \\
f(\alpha\cup\beta) & = & f(\alpha)\cup f(\beta) \\
f(\alpha\cap\beta) & = & f(\alpha)\cap f(\beta) \\
f(\alpha \mathbin{!} \beta) & = & f(\alpha) \mathbin{!} f(\beta) \\
f(L_B\alpha) & = & L_B f(\alpha)
\end{array}$$

LEMMA 4. Given a formula $\varphi \in \mathcal{L}_N$, we have that $f(\varphi) \in \mathcal{L}_N^f$, where $\mathcal{L}_N^f$ the following BNF:

$$\varphi ::= p \mid \neg\varphi \mid \varphi\wedge\varphi \mid K_n\varphi \mid C_B\varphi \mid [L_B\alpha]C_B\varphi$$

where all formulas that occur in $L_B\alpha$ are also in $\mathcal{L}_N^f$.

PROOF. By induction on $\varphi \in \mathcal{L}_N(P)$. □

The next lemma shows, that if we can prove by induction that something holds for every formula $\varphi \in \mathcal{L}_N^f$, then it also applies to every $\varphi \in \mathcal{L}_N$.

LEMMA 5. (WELL-FOUNDED ORDER) There exists a well-founded order $<$ on the language $\mathcal{L}_N \cup \mathcal{L}_N^{act}$ with the following properties:

1. $\psi < \varphi$, for any subformula ψ of φ
2. $<$ is transitive
3. $f(\varphi) \leq \varphi$

PROOF. The proof is very much like a similar proof given in the appendix of (173), where a theorem about lexicographic path orders is used. We apply the same technique but there is a key difference. A formula of the form $[\alpha]\varphi$ can be viewed as a function $[\cdot]\cdot$ on α and φ. The order of the arguments is important for a lexicographic path order. In (173) the order of the arguments is switched in the definition of the lexicographic path order. Here we do not switch the arguments.

Let Σ be the signature of $\mathcal{L}_N$, where atomic propositions are viewed as 0-ary functions, where negations, individual epistemic operators, common knowledge operators, tests, and learn operators are viewed as unary functions, and where conjunctions, sequential composition, non-deterministic choice, concurrent knowledge action, and the $[\cdot]\cdot$ operators are viewed as binary operators.

Now consider the lexicographical path order $<$ that is induced by fixing an order on these such that $[\cdot]\cdot$ is the greatest and the rest of the signature is unordered. It follows directly from the theorem cited in (173) that:

1. $<$ is transitive.
2. $<$ has the subterm property.
3. $<$ is monotonic.
4. $<$ is well-founded.

We now prove that $f(\varphi) \leq \varphi$ by induction on φ. The cases for atoms, negation, conjunction, individual epistemic operators, and common knowledge operators is straightforward.

Suppose φ is of the form $[?\psi]\chi$. Now we can show that $f(\psi) \to f(\chi) < [?\psi]\chi$, because $[\cdot]\cdot$ is greater than $\to$ and because $f(\psi) \leq \psi$ and $f(\chi) \leq \chi$ by the induction hypothesis. Now ψ and χ are both subterms of $[?\psi]\chi$. Therefore $f(\psi) \to f(\chi) < [?\psi]\chi$.

Suppose φ is of the form $[\alpha\ ;\ \beta]\psi$. Now we can show that $f([\alpha]f([\beta]\psi)) < [\alpha\ ;\ \beta]\psi$, because $[\alpha][\beta]\psi < [\alpha\ ;\ \beta]\psi$. Note that $\alpha < \alpha\ ;\ \beta$, because of the subterm property. For the same reason we have $\alpha < [\alpha\ ;\ \beta]\psi$. Now we need to show that $[\beta]\psi < [\alpha\ ;\ \beta]\psi$. And again this is induced by the subterm property. The cases for nondeterministic choice, concurrent execution, and local choice are analogous.

Now we turn to formulas of the form $[L_B\alpha]\psi$. If ψ is an atom p, note that $\mathsf{pre}(\alpha) < [\alpha]\psi$ for all actions α, and p is obviously a subterm of $[L_B\alpha]p$.

If ψ is a negation, we again use the observation that $[\cdot]\cdot$ is greater than disjunctions, and negations. Then we can simply apply the induction hypothesis. The case for conjunctions and individual epistemic operators is analogous.

In case ψ is of the form $C_B\chi$, we observe that the induction hypothesis immediately implies that $f(\alpha) \leq \alpha$. This together with applying the induction hypothesis to χ shows that $[f(L_B\alpha)]C_B f(\chi) \leq [L_B\alpha]C_B\chi$.

The case where ψ is of the form $[\beta]\chi$, follows immediately from the induction hypothesis. □

LEMMA 6. We have both (a) and (b):

(a) $\vdash f(\varphi) \leftrightarrow \varphi$

(b) $\models f(\varphi) \leftrightarrow \varphi$

PROOF. (a) follows immediately from the axioms given in Definition 8 whereas (b) follows from (a) and the soundness Theorem 3. □

We can now start constructing the canonical model. Because logics with reflexive transitive closure operators are generally not compact we need to construct a finite canonical model for every formula. That means we only look at maximally consistent sets with respect to some finite set of sentences. This set of sentences is called the closure.

DEFINITION 11. (CLOSURE) Let $\varphi \in \mathcal{L}_N^f$. The *closure* of φ is the minimal set $\mathcal{C}l(\varphi) \subseteq \mathcal{L}_N^f$ such that

1. $\varphi \in \mathcal{C}l(\varphi)$.
2. If $\psi \in \mathcal{C}l(\varphi)$ and χ is a subformula of ψ, then $\chi \in \mathcal{C}l(\varphi)$.
3. If $\psi \in \mathcal{C}l(\varphi)$ and ψ itself is not a negation, then $\neg\psi \in \mathcal{C}l(\varphi)$
4. If $C_B\psi \in \mathcal{C}l(\varphi)$, then $K_n C_B\psi \in \mathcal{C}l(\varphi)$, for all $a \in B$
5. If $[\alpha]C_B\psi \in \mathcal{C}l(\varphi)$, then for all β such that $\alpha =_T \beta$: $K_n[\beta]C_B\psi, [\beta]\psi \in \mathcal{C}l(\varphi)$.

LEMMA 7. For any formula $\varphi \in \mathcal{L}_N^f$, the closure of φ is finite.

PROOF. One can first apply the clauses 1 and 2. This yields a finite set. To this set, the clauses 4 and 5 can be applied, which preserves finiteness (by Lemma 1 we know that there are only finitely many β such that $\alpha \sim_n \beta$). Finally, applying clause 3 to this set at most doubles its size. □

From now on, we will often write Φ for $\mathcal{C}l(\varphi)$.

DEFINITION 12. (MAXIMALLY CONSISTENT IN Φ) A finite set of sentences Γ such that $\Gamma \subseteq \Phi$, is maximally consistent in Φ iff:

1. Γ is consistent, i.e. $\not\vdash \neg(\bigwedge_{\psi\in\Gamma}\psi)$.
2. There is no $\Gamma' \subset \Phi$, such that $\Gamma' \supset \Gamma$ and Γ' is consistent.

LEMMA 8. (LINDENBÄUMCHEN) Let Φ be the closure of a consistent $\varphi \in \mathcal{L}_N^f$. If $\Gamma \subseteq \Phi$ is consistent in Φ, then there is a set $\Gamma' \supseteq \Gamma$ which is maximally consistent in Φ.

PROOF. As Φ is finite, the members of Φ can be enumerated. Let us suppose $\#(\Phi) = k$ and that φ_i $(1 \leq i \leq k)$is the i-th formula sentence of this enumeration. Now define Γ_i $(0 \leq i \leq k)$ as follows:

$$\begin{array}{lcl}\Gamma_0 & = & \Gamma \\ \Gamma_{i+1} & = & \left\{\begin{array}{ll}\Gamma_i & \text{if } \Gamma_i \cup \{\varphi_{i+1}\} \text{ is inconsistent} \\ \Gamma_i \cup \{\varphi_{i+1}\} & \text{otherwise}\end{array}\right.\end{array}$$

It is easily seen that Γ_k is maximally consistent in Φ.

□

DEFINITION 13. (Φ-CANONICAL MODEL) $M^\Phi = (W^\Phi, R^\Phi, V^\Phi)$

- $W^\Phi = \{\Gamma \subseteq \Phi \,|\, \Gamma \text{ is maximally } \Phi\text{-consistent}\}$
- $\Gamma R_n^\Phi \Delta$ iff $\{\psi \in \Phi \mid K_n\psi \in \Gamma\} = \{\psi \in \Phi \mid K_n\psi \in \Delta\}$ for all $n \in N$

- $V^\Phi(p) = \{\Gamma \mid p \in \Gamma\}$

We can think of $\Gamma \in W^\Phi$ both as a set of formulas of Φ and as its conjunction: if we mean the latter we write $\underline{\Gamma} = \bigwedge_{\varphi \in \Gamma} \gamma$. Note that M^Φ is finite: it contains at most $2^{|\Phi|}$ elements. Moreover, note that it is a model in $\mathcal{S}5_B$, where B is the group of agents that occur in φ, because the accessibility relations R_n^Φ are all equivalence relations.

DEFINITION 14. (GOOD PATH) A good path from $\Gamma \in M^\Phi$ for $\langle\alpha\rangle\hat{C}_B\psi$ is a path in M^Φ

$$\Gamma = \Gamma_0 \sim_{n_1} \Gamma_1 \sim_{n_2} \cdots \sim_{n_k} \Gamma_k$$

such that $k \geq 0$, $n_i \in B$ and there are actions α_i such that

$$\alpha = \alpha_0 \sim_{n_1} \alpha_1 \sim_{n_2} \cdots \sim_{n_k} \alpha_k$$

such that $\langle\alpha_i\rangle\top \in \Gamma_i$ $(0 \leq i \leq k)$ and $\langle\alpha_k\rangle\psi \in \Gamma_k$.

The relationship of a 'good path' to the semantically motivated 'witness path' (Definition 9) will be obvious.

LEMMA 9. Suppose $[\alpha]C_B\psi \in \Phi$. Then: if there is a good path from Γ_0 for $\langle\alpha\rangle\hat{C}_B\neg\psi$, then $\langle\alpha\rangle\hat{C}_B\neg\psi \in \Gamma_0$.

PROOF. By induction on the length k of the path. If $k = 0$, then, since $\alpha_0 = \alpha$, we have $\langle\alpha\rangle\neg\psi \in \Gamma_0$. If $\langle\alpha\rangle\hat{C}_B\neg\psi \notin \Gamma_0$ then, we have $[\alpha]C_B\chi \in \Gamma_0$, and hence, by clause 5 of Definition 11, and the fact that $\vdash [\alpha]C_B\psi \rightarrow [\alpha]\psi$, we have that $[\alpha]\psi \in \Gamma_0$; a contradiction.

Now suppose we have proven the result for k, and suppose that there is a good path from Γ_0 for $\langle\alpha\rangle\hat{C}_B\neg\psi$ of length $k+1$. This gives us a good path of length k from Γ_1 for $\langle\alpha_1\rangle\hat{C}_B\neg\psi$. We also have $[\alpha_1]C_B\psi \in \Phi$, and hence, by using the induction hypothesis, we have $\langle\alpha_1\rangle\hat{C}_B\neg\psi \in \Gamma_1$. Now suppose $\langle\alpha\rangle\hat{C}_B\neg\psi \notin \Gamma_0$, then $[\alpha]C_B\psi \in \Gamma_0$. By Lemma 10 below and the action use axiom we know that $\Gamma_0 \vdash [\alpha]C_B\psi \wedge \mathsf{pre}(\alpha) \rightarrow K_n[\alpha_1]C_B\psi$ and hence $K_n[\alpha_1]C_B\psi \in \Gamma_0$. So $[\alpha_1]C_B\psi \in \Gamma_1$, which contradicts $\langle\alpha_1\rangle\hat{C}_B\neg\psi \in \Gamma_1$. □

LEMMA 10. The precondition of an action α is provably equivalent to $\langle\alpha\rangle\top$.

PROOF. By induction on α. The case for test follows from the test axiom. Using the induction hypothesis the cases for sequential composition, non-deterministic choice, concurrent action, local choice follow directly using the appropriate axioms. The case for the learn operator follows from the Learning axiom. □

LEMMA 11. If $\langle\alpha\rangle\hat{C}_B\neg\psi \in \Gamma$ then there is a good path from Γ for $\langle\alpha\rangle\hat{C}_B\neg\psi$.

PROOF. Suppose $\langle\alpha\rangle\hat{C}_B\neg\psi \in \Gamma$. For each β such that $\alpha \sim_B \beta$, let S_β be the (finite) set of all $\Gamma \in M_\Phi$ such that there is *no* good path from Γ for $\langle\beta\rangle\hat{C}_B\neg\psi$. We need to see that $\Gamma \notin S_\alpha$. Suppose toward a contradiction that $\Gamma \in S_\alpha$. Let

$$\chi_\beta = \bigvee_{\Delta \in S_\beta} \underline{\Delta}$$

Note that $\neg\psi_\beta$ is logically equivalent to $\bigvee_{\Delta' \notin S_\beta} \underline{\Delta'}$. Since we assumed $\Gamma \in S_\alpha$, we have $\vdash \underline{\Gamma} \rightarrow \psi_\alpha$.

We first claim that $\psi_\beta \wedge \langle\beta\rangle\psi$ is inconsistent. Otherwise, there would be a $\Delta \in S_\beta$ such that $\vdash \underline{\Delta} \rightarrow \psi_\beta \wedge \langle\beta\rangle\psi$. Note that $\vdash \langle\beta\rangle\psi \rightarrow \langle\beta\rangle\top$, and, by Lemma 10, $\vdash \langle\beta\rangle\top \leftrightarrow \mathsf{pre}(\beta)$. But then the one point path Δ is a good path from Δ for $\langle\beta\rangle\hat{C}_B\psi$. Thus $\Delta \notin S_\beta$, and this is a contradiction. So indeed, $\psi_\beta \wedge \langle\beta\rangle\psi$ is inconsistent. Therefore, $\vdash \psi_\beta \rightarrow [\beta]\neg\psi$.

We will need the following standard claim: If $\underline{\Delta} \wedge \hat{K}_n\underline{\Delta'}$ is consistent, then $\Delta R_n^\Phi \Delta'$. To see this, suppose that not $\Delta R_n^\Phi \Delta'$. Then there must be a formula $K_n\chi$, such that $K_n\chi \in \Delta$ and $K_n\chi \notin \Delta'$. Therefore, $\Delta \vdash K_nK_n\chi$ and $\hat{K}_n\underline{\Delta'} \vdash \hat{K}_n\neg K_n\chi$. This implies that $\underline{\Delta} \wedge \hat{K}_n\underline{\Delta'}$ is inconsistent.

We next show that for all $n \in B$, and all β and μ such that $\beta \sim_B \mu$, the formula $\psi_\beta \wedge \mathsf{pre}(\beta) \wedge \hat{K}_n\neg\psi_\mu$ is inconsistent. Suppose that it is consistent. Because ψ_β is a disjunction, we can pick a disjunct $\underline{\Theta}$ for which $\underline{\Theta} \wedge \mathsf{pre}(\beta) \wedge \hat{K}_n\neg\psi_\mu$ is consistent. Note that $\Theta \in S_\beta$. Since Θ is maximally consistent in Φ, we have $\mathsf{pre}(\beta) \in \Theta$. Thus, we now have that $\underline{\Theta} \wedge \hat{K}_n\neg\psi_\mu$ is consistent. Note that $\neg\psi_\mu$ is logically equivalent to $\bigvee_{\Theta' \notin S_\mu} \underline{\Theta'}$. As $\hat{K}_n$ distributes over disjunction, we can now pick a disjunct $\hat{K}_n\underline{\Theta'}$ such that $\underline{\Theta} \wedge \hat{K}_n\underline{\Theta'}$ is consistent. Therefore, by the claim above, $\Theta \sim_n \Theta'$. Since $\mathsf{pre}(\beta) \in \Theta$ and $\beta \sim_n \mu$ and there is a good path for $\langle\mu\rangle\hat{C}_B\psi$ from Θ', there is a good path for $\langle\alpha\rangle\hat{C}_B\neg\psi$ from Θ. This contradicts that $\Theta \in S_\beta$. Therefore, $\vdash \psi_\beta \wedge \mathsf{pre}(\beta) \rightarrow K_n\psi_\mu$.

Now we can apply the Action induction rule to show that $\Gamma \vdash \psi_\alpha \rightarrow [\alpha]C_B\neg\psi$ and $\Gamma \vdash \psi_\alpha$. Therefore, $[\alpha]C_B\neg\psi \in \Gamma$. This contradicts our initial assumption, therefore, there *is* a good path for $\langle\alpha\rangle\hat{C}_B\neg\psi$ from Γ.

□

LEMMA 12. (TRUTH LEMMA) If $\Gamma \in W^\Phi$, then for all $\psi \in \Phi$ it holds that $(M^\Phi, \Gamma) \models \psi$ iff $\psi \in \Gamma$.

PROOF. By induction on ψ. Suppose $\psi \in \Phi$. For atoms p, negations, conjunctions, individual epistemic operators and common knowledge operators we refer to (181).

Let ψ be of the form $[\alpha]C_B\chi$. We have the following equivalences:

$(M^\Phi, \Gamma) \not\models [\alpha]C_B\chi$
$\Leftrightarrow$ {Definition of $\langle\alpha\rangle$}
$(M^\Phi, \Gamma) \models \langle\alpha\rangle\hat{C}_B\neg\chi$
$\Leftrightarrow$ {Lemma 3}
There exists a witness path for $\langle\alpha\rangle\hat{C}_B\neg\chi$ from Γ
$\Leftrightarrow$ {Induction Hypothesis}
There exists a good path for $\langle\alpha\rangle\hat{C}_B\neg\chi$ from Γ
$\Leftrightarrow$ {Lemma's 11 and 9}
$\langle\alpha\rangle\hat{C}_B\neg\chi \in \Gamma$
$\Leftrightarrow$ {Γ is maximally consistent in Φ}
$[\alpha]C_B\chi \notin \Gamma$

□

THEOREM 4. (COMPLETENESS) If $\not\vdash \varphi$, then there is a model (M, w) such that $(M, w) \not\models \varphi$

PROOF. Suppose $\not\vdash \varphi$. Then, $\neg\varphi$ is consistent. Take $f(\neg\varphi)$. Note that $\neg\varphi$ and $f(\neg\varphi)$ are provably equivalent (Lemma 6). Now, there is a maximally consistent set Γ in the closure Φ of $f(\neg\varphi)$ such that $f(\neg\varphi) \in \Gamma$. Because of the truth lemma we may conclude that $(M^\Phi, \Gamma) \models f(\neg\varphi)$, and therefore (Lemma 6), $(M^\Phi, \Gamma) \models \neg\varphi$ and thus $(M^\Phi, \Gamma) \not\models \varphi$ □

COROLLARY 4. (DECIDABILITY) The validity problem for concurrent dynamic epistemic logic is decidable.

PROOF. As we noted earlier the canonical model for a formula φ has at most $2^{|\Phi|}$ worlds. There are finitely many models with $2^{|\Phi|}$ worlds. As we can check whether φ holds in a model in finite time, we can check for all these models whether they satisfy φ. If they all satisfy φ, then we can conclude that $\models \varphi$. □

5. APPLICATIONS

In various publications this language has been applied to describe the dynamics of concrete multiagent systems (200; 203; 202; 204). We give an overview of application areas by examples.

EXAMPLE 11. (CARD GAME ACTIONS)
Assume three players $1, 2, 3$ and three cards a, b, c. Each player is dealt one card. Atom a_1 represents the fact where card a is held by player 1, etc. The action where player 1 picks up his card, so that the others cannot see which card it is, is described by the action

$$\mathsf{pickup} = L_{123}(L_1?a_1 \cup L_1?b_1 \cup L_1?c_1)$$

In some epistemic state s where each player is dealt one card and all players have picked up their cards (for details, see (203)), player 1 puts his card face up on the table. This is described by the action

$$\mathsf{table} = L_{123}?a_1 \cup L_{123}?b_1 \cup L_{123}?c_1$$

Note that in a given epistemic state only one of these alternatives can be executed. Now in that same epistemic state s we can also execute two rather different actions: firstly, player 1 can show his card to player 2 without player 3 seeing which card is shown. This action is described by

$$\mathsf{show} = L_{123}(L_{12}?a_1 \cup L_{12}?b_1 \cup L_{12}?c_1)$$

Next, player 2 can ask player 1 "please whisper in my ear the name of a card that you do not have," after which player 1 responds to 2's request. That action is described by

$$\mathsf{whisper} = L_{123}(L_{12}?\neg a_1 \cup L_{12}?\neg b_1 \cup L_{12}?\neg c_1)$$

In this case, whatever the actual epistemic state, 1 can choose one of two cards to whisper (and indeed, the complexity of the resulting epistemic state has now increased).

EXAMPLE 12. (CLUEDO) The 'murder game' Cluedo is a card game where actions as in the previous example can take place. Other typical actions in Cluedo are 'ending your move' and 'winning the game'. For a perfect logician, ending a move in Cluedo is publicly announcing that you cannot win the game yet. This is the action $L_N?\neg\mathsf{win}_n$, where win_n is an epistemic formula describing knowledge of the 'murder cards', the cards 'held by the table' (agent 0) so to speak, i.e. $\mathsf{win}_n = K_n(\mathsf{scarlett}_0 \wedge \mathsf{knife}_0 \wedge \mathsf{kitchen}_0) \vee K_n \ldots$ (all murder cards combinations).

EXAMPLE 13. (DIFFERENT CARDS)
Two players $1, 2$ face three cards a, b, c lying face-down in two stacks on the table. Let a be the atom describing 'card a is in the stack with two cards', etc. Consider the following two actions:

- Player 1 draws a card from the two-cards stack, looks at it, returns it, and then player 2 draws a card from the two-cards stack and looks at it.
- Player 1 draws a card from the two-cards stack, and then player 2 takes the remaining card from that stack. They both look at their card.

The first action is described by the sequence

$$L_{12}(L_1?p \cup L_1?q \cup L_1?r) \ ; \ L_{12}(L_2?p \cup L_2?q \cup L_2?r)$$

Alternatively, the first action could have been described by

$$L_{12}(\bigcup_{x,y=a,b,c} (L_1?x \cap L_2?y))$$

The second action is described by

$$L_{12}(\bigcup_{x\neq y=a,b,c}(L_1?x\cap L_2?y))$$

The first action has nine different executions, the second one six only. The second action, where the alternatives chosen by 1 and 2 depend on each other, has also a different description as a sequence of two actions, namely:

$$L_{12}(L_1?p\cup L_1?q\cup L_1?r)\ ;$$
$$L_{12}(L_2?(p\wedge\neg K_1p)\cup L_2?(q\wedge\neg K_1q)\cup L_2?(r\wedge\neg K_1r))$$

For example, $L_2?(p\wedge\neg K_1p)$ expresses that player 2 only learns p when player 1 has not learnt p already (after which 1 knows that p). That dependence could also have been put explicitly in local choices, which would have resulted in:

$$\begin{array}{l}L_{12}(\\ \quad L_{12}(!L_1?p\cup L_1?q\cup L_1?r)\ ;\ L_{12}(L_2?p\cup\ !L_2?q\cup L_2?r)\ \cup\\ \quad L_{12}(!L_1?p\cup L_1?q\cup L_1?r)\ ;\ L_{12}(L_2?p\cup L_2?q\cup\ !L_2?r)\ \cup\\ \quad L_{12}(L_1?p\cup\ !L_1?q\cup L_1?r)\ ;\ L_{12}(!L_2?p\cup L_2?q\cup L_2?r)\ \cup\\ \quad L_{12}(L_1?p\cup\ !L_1?q\cup L_1?r)\ ;\ L_{12}(L_2?p\cup L_2?q\cup\ !L_2?r)\ \cup\\ \quad L_{12}(L_1?p\cup L_1?q\cup\ !L_1?r)\ ;\ L_{12}(!L_2?p\cup L_2?q\cup L_2?r)\ \cup\\ \quad L_{12}(L_1?p\cup L_1?q\cup\ !L_1?r)\ ;\ L_{12}(L_2?p\cup\ !L_2?q\cup L_2?r)\\ )\end{array}$$

EXAMPLE 14. (SUSPICION) Suppose that an action α *may have* taken place. In what sense? Some agents are involved in that action, others aren't, and the agents not involved can imagine one of two things to have taken place: either that action, or nothing. They cannot distinguish one from the other. One might say that they only *suspect* but do not know that the action has taken place, or that they *consider* the action to have taken place (which is less biased towards one of the alternatives). The result can be described as

$$\mathsf{consider}(\alpha) := L_N(\alpha\cup\ ?\top)$$

In words: group N learn that either α happens or that nothing happens (that the 'test on verity succeeds': always).

It is a generalization of Action Scenario 3, where Bert can imagine Anne to have read the letter. This action was described as $L_{12}(L_1?p\cup L_1?\neg p\cup\ ?\top)$.

EXAMPLE 15. (MUDDY CHILDREN) We assume familiarity with the 'muddy children problem' (181). All actions taking place in the 'muddy children problem' are public announcements. Public announcement of φ corresponds in $\mathcal{L}_N$ to a knowledge action $L_N?\varphi$. Suppose there are three children 1, 2, and 3. First 'father' tells them that at least one of them is muddy. This is described by $L_{123}?(m_1 \vee m_2 \vee m_3)$ (where m_i stand for 'child i is muddy'). And then father tells them, that who knows whether (s)he is muddy may step forward. When nobody steps forward, that action noforward is generally (196; 183; 178) analysed as the public announcement of a conjunction describing that none of the children knows whether he/she is muddy: $L_{123}?((\neg K_1 m_1 \wedge \neg K_1 \neg m_1) \wedge (\neg K_2 m_2 \wedge \neg K_2 \neg m_2) \wedge (\neg K_3 m_3 \wedge \neg K_3 \neg m_3))$. Although correct, this description is more from an external observer's point of view than from the point of view of a child having decided not to step forward. We prefer an analysis where this is clear, in other words, where the action 'nobody steps forward' is composed of subactions '1 does not step forward', '2 does not step forward' and '3 does not step forward':

$$\begin{aligned}\textsf{noforward} \;=\; L_{123}(\; & L_{123}?(\neg K_1 m_1 \wedge \neg K_1 \neg m_1) \cap \\ & L_{123}?(\neg K_2 m_2 \wedge \neg K_2 \neg m_2) \cap \\ & L_{123}?(\neg K_3 m_3 \wedge \neg K_3 \neg m_3) \;)\end{aligned}$$

Suppose that child 1 and 2 are actually muddy, and let this epistemic state be described by $(Cube, 110)$. Then after the execution of $L_{123}?(m_1 \vee m_2 \vee m_3)$ and noforward the epistemic state of Figure 3 results, where it is the case that child 1 and 2 know that they are muddy (so *will* step forward at the next stage).

In Figure 3 we have visualized the precise structure of one of the worlds of the resulting epistemic state, namely 101. The world named 101 is actually a set of three epistemic states, corresponding to, from left to right, 2, 1, and 3 making public that they do not know whether they are muddy:

$$\begin{aligned}&(Cube, 101)[\![L_{123}?(\neg K_2 m_2 \wedge \neg K_2 \neg m_2)]\!]\\ &(Cube, 101)[\![L_{123}?(\neg K_1 m_1 \wedge \neg K_1 \neg m_1)]\!]\\ &(Cube, 101)[\![L_{123}?(\neg K_3 m_3 \wedge \neg K_3 \neg m_3)]\!]\end{aligned}$$

Note that this set of three epistemic states is indeed merely a complex name for that world in the resulting model: the only thing that counts is 'its valuation', namely that child 1 and 3 are muddy in that world and that child 2 is not muddy (and of course, all three epistemic states in the set already corresponded on that!).

EXAMPLE 16. (SECURITY PROTOCOLS) From a pack of seven known cards (0, 1, 2, 3, 4, 5, 6) two players Anne (a) and Bill (b) each draw three cards and a third player Crow (c) gets the remaining card. How can Anne and Bill openly (publicly) inform each other about their cards, without Crow learning from any of their cards who holds it? There are many solutions to this problem (204). Suppose Anne actually holds {0,1,2} (012_a), Bill {3,4,5}, and Crow card 6. One of the solutions consists of Anne saying "My hand is one of $012, 034, 056, 135, 246$" after which Bill

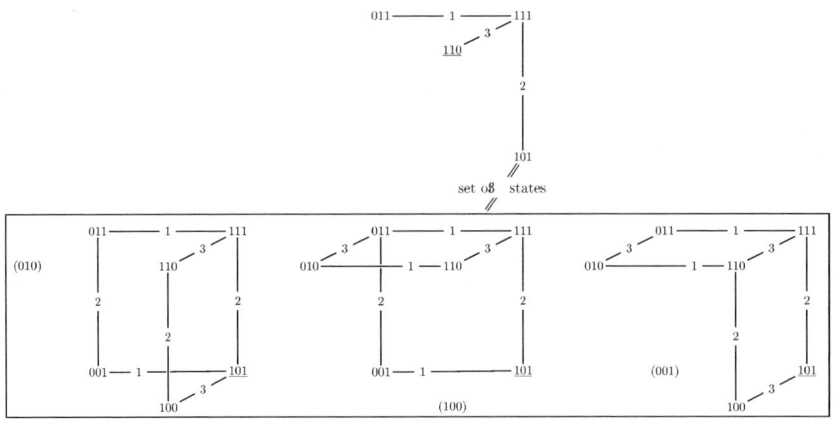

FIGURE 3. None of the children has stepped forward after father has told that at least one of them is muddy. The actual epistemic state is 110: 1 and 2 muddy. Each world of the resulting epistemic state is actually a set of three epistemic states. This is visualized for world 101.

says "Crow has card 6". This is described by the sequence of two public announcements

$$L_{abc}?K_a(012_a \vee 034_a \vee 056_a \vee 135_a \vee 246_a)\ ;\ L_{abc}?K_b6_c$$

Hereafter, it is common knowledge that Anne knows Bill's cards, Bill knows Anne's cards, and Crow doesn't know any of Anne's or Bill's cards.

6. CONCLUSIONS

We have presented a proof system, and proved it to be sound and complete, for a dynamic epistemic logic in which higher-order information and belief change, and even higher-order belief change, can all be elegantly expressed. The crucial technical features of the language are, (1) that the notion of epistemic accessibility is lifted from one between worlds of an epistemic state to one between more complex semantic objects, such as sets of epistemic states, (2) the notion of the group of models, of epistemic states, and of actions, and (3) that actions are interpreted as a relation between epistemic states and sets of epistemic states. In view of proving completeness, we introduced a tentative notion of syntactic access between actions. We gave an overview of the wide range of applications of this language for concrete multiagent system specification. We intend to continue this research by generalizing the semantics to include (not just knowledge but also) belief.

ACKNOWLEDGMENTS

Wiebe van der Hoek carried out part of this research while visiting the University of Otago as a William Evans fellow. Barteld Kooi carried out this research with the assistance of the Netherlands Organization for Scientific Research (NWO) while visiting the University of Otago.

H. van Ditmarsch
Department of Computer Science
University of Otago
New Zealand

W. van der Hoek
Department of Computer Science
University of Liverpool
United Kingdom

B. Kooi
Department of Computing Science
University of Groningen
The Netherlands

REFERENCES

[173] L.S. Moss A. Baltag and S. Solecki. The logic of public announcements, common knowledge and private suspicions. Originally presented at TARK 98, accepted for publication in Annals of Pure and Applied Logic, 2002.

[174] C.E. Alchourrón, P. Gärdenfors, and D. Makinson. On the logic of theory change: partial meet contraction and revision functions. *Journal of Symbolic Logic*, 50:510–530, 1985.

[175] R. Alur, T. A. Henzinger, and O. Kupferman. Alternating-time temporal logic. In *Proceedings of the 38th IEEE Symposium on Foundations of Computer Science*, pages 100–109, Florida, October 1997.

[176] R.J. Aumann and A. Brandeburger. Epistemic conditions for Nash equilibrium. *Econometrica*, (63):1161–1180, 1995.

[177] A. Baltag. A logic of epistemic actions. In J.-J. Meyer W. van der Hoek and C. Witteveen, editors, *(Electronic) Proceedings of the ESSLLI 1999 workshop on Foundations and Applications of Collective Agent-Based Systems*. Utrecht University, 1999.

[178] A. Baltag. A logic for suspicious players: Epistemic actions and belief updates in games. *Bulletin of Economic Research*, 54(1):1–45, 2002.

[179] S. Benferhat, D. Dubois, H. Prade, and M.A. Williams. A practical approach to revising prioritized knowledge bases. *Studia Logica*, 70(1), 2002.

[180] A. Darwiche and J. Pearl. On the logic of iterated belief revision. *Artificial Intelligence*, 89(1-2):1–29, 1997.

[181] R. Fagin, J. Y. Halpern, Y. Moses, and M. Y. Vardi. *Reasoning About Knowledge*. MIT Press, Cambridge MA, 1995.

[182] J.D. Gerbrandy. *Bisimulations on Planet Kripke*. Phd thesis, University of Amsterdam, 1999. ILLC Dissertation Series DS-1999-01.

[183] J.D. Gerbrandy and W. Groeneveld. Reasoning about information change. *Journal of Logic, Language, and Information*, 6:147–169, 1997.

[184] R. Goldblatt. *Logics of Time and Computation*. CSLI Publications, Stanford, 2nd edition, 1992. CSLI Lecture Notes No. 7.

[185] D. Harel, D. Kozen, and J. Tiuryn. *Dynamic Logic*. Foundations of Computing Series. MIT Press, Cambridge MA, 2000.

[186] J. Hintikka. *Knowledge and Belief*. Cornell University Press, Ithaca, NY, 1962.

[187] J. Hintikka. Reasoning about knowledge in philosophy. In J. Y. Halpern, editor, *Proceedings of the 1986 Conference on Theoretical Aspects of Reasoning About Knowledge*, pages 63–80, San Mateo, CA, 1986. Morgan Kaufmann Publishers.

[188] H. Katsuno and A. Mendelzon. On the difference between updating a knowledge base and revising it. In *Proceedings of the Second International Conference on Principles of Knowledge Representation and Reasoning*, pages 387–394, 1991.

[189] A.R. Lomuscio and M. D. Ryan. An algorithmic approach to knowledge evolution. *Artificial Intelligence for Engineering Design, Analysis and Manufacturing (AIEDAM)*, 13(2), 1999. Special issue on Temporal Logic in Engineering.

[190] J.-J.Ch. Meyer and W. van der Hoek. *Epistemic Logic for AI and Computer Science*, volume 41 of *Cambridge Tracts in Theoretical Computer Science*. Cambridge University Press, Cambridge, 1995.

[191] T.A. Meyer, W.A. Labuschagne, and J. Heidema. Refined epistemic entrenchment. *Journal of Logic, Language and Information*, 9:237–259, 2000.

[192] M. de Rijke P. Blackburn and Y. Venema. *Modal Logic*, volume 53 of *Cambridge Tracts in Theoretical Computer Science*. Cambridge University Press, Cambridge, 2001.

[193] R. Parikh. The logic of games and its applications. In M. Karpinski and J. van Leeuwen, editors, *Topics in the theory of computation*, volume 24 of *Annals of Discrete Mathematics*, pages 111–139. Elsevier Science, Amsterdam, 1985.

[194] M. Pauly. Game logic for game theorists. Technical report, CWI, Amsterdam, 2000. CWI Technical Report INS-R0017.

[195] D. Peleg. Concurrent dynamic logic. *Journal of the ACM*, 34(2):450–479, 1987.

[196] J.A. Plaza. Logics of public communications. In M.L. Emrich, M.S. Pfeifer, M. Hadzikadic, and Z.W. Ras, editors, *Proceedings of the 4th International Symposium on Methodologies for Intelligent Systems*, pages 201–216, 1989.

[197] B. ten Cate. Internalizing epistemic actions. In Maricarmen Martinez, editor, *Proceedings of the NASSLLI-2002 student session*, Stanford University, 2002.

[198] J.F.A.K. van Benthem. Logics for information update. In J.F.A.K. van Benthem, editor, *Proceedings of TARK VIII*, pages 51–88, Los Altos, 2001. Morgan Kaufmann.

[199] W. van der Hoek and M.J. Wooldridge. Tractable multi agent planning for epistemic goals. In C. Castelfranchi and W.L. Johnson, editors, *Proceedings of the First Internation Joint Conference on Autonomous Agents and Multi Agent Systems (AAMAS)*, pages 1167–1174, New York, USA, 2002. ACM Press.

[200] H.P. van Ditmarsch. *Knowledge games.* Phd thesis, University of Groningen, 2000. ILLC Dissertation Series DS-2000-06.

[201] H.P. van Ditmarsch. The semantics of concurrent knowledge actions. In M. Pauly and G. Sandu, editors, *ESSLLI 2001 workshop on Logic and Games*, 2001.

[202] H.P. van Ditmarsch. The description of game actions in cluedo. In L.A. Petrosian and V.V. Mazalov, editors, *Game Theory and Applications*, volume 8, pages 1–28. Nova Science Publishers, Commack, NY, USA, 2002.

[203] H.P. van Ditmarsch. Descriptions of game actions. *Journal of Logic, Language and Information*, 11:349–365, 2002.

[204] H.P. van Ditmarsch. The russian cards problem, 2002. To appear in *Studia Logica.*

JOHN F. SOWA

LAWS, FACTS, AND CONTEXTS: FOUNDATIONS FOR MULTIMODAL REASONING

ABSTRACT

Leibniz's intuition that necessity corresponds to truth in all possible worlds enabled Kripke to define a rigorous model theory for several axiomatizations of modal logic. Unfortunately, Kripke's model structures lead to a combinatorial explosion when they are extended to all the varieties of modality and intentionality that people routinely use in ordinary language. As an alternative, any semantics based on possible worlds can be replaced by a simpler and more easily generalizable approach based on Dunn's semantics of laws and facts and a theory of contexts based on the ideas of Peirce and McCarthy. To demonstrate consistency, this article defines a family of *nested graph models*, which can be specialized to a wide variety of model structures, including Kripke's models, situation semantics, temporal models, and many variations of them. An important advantage of nested graph models is the option of partitioning the reasoning tasks into separate metalevel stages, each of which can be axiomatized in classical first-order logic. At each stage, all inferences can be carried out with well-understood theorem provers for FOL or some subset of FOL. To prove that nothing more than FOL is required, Section 6 shows how any nested graph model with a finite nesting depth can be *flattened* to a conventional Tarski-style model. For most purposes, however, the nested models are computationally more tractable and intuitively more understandable.

1. REPLACING POSSIBLE WORLDS WITH CONTEXTS

Possible worlds have been the most popular semantic foundation for modal logic since (219) adopted them for his version of model structures. (221), for example, argued that "We ought to believe in other possible worlds and individuals because systematic philosophy goes more smoothly in many ways if we do." Yet computer implementations of modal reasoning replace possible worlds with "ersatz worlds" consisting of collections of propositions that more closely resemble (212)'s *model sets.* By dividing the model sets into necessary laws and contingent facts, (208) defined a conservative refinement of Kripke's semantics that eliminated the need for a "realist" view of possible worlds. Instead of assuming Kripke's accessibility relation as an unexplained primitive, Dunn derived it from the selection of laws and facts.

Since Dunn's semantics is logically equivalent to Kripke's for conventional modalities, most logicians ignored it in favor of Kripke's. For multimodal reasoning, however, Dunn's approach simplifies the reasoning process by separating the metalevel reasoning about laws and facts from

V.F. Hendricks, K.F. Jørgensen and S.A. Pedersen (eds.), Knowledge Contributors, 145–184.

the object-level reasoning in ordinary first-order logic. For each modality, Kripke semantics supports two operators such as $\Box$ for necessity and $\Diamond$ for possibility. For temporal logic, the same two operators are interpreted as always and sometimes. For deontic logic, they are reinterpreted as obligation and permission. That approach cannot represent, much less reason about a sentence that mixes all three modalities, such as *You are never obligated to do anything impossible.* The limitation to just one modality is what Scott (1970) considered "one of the biggest mistakes of all in modal logic":

> The only way to have any philosophically significant results in deontic or epistemic logic is to combine these operators with: Tense operators (otherwise how can you formulate principles of change?); the logical operators (otherwise how can you compare the relative with the absolute?); the operators like historical or physical necessity (otherwise how can you relate the agent to his environment?); and so on and so on. (p. 143)

These philosophical considerations are even more pressing for linguistics, which must relate different modalities in the same sentence. Dunn's semantics facilitates multimodal interactions by allowing each modal operator or each verb that implies a modal operator to have its own associated laws. At the metalevel, laws can be distinguished from facts and from the laws associated with different verbs or operators. At the object level, however, the reasoning process can use first-order logic without distinguishing laws from facts or the laws of one modality from the laws of another.

To take advantage of Dunn's semantics, the metalevel reasoning should be performed in a separate context from the object-level reasoning. This separation requires a formal theory of contexts that can distinguish different metalevels. But as Rich Thomason (241) observed, "The theory of context is important and problematic – problematic because the intuitions are confused, because disparate disciplines are involved, and because the chronic problem in cognitive science of how to arrive at a productive relation between formalizations and applications applies with particular force to this area." The version of contexts adopted for this article is based on a representation that Peirce introduced for *existential graphs* (EGs) and (237) adopted as a foundation for *conceptual graphs* (CGs). That approach is further elaborated along the lines suggested by (223) and developed by (238), (239).

Sections 2, 3, and 4 of this article summarize Dunn's semantics of laws and facts, a theory of contexts based on the work of Peirce and McCarthy, and Tarski's hierarchy of metalevels. Then Section 5 introduces *nested graph models* (NGMs) as a general formalism for a family of models that can be specialized for various theories of modality and intentionality. Section 6 shows how any NGM with a finite depth of nesting can be flattened to a Tarski-style model consisting of nothing but a set $\boldsymbol{D}$ of individuals and a set $\boldsymbol{R}$ of relations over $\boldsymbol{D}$. Although the process of flattening shows that modalities can be represented in first-order logic, the flattening comes at the expense of adding extra arguments to each relation to indicate every context in which it is nested. Finally, Section 7 shows how Peirce's semeiotic, Dunn's semantics, Tarski's metalevels, and nested graph models provide a powerful combination of tools for analyzing and formalizing semantic relationships.

2. DUNN'S LAWS AND FACTS

Philosophers since Aristotle have recognized that modality is related to laws; Dunn's innovation made the relationships explicit. Instead of Kripke's primitive accessibility relation between worlds, (208) replaced each possible world with two sets of propositions called *laws* and *facts*. For every Kripke world w, Dunn assumed an ordered pair $(\boldsymbol{M},\boldsymbol{L})$, where $\boldsymbol{M}$ is a Hintikka-style model set called the *facts* of w and $\boldsymbol{L}$ is a subset of $\boldsymbol{M}$ called the *laws* of w. For this article, the following conventions are assumed:

- *Axioms.* Any subset $\boldsymbol{A}$ of $\boldsymbol{L}$ whose deductive closure is the laws $(\boldsymbol{A} \vdash \boldsymbol{L})$ is called an *axiom set* for $(\boldsymbol{M},\boldsymbol{L})$.
- *Facts.* The set of all facts $\boldsymbol{M}$ is maximally consistent: for any proposition p, either $p \in \boldsymbol{M}$ or $\sim p \in \boldsymbol{M}$, but not both.
- *Contingent facts.* The set $\boldsymbol{M}$-$\boldsymbol{L}$ of all facts that are not laws is called the *contingent facts.*
- *Closure.* The facts are the deductive closure of any axiom set $\boldsymbol{A}$ and the contingent facts: $\boldsymbol{A} \cup (\boldsymbol{M} - \boldsymbol{L}) \vdash \boldsymbol{M}$.

With this formulation, Kripke's accessibility relation is no longer primitive, and the modal semantics does not depend on imaginary worlds. Instead, modality depends on the choice of laws, which could be laws of nature or merely human rules and regulations.

To show how the accessibility relation from one world to another can be derived from the choice of laws, let $(\boldsymbol{M}_1,\boldsymbol{L}_1)$ be a pair of facts and laws that describe a possible world w_1, and let the pair $(\boldsymbol{M}_2,\boldsymbol{L}_2)$ describe a world w_2. Dunn defined accessibility from the world w_1 to the world w_2 to mean that the laws $\boldsymbol{L}_1$ are a subset of the facts in $\boldsymbol{M}_2$:

$$\mathrm{R}(w_1,w_2) \equiv \boldsymbol{L}_1 \subset \boldsymbol{M}_2.$$

According to this definition, the laws of the first world w_1 remain true in the second world w_2, but they may be demoted from the status of laws to merely contingent facts. In Kripke's semantics, possibility $\Diamond p$ means that p is true of some world w accessible from the real world w_0:

$$\Diamond p \equiv (\exists w{:}\mathrm{World})(\mathrm{R}(w_0,w) \wedge w \models p).$$

By substituting the laws and facts for the possible worlds, Dunn restated the definitions of possibility and necessity:

$$\Diamond p \equiv (\exists \boldsymbol{M}{:}\text{ModelSet})\ (\boldsymbol{L}_0 \subset \boldsymbol{M} \wedge p \in \boldsymbol{M}).$$

Now possibility $\Diamond p$ means that there exists a model set $\boldsymbol{M}$ that contains the laws of the real world $\boldsymbol{L}_0$ and p is a fact in $\boldsymbol{M}$. Since $\boldsymbol{M}$ is consistent and it contains the laws $\boldsymbol{L}_0$, possibility implies that p must be consistent with the laws of the real world. By the same substitutions, the definition of necessity becomes

$$\Box p \equiv (\forall \boldsymbol{M}{:}\text{ModelSet})(\boldsymbol{L}_0 \subset \boldsymbol{M} \supset p \in \boldsymbol{M}).$$

Necessity $\Box p$ means that every model set $\boldsymbol{M}$ that contains the laws of the real world also contains p.

Dunn performed the same substitutions in Kripke's constraints on the accessibility relation. The result is a restatement of the constraints in terms of the laws and facts:

- **System T**. The two axioms $\Box p \supset p$ and $p \supset \Diamond p$ require every world to be accessible from itself. That property follows from Dunn's definition because the laws $\boldsymbol{L}$ of any world are a subset of the facts: $\boldsymbol{L} \subset \boldsymbol{M}$.
- **System S4**. System T with axiom S4, $\Box p \supset \Box\Box p$, requires that R must also be transitive. It imposes the tighter constraint that the laws of the first world must be a subset of the laws of the second world: $\boldsymbol{L}_1 \subset \boldsymbol{L}_2$.
- **System S5**. System S4 with axiom S5, $\Diamond p \supset \Diamond\Box p$, requires that R must also be symmetric. It constrains both worlds to have exactly the same laws: $\boldsymbol{L}_1 = \boldsymbol{L}_2$.

In Dunn's theory, the term *possible world* is an informal metaphor that does not appear in the formalism: the semantics of $\Box p$ and $\Diamond p$ depends only on the choice of laws and facts. All formulas in $\boldsymbol{M}$ and $\boldsymbol{L}$ are purely first order, and the symbols $\Box$ and $\Diamond$ never appear in any of them.

Dunn's theory is a conservative refinement of Kripke's theory, since any Kripke model structure (K,R,Φ) can be converted to one of Dunn's model structures in two steps:

1. Replace every world w in K with the set $\boldsymbol{M}$ of propositions that are true in w and the set $\boldsymbol{L}$ of propositions that are necessary in w.
   $\boldsymbol{M} = \{p \mid \Phi(p,w) = \text{true}\}$.
   $\boldsymbol{L} = \{p \mid (\forall u{:}\text{World})(\text{R}(w,u) \supset \Phi(p,u) = \text{true})\}$.
2. Define Kripke's primitive accessibility relation $\text{R}(u,v)$ by the constraint that the laws of u are true in v:

$$\text{R}(u,v) \equiv (\forall p{:}\text{Proposition})(p \in \boldsymbol{L}_u \supset p \in \boldsymbol{M}_v).$$

This construction generates a model in Dunn's sense for every model in Kripke's sense. It holds for the normal models defined by Kripke (219) and for the non-normal models by Kripke (220). In an normal world, every law is also a fact, but that constraint is dropped for non-normal

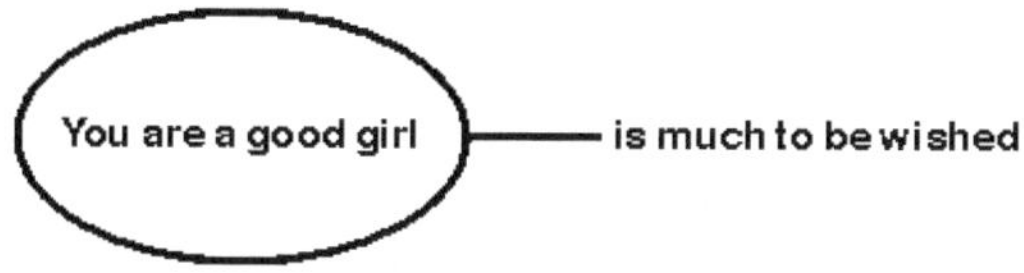

FIGURE 1. One of Peirce's graphs for talking about a proposition

worlds. Dunn's definition of the accessibility relation, however, remains unchanged; therefore, a non-normal world is not accessible from itself.

Every axiom and theorem of Kripke's theory remains true in Dunn's version, but Dunn's theory makes the reasons for modality available for further inferences. For theories of intentionality, Dunn's approach can relate the laws to the goals and purposes of some agent, who in effect *legislates* which propositions are to be considered laws. This approach formalizes an informal suggestion by (215): "a world, w_2, is accessible to a world, w_1, if w_2 is conceivable by someone living in w_1." In Dunn's terms, the laws that determine what is necessary in the world w_1 are the propositions that are not conceivably false for someone living in w_1.

3. CONTEXTS BY PEIRCE AND MCCARTHY

In first-order logic, laws and facts are propositions, and there is no special mark that distinguishes a law from a fact. To distinguish them, a context mechanism is necessary to separate first-order reasoning with the propositions from metalevel reasoning about the propositions and about the distinctions between laws and facts. (228), (229) invented the algebraic notation for predicate calculus, which with a change of symbols by Peano became today's most widely used notation for logic. A dozen years later, Peirce developed a graphical notation for logic that more clearly distinguishes contexts. Figure 1 shows his graph notation for delimiting the context of a proposition. In explaining that graph, Peirce (1898) said "When we wish to assert something about a proposition without asserting the proposition itself, we will enclose it in a lightly drawn oval." The line attached to the oval links it to a relation that makes a *metalevel* assertion about the nested proposition.

The oval serves the syntactic function of grouping related information in a package. Besides notation, Peirce developed a theory of the semantics and pragmatics of contexts and the rules of inference for importing and exporting information into and out of contexts. To support first-order logic, the only metalevel relation required is *negation*. By combining negation with the existential-conjunctive subset of logic, Peirce developed his *existential graphs* (EGs), which are based on three logical operators and an open-ended number of relations:

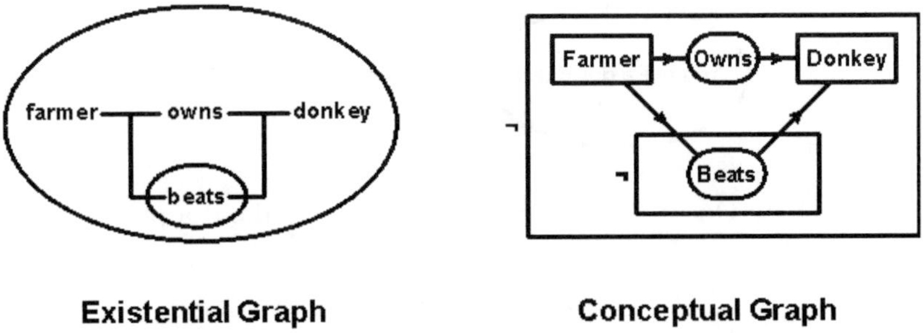

FIGURE 2. EG and CG for "If a farmer owns a donkey, then he beats it."

1. Existential quantifier: A bar or linked structure of bars, called a *line of identity*, represents $\exists$.
2. Conjunction: The *juxtaposition* of two graphs in the same context represents $\wedge$.
3. Negation: An *oval enclosure* with no lines attached to it represents $\sim$ or the denial of the enclosed proposition.
4. Relation: Character strings represent the names of propositions, predicates, or relations, which may be attached to zero or more lines of identities.

In Figure 1, the character string "You are a good girl" is the name of a *medad*, which represents a proposition or 0-adic relation; the string "is much to be wished" is the name of a *monad* or monadic predicate or relation. In the EG on the left of Figure 2, "farmer" and "donkey" are monads; "owns" and "beats" are *dyads*, which represent dyadic relations. When combined with relations in all possible ways, the three logical operators can represent full first-order logic. When used to state propositions about nested contexts, they form a metalanguage that can be used to define the version of modal logic used in some nested context. For Peirce's own tutorial on existential graphs and their rules of inference, see his MS 514 (1909).

To illustrate the use of negative contexts for representing FOL, Figure 2 shows an existential graph and a conceptual graph for the sentence *If a farmer owns a donkey, then he beats it.* This sentence is one of a series of examples used by medieval logicians to illustrate issues in mapping language to logic. The EG on the left has two ovals with no attached lines; by default, they represent negations. It also has two lines of identity, represented as linked bars: one line, which connects *farmer* to the left side of *owns* and *beats*, represents an existentially quantified variable $(\exists x)$; the other line, which connects *donkey* to the right side of *owns* and *beats* represents another variable $(\exists y)$.

When the EG of Figure 2 is translated to predicate calculus, *farmer* and *donkey* map to monadic predicates; *owns* and *beats* map to dyadic predicates. If a relation is attached to more than one line of identity, the lines are ordered from left to right by their point of attachment to the name of the relation. With the implicit conjunctions represented by the $\wedge$ symbol, the result is an untyped formula:

$$\sim (\exists \mathrm{x})(\exists y)(\mathrm{farmer}(x) \wedge \mathrm{donkey}(y) \wedge \mathrm{owns}(x,y) \wedge \sim\mathrm{beats}(x,y)).$$

A nest of two ovals, as in Figure 2, is what Peirce called a *scroll*. It represents implication, since $\sim (p \wedge \sim q)$ is equivalent to $p \supset q$. Using the $\supset$ symbol, the formula may be rewritten

$$(\forall x)(\forall y)((\mathrm{farmer}(x) \wedge \mathrm{donkey}(y) \wedge \mathrm{owns}(x,y)) \supset \mathrm{beats}(x,y)).$$

The CG on the right of Figure 2 may be considered a typed or sorted version of the EG. The boxes [**Farmer**] and [**Donkey**] represent a notation for sorted quantification ($\exists x$:Farmer) and ($\exists y$:Donkey). The ovals **(Owns)** and **(Beats)** represent relations, whose attached arcs link to the boxes that represent the arguments. The large boxes with the symbol $\neg$ in front correspond to Peirce's ovals that represent negation. As a result, the CG corresponds to the following formula, which uses sorted or restricted quantifiers:

$$(\forall x{:}\mathrm{Farmer})(\forall y{:}\mathrm{Donkey})(\mathrm{owns}(x,y) \supset \mathrm{beats}(x,y)).$$

The algebraic formulas with the $\supset$ symbol illustrate a peculiar feature of predicate calculus: in order to keep the variables x and y within the scope of the quantifiers, the existential quantifiers for the phrases *a farmer* and *a donkey* must be moved to the front of the formula and be translated to universal quantifiers. This puzzling feature of logic has been a matter of debate among linguists and logicians since the middle ages.

The nested graph models defined in Section 5 are based on the CG formalism, but with one restriction: every graph must be wholly contained within a single context. The relation **(Beats)** in Figure 2 could not be linked to concept boxes outside its own context. To support that restriction, Figure 3 shows an equivalent CG in which concept boxes in different contexts are connected by dotted lines called *coreference links*, which indicate that the two concepts refer to exactly the same individual. A set of boxes connected by coreference links corresponds to what Peirce called a line of identity.

The symbol $\top$, which is a synonym for the type **Entity**, represents the most general type, which is true of everything. Therefore, concepts of the form [$\top$] correspond an unrestricted quantifier, such as ($\exists z$). The dotted lines correspond to equations of the form $x = z$. Therefore, Figure 3 is equivalent to the following formula:

$$\begin{array}{l}(\forall x{:}\mathrm{Farmer})(\forall y{:}\mathrm{Donkey})(\mathrm{owns}(x,y) \supset \\ \quad (\exists z)(\exists w)(\mathrm{beats}(z,w) \wedge x = z \wedge y = w))).\end{array}$$

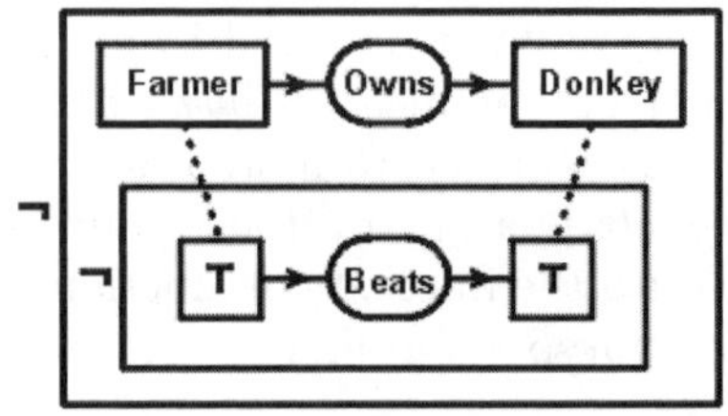

FIGURE 3. A conceptual graph with coreference links

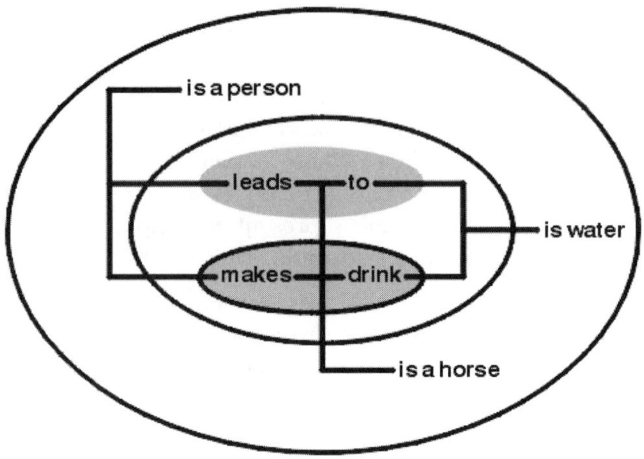

FIGURE 4. EG for "You can lead a horse to water, but you can't make him drink."

By the rules of inference for predicate calculus, this formula is provably equivalent to the previous one.

Besides attaching a relation to an oval, Peirce also used colors or *tinctures* to distinguish contexts other than negation. Figure 4 shows one of his examples with red (or shading) to indicate possibility. The graph contains four ovals: the outer two form a scroll for *if-then*; the inner two represent possibility (shading) and impossibility (shading inside a negation). The outer oval may be read *If there exist a person, a horse, and water*; the next oval may be read *then it is possible for the person to lead the horse to the water and not possible for the person to make the horse drink the water.*

The notation "—leads—to—" represents a *triad* or triadic relation

$$\text{leadsTo}(x, y, z),$$

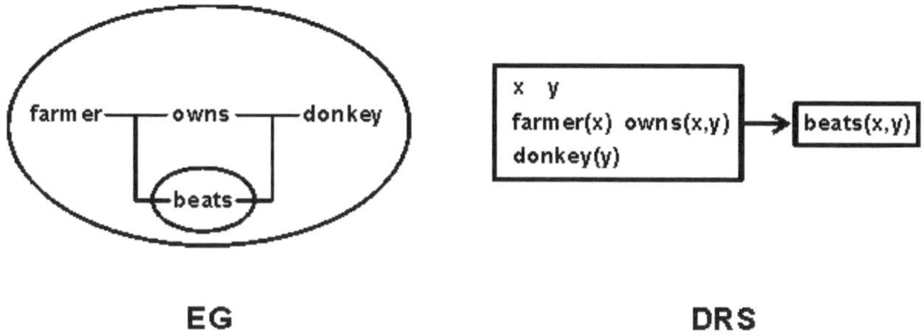

FIGURE 5. EG and DRS for "If a farmer owns a donkey, then he beats it".

and "—makes—drink—" represents makesDrink(x, y, z). In the algebraic notation with the symbol $\Diamond$ for possibility, Figure 4 maps to the following formula:

$$\sim (\exists \mathrm{x})(\exists y)(\exists z)(\mathrm{person}(x) \wedge \mathrm{horse}(y) \wedge \mathrm{water}(z) \wedge \\ \sim (\Diamond \mathrm{leadsTo}(x, y, z) \wedge \sim \Diamond \mathrm{makesDrink}(x, y, z))).$$

With the symbol $\supset$ for implication, this formula becomes

$$(\forall x)(\forall y)(\forall z)((\mathrm{person}(x) \wedge \mathrm{horse}(y) \wedge \mathrm{water}(z)) \supset \\ (\Diamond \mathrm{leadsTo}(x, y, z) \wedge \sim \Diamond \mathrm{makesDrink}(x, y, z))).$$

This version may be read *For all x, y, and z, if x is a person, y is a horse, and z is water, then it is possible for x to lead y to z, and not possible for x to make y drink z.* These readings, although logically explicit, are not as succinct as the proverb *You can lead a horse to water, but you can't make him drink.*

Discourse representation theory. The logician Hans Kamp once spent a summer translating English sentences from a scientific article to predicate calculus. During the course of his work, he was troubled by the same kinds of irregularities that puzzled the medieval logicians. In order to simplify the mapping from language to logic, (216) developed *discourse representation structures* (DRSs) with an explicit notation for contexts. In terms of those structures, Kamp defined the rules of *discourse representation theory* for mapping quantifiers, determiners, and pronouns from language to logic ((217)).

Although Kamp had not been aware of Peirce's existential graphs, his DRSs are structurally equivalent to Peirce's EGs. The diagram on the right of Figure 5 is a DRS for the donkey sentence, *If there exist a farmer x and a donkey y and x owns y, then x beats y.* The two boxes connected by an arrow represent an implication where the antecedent includes the consequent within its scope.

The DRS and EG notations look quite different, but they are exactly isomorphic: they have the same primitives, the same scoping rules for variables or lines of identity, and the same translation to predicate calculus. Therefore, the EG and DRS notations map to the same formula:

$$\sim (\exists \mathrm{x})(\exists y)(\mathrm{farmer}(x) \land \mathrm{donkey}(y) \land \mathrm{owns}(x,y) \land \ \sim\!\mathrm{beats}(x,y)).$$

Peirce's motivation for the EG contexts was to simplify the logical structures and rules of inference. Kamp's motivation for the DRS contexts was to simplify the mapping from language to logic. Remarkably, they converged on isomorphic representations. Therefore, Peirce's rules of inference and Kamp's discourse rules apply equally well to contexts in the EG, CG, or DRS notations. For notations with a different structure, such as predicate calculus, those rules cannot be applied without major modifications.

McCarthy's contexts. In his "Notes on Formalizing Context," (223) introduced the predicate ist($\boldsymbol{C}$,p), which may be read "the proposition p is true in context $\boldsymbol{C}$." For clarity, it will be spelled out in the form isTrueIn($\boldsymbol{C}$, p). As illustrations, McCarthy gave the following examples:

- isTrueIn(contextOf("Sherlock Holmes stories"), "Holmes is a detective").
- isTrueIn(contextOf("U.S. legal history"), "Holmes is a Supreme Court Justice").

In these examples, the context *disambiguates* the referent of the name *Holmes* either to the fictional character Sherlock Holmes or to Oliver Wendell Holmes, Jr., the first appointee to the Supreme Court by President Theodore Roosevelt. In effect, names behave like indexicals whose referents are determined by the context.

One of McCarthy's reasons for developing a theory of context was his uneasiness with the proliferation of new logics for every kind of modal, temporal, epistemic, and nonmonotonic reasoning. The ever-growing number of modes presented in AI journals and conferences is a throwback to the scholastic logicians who went beyond Aristotle's two modes *necessary* and *possible* to *permissible, obligatory, doubtful, clear, generally known, heretical, said by the ancients,* or *written in Holy Scriptures.* The medieval logicians spent so much time talking about modes that they were nicknamed the *modistae.* The modern logicians have axiomatized their modes and developed semantic models to support them, but each theory includes only one or two of the many modes. (222) observed, 'For AI purposes, we would need all the above modal operators in the same system. This would make the semantic discussion of the resulting modal logic extremely complex.'

Instead of an open-ended number of modes, McCarthy hoped to develop a simple, but universal mechanism that would replace modal logic with first-order logic supplemented with metalanguage about contexts. That approach can be adapted to Dunn's semantics by adding another predicate isLawOf($\boldsymbol{C}$,p), which states that proposition p is a law of context $\boldsymbol{C}$. Then Dunn's laws and facts can be defined in terms of McCarthy's contexts:

- The facts of a context are determined by metalevel reasoning with the isTrueIn predicate:

$$\boldsymbol{M} = \{p \mid \text{isTrueIn}(\boldsymbol{C},p)\}.$$

- The laws of a context are determined by metalevel reasoning with the isLawOf predicate:

$$\boldsymbol{L} = \{p \mid \text{isLawOf}(\boldsymbol{C},p)\}.$$

Metalevel reasoning about the laws and facts of a context determines the kind of modality it is capable of expressing. Multimodal reasoning involves metalevel reasoning about the sources that have legislated the various laws. But within a context, there is no difference between laws and contingent facts, and an ordinary first-order theorem prover can be used to reason about them.

4. TARSKI'S METALEVELS

The semantics for multiple levels of nested contexts is based on the method of *stratified metalevels* by (240). Each context in a nest is treated as a metalevel with respect to every context nested within it. The propositions in some context that has no nested levels beneath it may be considered as an *object language* $\boldsymbol{L}_0$, which refers to entities in some universe of discourse $\boldsymbol{D}$. The *metalanguage* $\boldsymbol{L}_1$ refers to the symbols of $\boldsymbol{L}_0$ and their relationships to $\boldsymbol{D}$. Tarski showed that the metalanguage is still first order, but its universe of discourse is enlarged from $\boldsymbol{D}$ to $\boldsymbol{L}_0 \cup \boldsymbol{D}$. The *metametalanguage* $\boldsymbol{L}_2$ is also first order, but its universe of discourse is $\boldsymbol{L}_1 \cup \boldsymbol{L}_0 \cup \boldsymbol{D}$. To avoid paradoxes, Tarski insisted that no metalanguage $\boldsymbol{L}_n$ could refer to its own symbols, but it could refer to the symbols or individuals in the domain of any language $\boldsymbol{L}_i$ where $0 \leq i < n$.

In short, metalevel reasoning is first-order reasoning about the way statements may be sorted into contexts. After the sorting has been done, reasoning with the propositions in a context can be handled by the usual FOL rules. At every level of the Tarski hierarchy of metalanguages, the reasoning process is governed by first-order rules. But first-order reasoning in language $\boldsymbol{L}_n$ has the effect of higher-order or modal reasoning for every language below n. At every level n, the model theory that justifies the reasoning in $\boldsymbol{L}_n$ is a conventional first-order Tarskian semantics, since the nature of the objects in the domain $\boldsymbol{D}_n$ is irrelevant to the rules that apply to $\boldsymbol{L}_n$.

Example. To illustrate the interplay of the metalevel and object-level inferences, consider the following statement, which includes direct quotation, indirect quotation, indexical pronouns, and metalanguage about belief:

Joe said "I don't believe in astrology, but everybody knows that it works even if you don't believe in it."

This statement could be translated word-for-word to a conceptual graph in which the indexicals are represented by the symbols #I, #they, #it, and #you. Then the resolution of the indexicals could be performed by metalevel transformations of the graph. Those transformations could also be written in stylized English:

1. First mark the indexicals with the # symbol, and use square brackets to mark the multiple levels of nested contexts:
   Joe said
       [#I don't believe [in astrology]
           but everybody knows
               [[#it works]
                   even if #you don't believe [in #it]]].
2. The indexical #I can be resolved to the speaker Joe, but the other indexicals depend on implicit background knowledge. The pronoun *everybody* is a universal quantifier that could be translated to "every person." The two occurrences of #it refer to astrology, but the three nested contexts about astrology have different forms; for simplicity, they could all be rewritten "astrology works." When no explicit person is being addressed, the indexical #you can be interpreted as a reference to any or every person who may be listening. For this example, it could be assumed to be coreferent with "every person" in the community. With these substitutions, the statement becomes
   Joe said
       [Joe doesn't believe [astrology works]
           but every person x knows
               [[astrology works]
                   even if x doesn't believe
                       [astrology works]]].
3. If Joe's statement was sincere, Joe believes what he said. The word *but* could be replaced with the word *and*, which preserves the propositional content, but omits the contrastive emphasis. A statement of the form "p even if q" means that p is true independent of the truth value of q. It is equivalent to $((q \supset p) \wedge ((\sim q) \supset p))$, which implies p by itself. The statement can therefore be rewritten
   Joe believes
       [Joe doesn't believe [astrology works]
           and every person x knows [astrology works]].

4. Since Joe is a person in Joe's community, the constant "Joe" may be substituted for the quantifier "every person x":
   Joe believes
   [Joe doesn't believe [astrology works]
   and Joe knows [astrology works]].
5. By the axioms of epistemic logic, everything known is believed. Therefore, the verb **knows** in the third line can be replaced by the implicit **believes**:
   Joe believes
   [Joe doesn't believe [astrology works]
   and Joe believes [astrology works]].
   This statement shows that Joe believes a contradiction of the form $(\sim p \wedge p)$.

For computer analysis of language, the most difficult task is to determine the conversational implicatures and the background knowledge needed for resolving indexicals. After the implicit assumptions have been made explicit, the translation to logic and further deductions in logic are straightforward.

In the process of reasoning about Joe's beliefs, the context [**astrology works**] is treated as an encapsulated object, whose internal structure is ignored. When the levels interact, however, further axioms are necessary to relate them. Like the iterated modalities $\Diamond\Diamond p$ and $\Diamond\Box p$, iterated beliefs occur in statements like *Joe believes that Joe doesn't believe that astrology works*. One reasonable axiom is that if an agent a believes that a believes p, then a believes p:

$$(\forall a\text{:Agent})(\forall p\text{:Proposition})(\text{believe}(a,\text{believe}(a,p)) \supset \text{believe}(a,p)).$$

This axiom enables two levels of nested contexts to be collapsed into one. The converse, however, is less likely: many people act as if they believe propositions that they are not willing to admit. Joe, for example, might read the astrology column in the daily newspaper and follow its advice. His actions could be considered evidence that he believes in astrology. Yet when asked, Joe might continue to insist that he doesn't believe in astrology.

5. NESTED GRAPH MODELS

To prove that a syntactic notation for contexts is consistent, it is necessary to define a model-theoretic semantics for it. But to show that the model captures the intended interpretation, it is necessary to show how it represents the entities of interest in the application domain. For consistency, this section defines model structures called *nested graph models* (NGMs), which can serve as the denotation of logical expressions that contain nested contexts. Nested graph models are general enough to represent a variety of other model structures, including Tarski-style "flat" models, the possible

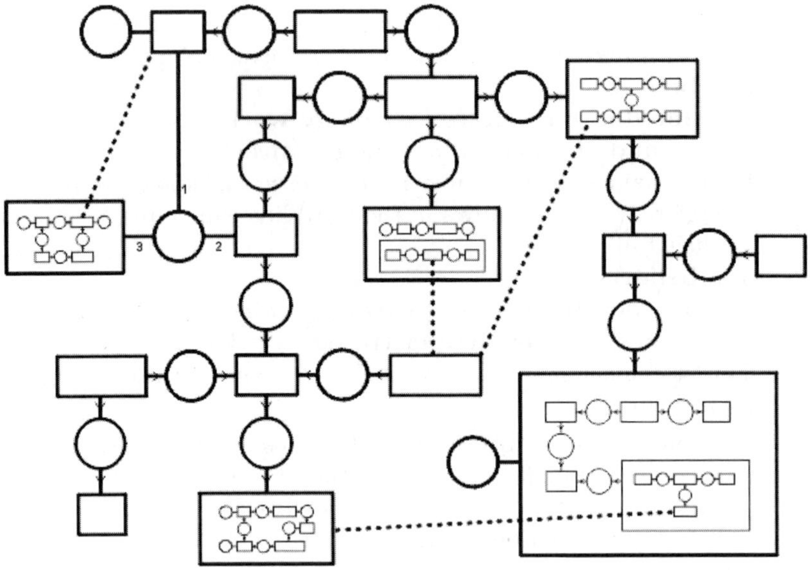

FIGURE 6. A nested graph model (NGM)

worlds of Kripke and Montague, and other approaches discussed in this article. The mapping from those model structures to NGMs shows that NGMs are at least as suitable for capturing the intented interpretation. Dunn's semantics allows NGMs to do more: the option of representing metalevel information in any context enables statements in one context to talk about the laws and facts of nested contexts and about the intentions of agents who may have legislated the laws.

To illustrate the formal definitions, Figure 6 shows an informal example of an NGM. Every box or rectangle in Figure 6 represents an individual entity in the domain of discourse, and every circle represents a property (monadic predicate) or a relation (predicate or relation with two or more arguments) that is true of the individual(s) to which it is linked. The arrows on the arcs are synonyms for the integers used to label the arcs: for dyadic relations, an arrow pointing toward the circle represents the integer 1, and an arrow pointing away from the circle represents 2; relations with more than two arcs must supplement the arrows with integers. Some boxes contain nested graphs: they represent individuals that have parts or aspects, which are individual entities represented by the boxes in the nested graphs.

The four dotted lines in Figure 6 are coreference links, which represent three lines lines of identity. Two lines of identity contain only two boxes, which are the endpoints of a single coreference link. The third line of identity contains three boxes, which are connected by two coreference links. In general, a line of identity with n boxes may be shown by $n-1$ coreference links, each of which corresponds to an equation that asserts the equality of the referents of the boxes it connects. A coreference link may connect two boxes of the same NGM, or it may connect a box of an NGM G to a box of another NGM that is nested directly or indirectly in G. But a coreference link may never connect a box of an NGM G to a box of another NGM H, where neither G nor H is nested in the other. As Figure 6 illustrates, coreference links may go from an outer NGM to a more deeply nested NGM, but they may not connect boxes in two independently nested NGMs.

For convenience in relating the formalism to diagrams such as Figure 6, the components of a nested graph model (NGM) are called *arcs, boxes, circles, labels*, and *lines of identity.* Formally, however, an NGM is defined as a 5-tuple G = (A,B,C,L,I), consisting of five abstract sets whose implications are completely determined by the following definitions:

1. **Arcs**. Every arc in A is an ordered pair (c, b), where c is a circle in C and b is a box in B.
2. **Boxes**. If b is any box in B, there may be a nested graph model H that is said to be *contained* in b and *directly nested* in G. An NGM is said to be *nested* in G if it is directly nested either in G itself or in some other NGM that is nested in G. The NGM G may not be nested in itself, and any NGM nested in G must be contained in exactly one box of G or of some NGM nested in G. No NGM may be contained in more than one box.
3. **Circles**. If c is any circle in C, any arc (c, b) in A is said to *belong* to c. For any circle c, the number n of arcs that belong to c is finite; and for each i from 1 to n, there is one and only one arc a_i, which belongs to c and for which $label(a_i) = i$. (If no arcs belong to c, then c represents a proposition constant, which Peirce called a *medad.*)
4. **Labels**. L is a set of entities called *labels*, for which there exists a function *label*: A∪B∪C⟶L. If a is any arc in A, $label(a) = i$ is a positive integer. If b is any box in B, $label(b)$ is said to be an *individual identifier*; no two boxes in B may have identical labels. If c is any circle in C, $label(c)$ is said to be a *relation identifier*; any number of circles in C may have identical labels.
5. **Lines of Identity**. Every line of identity is a set of two or more boxes. For each i in I, there must exist exactly one NGM H, where either H=G or H is nested in G; one or more boxes of i must be boxes of H, and all other boxes of i must be boxes of some NGM nested in H. (Note: coreference links, which appear in informal diagrams such as Figures 3 and 6, are not mentioned in the formal

definition of lines of identity. Alternative notations, such as variable names, could be used to indicate the boxes that belong to each line of identity.)

6. **Outermost context**. The NGM G is said to be the *outermost context* of G. Any box that contains an NGM H nested in G is said to be a *nested context* of G.

The five sets A, B, C, L, and I must be disjoint. Any NGM that is drawn on paper or stored in a computer must be finite, but for generality, there is no theoretical limit on the cardinality of any of the sets A, B, C, L, or I. In computer implementations, character strings are usually chosen as names to label the boxes and circles, but in theory, any sets, including images or even uncountably infinite sets, could be used as labels.

An NGM may contain any number of levels of nested NGMs, but no NGM may be nested within itself, either directly or indirectly. If an NGM has an infinite nesting depth, it could be isomorphic to another NGM nested in itself; but the nested copy is considered to be distinct from the outer NGM.

Mapping other models to NGMs. Nested graph models are set-theoretical structures that can serve as models for a wide variety of logical theories. They can be specialized in various ways to represent other model structures. Tarski-style models require no nesting, Kripke-style models require one level of nesting, and models for multiple modalities, which will be discussed in Sections 6 and 7, require deeper nesting.

- **Tarski's flat models**. A Tarski-style model M = (D,R,Φ) consists of a nonempty set D called a *domain of individuals*, a set R of relations defined over D, and an evaluation function Φ. For any first-order proposition p stated in terms of D and R, $\Phi(p)$ is a truth value T or F. By the usual methods for representing relations as graphs, the model M can be represented as a *flat* NGM G = (A,B,C,L,I), for which no box in B contains a nested NGM. Informally, the individuals in D are represented by boxes, and the relations are represented by circles. The labels of the boxes are the names or identifiers of the individuals in D, and the labels of the circles are the names of the relations in R. Formally, the following construction defines an isomorphism from M to G:
    1. Each individual x in the domain D is represented by exactly one box b in B whose label is x: $label(b) = x$. For any x in D, the inverse $label^{-1}(x)$ is the box in B that represents x.
    2. Each tuple t=(x_1,...,x_n) of any n-adic relation r in R is represented by a circle c in C, and $label(c) = r$. The inverse $label^{-1}(r)$ is a subset of C, which contains exactly one circle for every tuple of r.

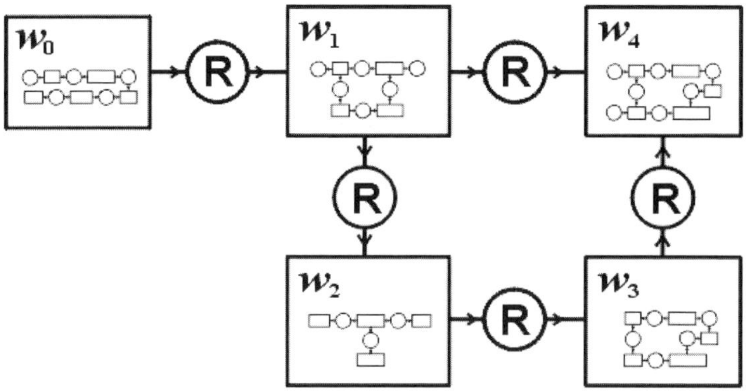

FIGURE 7. An NGM that represents a Kripke model structure

3. For each i from 1 to n, the i-th arc of the circle c for the tuple t is the pair $(c,\ label^{-1}(x_i))$. That arc is labeled with the integer i, and it is said to *link* c to the box labeled x_i.
4. The sets A, B, C, and L contain no elements other than those specified in steps 1, 2, and 3.
5. There are no lines of identity: the set I is empty.
6. Since this construction defines a unique NGM G that is isomorphic to M, the definition of $\Phi(p)$ in terms of D and R can be mapped to an equivalent evaluation function $\Psi(p)$ in terms of G.

For finite models, these steps can be translated to a computer program that constructs G from M and Ψ from Φ. For infinite models, they should be considered a specification rather than a construction. By this specification, D and R are subsets of L. Therefore, there would always be enough labels for the boxes and circles, even if D and R happen to be uncoutably infinite.

- **Kripke's possible worlds**. Any Kripke model structure M = (K,R,Φ) can be represented by a nested graph model with one level of nesting. The outermost context of G contains one box for every world w in K and one circle for every pair (w_i,w_j) in the accessibility relation R. Figure 7 shows such an NGM in which each of the five outer boxes contains a nested NGM that represents a Tarski-style model of some possible world.

  The box labeled w_0 represents the real world, and the boxes labeled w_1 to w_4 represent worlds that are accessible from the real world. The circles labeled **R** represent instances of the accessibility relation, and the arrows show which worlds are accessible from any

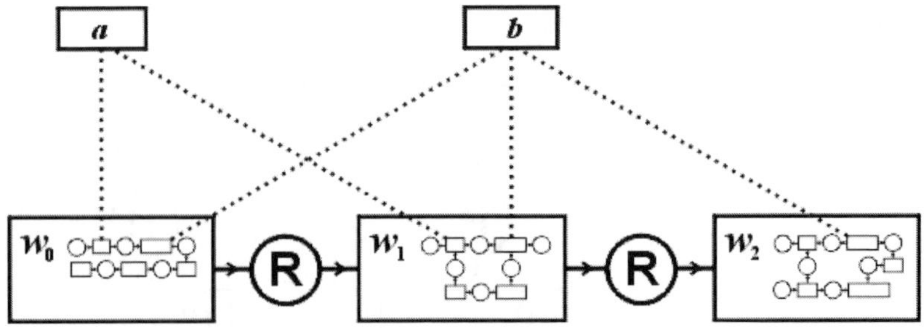

FIGURE 8. An NGM with counterparts in multiple worlds

other. Formally, the following construction defines an isomorphism from any Kripke model structure M to an NGM G = (A,B,C,L,I):

1. For each possible world w_i in K, let the set B have a box b_i, which contains a flat NGM W that represents a Tarski-style model for w_i. Let the label of the box b_i be the world w_i.
2. For each pair (w_i, w_j) in the accessibility relation R, let the set C have a circle c with the label "R", and let the set A have two arcs: an arc (c, b_i) with the label "1" and an arc (c, b_j) with the label "2". (In Figure 7, an arrow pointing toward the circle marks arc 1, and an arrow pointing away marks arc 2.)
3. The sets A, B, and C have no elements other than those specified in steps 1 and 2. Let the set L be the union of all the labels specified in those steps: L=K∪{"R","1","2"}. The arcs, boxes, circles, and labels in any NGM W nested in a box b_i in B are derived from the Tarski-style model for the world w_i.
4. There are no lines of identity: the set I is empty.
5. Since this construction defines a unique NGM G that is isomorphic to M, the definition of Φ for M can be mapped to an equivalent evaluation function Ψ for G.

- **Models for quantified modal logic**. Kripke's original model theory was designed for propositional modal logic, which does not support quantified variables that range over individuals. When quantification is added to modal logic, variables may refer to individuals that "exist" in more than one world. Figure 8 shows an extension to the Kripke models that allows individuals in one world to have *counterparts* in other worlds.

At the top of Figure 8, two individuals, represented by boxes labeled a and b, are connected by coreference links to some of the boxes of the nested graphs. The box labeled w_0 represents a Tarski-style model for the real world, in which two individuals are marked as identical to a and b by coreference links. The box labeled w_1 represents some possible world in which two individuals are marked as counterparts for a and b by coreference links, and w_2 represents another possible world in which only one individual has a counterpart for b. The two coreference links attached to box a represent a line of identity that contains three boxes, and the three coreference links attached to box b represent a line of identity that contains four boxes.

An NGM for quantified modal logic, G = (A,B,C,L,I), can be constructed by starting with the first three steps for an NGM for a Kripke-style model and continuing with the following:

1. For every individual x that has counterparts in two or more worlds, add x to the set of labels L.
2. Add a box b to B with label(b) = x.
3. For every world w that has a counterpart of x, there must be a nested NGM that has some box b_w that represents x.
4. Add a line of identity i to I consisting of the box b from step #2 and every b_w from step #3:
   $i = \{b\} \cup \{b_w \mid w \text{ is a world that has a counterpart of } x\}$.

If all the boxes in the line of identity i have the same label, then that label could be considered a *rigid identifier* of the individual across multiple worlds. This construction, however, does not require rigid identifiers: the boxes that represent the same individual in different worlds may have different labels.

- **Models for temporal logic**. (232) showed that the operators $\Box$ and $\Diamond$ could be interpreted as the temporal operators *sometimes* and *always*. That interpretation creates a modal-like version of temporal logic whose semantics can be formalized with Kripke-style models. For such logics, an NGM such as Figure 8 could be interpreted as a model of a sequence of events, in which each w_i represents a *snapshot* of one event in the sequence, and the relation **R** represents the *next* relation of each snapshot to its successor.

  As an example, Figure 8 might represent an encounter between a mouse a and a cat b. At time $t = 0$, the snapshot w_0 represents a model of an event in which the cat b catches the mouse a. In w_1, b eats a. In w_2, b is licking his lips, but a no longer exists. The cat b has a counterpart in all three snapshots, but the mouse a exists in just the first 2. The boxes in the snapshots that have no links to boxes outside their snapshot represent entities such as actions or aspects of actions, which exist only for the duration of one snapshot.

Figure 8 illustrates a version of temporal logic in which the snapshots are linearly ordered. An NGM could also represent *branching time*, in which the snapshots for the future lie on multiple branches, each of which represents a different option that the cat or the mouse might choose. Branching models are especially useful for game-playing programs that analyze options many steps into the future.

- **Barcan models.** With quantified modal logic, the quantifiers may interact with the modal operators in various ways. The Barcan formula imposes the strong constraint that the necessity operator commutes with universal quantifiers over individuals:

  $(\forall x)\Box P(\mathrm{x}) \;\equiv\; \Box\,(\forall x)\mathrm{P}(x)$.

  In terms of Kripke-style models or NGMs, the Barcan constraint implies that all worlds accessible from a given world must have exactly the same individuals. To enforce that constraint, a Barcan NGM can be defined as a G = (A,B,C,L,I) for quantified modal logic whose boxes B are partitioned in an equivalence class E with the following properties:

  1. Every e in equivalence class E is the union of two disjoint sets of boxes, $e = \mathrm{B}_1 \cup \mathrm{B}_2$, where the boxes in B_1 represent individuals and the boxes in B_2 represent worlds.
  2. For every box b in B_1, b contains no nested NGM, and the label(b) $= x$ for some individual x.
  3. For every box b in B_2, b contains a nested NGM H that represents some world w, label(b) $= w$, and there is an isomorphism f that maps the boxes of H to the boxes in B_1.
  4. For every box b in B_1, there exists a line of identity i in I that consists of the box b and the boxes of each nested NGM that are isomorphic to b:

     $i = \{b\} \cup \{d \mid d$ is a box of some NGM nested in a box of B_2 for which $f(d) = b\}$.
  5. There are no lines of identity in I other than those determined in step #4.

  In short, each equivalence class contains a set of individual boxes B_1 and a set of world boxes B_2. Each world box contains a nested NGM whose boxes are in a one-to-one correspondence with the individual boxes of B_1. Each individual box has a coreference link to the corresponding box of each NGM nested in a world box of B_2.

This discussion shows how various Kripke-style models can be converted to isomorphic NGMs. That conversion enables different kinds of model structures to be compared within a common framework. The next two sections of this paper show that NGMs combined with Dunn's semantics can represent a wider range of semantic structures and methods of reasoning.

6. BEYOND KRIPKE SEMANTICS

As the examples in Section 5 show, nested graph models can represent the equivalent of Kripke models for a wide range of logics. But Kripke models, which use only a single level of nesting, do not take full advantage of the representational options of NGMs. The possibility of multiple levels of nesting makes NGMs significantly more expressive than Kripke's model structures, but questions arise about what they actually express. In criticizing Kripke's models, (233) noted that models can be used to prove that certain axioms are consistent, but they don't explain the intended meaning of those axioms:

> The notion of possible world did indeed contribute to the semantics of modal logic, and it behooves us to recognize the nature of its contribution: it led to Kripke's precocious and significant theory of models of modal logic. Models afford consistency proofs; also they have heuristic value; but they do not constitute explication. Models, however clear they be in themselves, may leave us at a loss for the primary, intended interpretation.

Quine's criticisms apply with equal or greater force to NGMs. Although the metaphor of possible worlds raises serious ontological questions, it lends some aura of meaningfulness to the entities that make up the models. As purely set theoretical constructions, NGMs dispense with the dubious ontology of possible worlds, but their networks of boxes and circles have even less intuitive meaning.

To illustrate the issues, Figure 9 shows a conceptual graph with two levels of nesting to represent the sentence *Tom believes that Mary wants to marry a sailor.* The type labels of the contexts indicate how the nested CGs are interpreted: what Tom believes is a proposition stated by the CG nested in the context of type **Proposition**; what Mary wants is a situation described by the proposition stated by the CG nested in the context of type **Situation**. Relations of type **(Expr)** show that Tom and Mary are the experiencers of states of believing or wanting, and relations of type **(Thme)** show that the themes of those states are propositions or situations.

When a CG is in the outermost context or when it is nested in a concept of type **Proposition**, it states a proposition. When a CG is nested inside a concept of type **Situation**, the stated proposition describes the situation. When a context is translated to predicate calculus, the result depends on the type label of the context. In the following translation, the first line represents the subgraph outside the nested contexts, the second

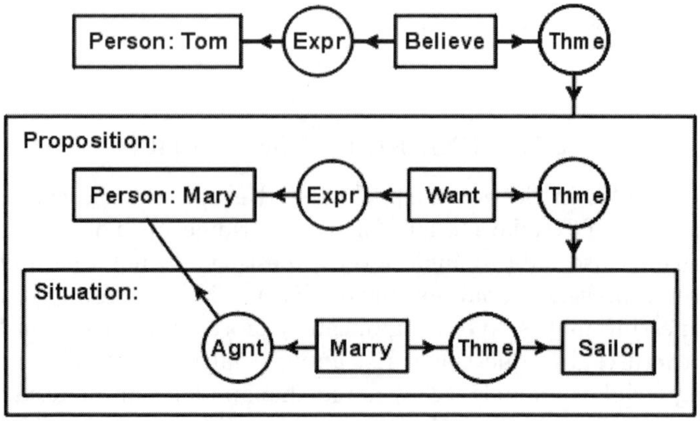

FIGURE 9. A conceptual graph with two nested contexts

and third lines represent the subgraph for Tom's belief, and the fourth line represents the subgraph for Mary's desire:

$(\exists a\text{:Person})(\exists b\text{:Believe})(\text{name}(a,\text{'Tom'}) \wedge \text{expr}(a,b) \wedge \text{thme}(b,$
$(\exists c\text{:Person})(\exists d\text{:Want})(\exists e\text{:Situation})$
$(\text{name}(c,\text{'Mary'}) \wedge \text{expr}(d,c) \wedge (\text{thme}(d,e) \wedge \text{dscr}(e,$
$(\exists f\text{:Marry})(\exists g\text{:Sailor})(\text{agnt}(f,c) \wedge \text{thme}(f,g))))))$

If a CG is outside any context, the default translation treats it as a statement of a proposition. Therefore, the part of Figure 9 inside the context of type **Proposition** is translated in the same way as the part outside that context. For the part nested inside the context of type **Situation**, the *description predicate* dscr relates the situation e to the statement of the proposition.

As the translation to predicate calculus illustrates, the nested CG contexts map to formulas that are nested as arguments of predicates, such as thme or dscr. Such graphs or formulas can be treated as examples of Tarski's stratified metalevels, in which a proposition expressed in the outer context can make a statement about a proposition in the nested context, which may in turn make a statement about another proposition nested even more deeply. A nested graph model for such propositions would have the same kind of nested structure.

To show how the denotation of the CG in Figure 9 (or its translation to predicate calculus) is evaluated, consider the NGM in Figure 10, which represents some aspect of the world, including some of Tom's beliefs. The outermost context of Figure 10 represents some information known to an outside observer who uttered the original sentence *Tom believes that Mary wants to marry a sailor.* The context labeled #4 contains some of Tom's beliefs, including his mistaken belief that person #5 is named Jane, even

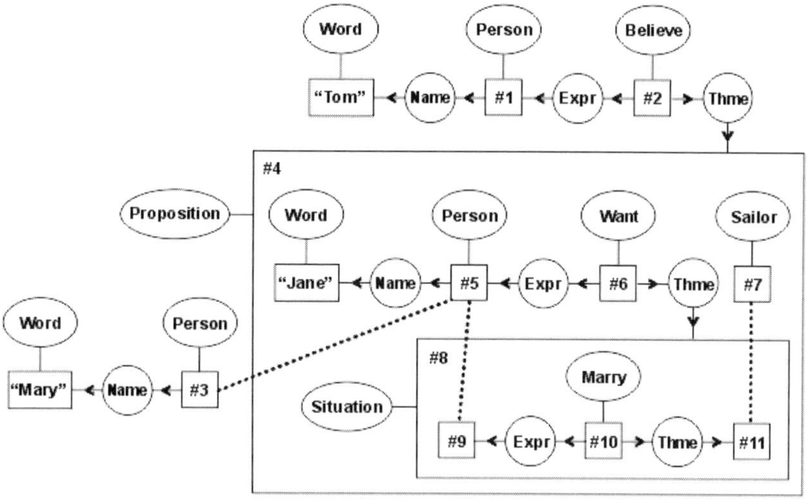

FIGURE 10. An NGM for which Figure 9 has denotation true.

though #5 is coreferent with person #3, who is known to the outside observer as Mary. The evaluation of Figure 9 in terms of Figure 10 is based on the method of *outside-in evaluation*, which (231) called *endoporeutic.*

Syntactically, Figure 10 is a well formed CG, but it is limited to a more primitive subset of features than Figure 9. Before the denotation of Figure 9 can be evaluated in terms of Figure 10, each concept node of the CG must be replaced by a subgraph that uses the same features. The concept [**Person: Tom**], for example, may be considered an abbreviation for a CG that uses only the primitive features:

(Person)—[∃]→(Name)→["Tom"]—(Word)

This graph says that there exists something [∃] for which the monadic predicate **(Person)** is true, and it has as name the character string **"Tom"**, for which the monadic predicate **(Word)** is true. This graph has denotation true in terms of Figure 10 because every part of it is either identical to or implied by a matching part of Figure 10; the only part that is not identical is the existential quantifier ∃, which is implied by the constant **#1**. In general, a conceptual graph g with no nested contexts is true in terms of a flat model m if and only if there exists a *projection* of g into m ((237)), where a projection is defined as a mapping from g into some subgraph of m for which every node of g is either identical to or a generalization of the corresponding node of m.

For nested CGs, projections are used to evaluate the denotations of subgraphs in each context, but more information must be considered: the nesting structure, the types of contexts, and the relations attached to the contexts. Figures 9 and 10 illustrate an important special case in which there are no negations, the nesting struture is the same, and the corresponding contexts have the same types and attached relations. For that case, the denotation is true if the subgraph of Figure 9 in each context has a projection into the corresponding subgraph of Figure 10. The evaluation starts from the outside and moves inward:

1. The first step begins by matching the outermost context of Figure 9 to the outermost context of Figure 10. When Figure 9 is converted to the same primitives as Figure 10, the projection succeeds. If the projection had failed, the denotation would be false, and further evaluation of the nested contexts would be irrelevant.
2. The evaluation continues by determining whether the part of Figure 9 nested one level deep has a projection into the corresponding part of Figure 10. In this case, the projection is blocked because Tom falsely believes that Mary has the name Jane. Nevertheless, the node [**#5**], which represents Jane in Tom's belief, is coreferent with the outer node [**#3**], which represents the person whose actual name is Mary. The projection can succeed if the subgraph with the name Mary may be imported (copied) from the outer context to the inner context. Since the original sentence was uttered by somebody who knew Mary's name, the speaker used the name Mary in that context, even though Tom believed she was named Jane. Therefore, the correct name may be used to evaluate the denotation. When the subgraph →**(Name)**→[**"Mary"**]—**(Word)** is imported into the context and attached to node [**#5**], the projection succeeds.
3. Finally, the part of Figure 9 nested two levels deep must have a projection into the corresponding part of Figure 10. In this case, the projection is blocked because concept [**#11**] is not marked as a sailor. Nevertheless, that node is coreferent with concept [**#7**], which is marked as a sailor. Since the scope of Tom's belief includes both contexts #4 and #8, the subgraph —**(Sailor)** may be imported from context #4 and attached to concept [**#11**]. As a result, the modified version Figure 9 can be projected into the modified version of Figure 10, and the denotation is true.

As this example illustrates, additional information may have to be imported into a context when the evaluation process reaches it. The import conditions may depend on the knowledge, belief, or intention of some agent who knows, believes, or intends the context to be true. For this example, the mental attitudes of two agents are significant: Tom's belief and some outside observer's knowledge; although Tom's belief about Mary's desire is relevant, Mary's actual desire is not. The type of context, the attached relations, and the attitudes of the agents determines what information can be imported.

By supporting multiple levels of nesting, NGMs can represent structures that are significantly richer than Kripke models. But the intended meaning of those structures and the methods for evaluating denotations raise seven key questions:

1. How does Peirce's method of endoporeutic relate to Tarski's method for evaluating the denotation of a formula in first-order logic?
2. To what extent does the nesting increase the expressive power of an NGM in comparison to a Tarski-style relational structure or a Kripke-style model structure?
3. Import rules add a feature that is not present in any version of Tarski's or Kripke's evaluation function. What is their model-theoretic justification?
4. How are NGMs related to Dunn's semantics, Tarski's stratified metalevels, and other semantic theories? How is the NGM formalism related to other graph formalisms, such as SNePS ((235); (236))?
5. The nested contexts are governed by concepts such as **Believe** and **Want**, which represent two kinds of propositional attitudes. But natural languages have hundreds or thousands of verbs that express some kind of mental attitude about a proposition stated in a subordinate clause. How could the evaluation function take into account all the conditions implied by each of those verbs or the events they represent?
6. The evaluation of Figure 9 depends on the mental attitudes of several agents, such as Tom, Mary, and an outside observer who presumably uttered the original sentence. Is it always necessary to consider multiple agents and the structure of the linguistic discourse? How can the effects of such interactions be analyzed and formalized in the evaluation function?
7. Finally, what is the ontological status of entities that are supposed to "exist" within a context? What is their "intended interpretation" in Quine's sense? If they don't represent things in possible worlds, what do they represent or correspond to in the real world?

These questions lead to open research issues in logic, linguistics, and philosophy. A definitive answer to all of them is far beyond the scope of this article, but a brief discussion of each of them is sufficient to show that the formalism of NGMs combined with Dunn's semantics and Peirce's endoporeutic provides a powerful method for addressing them.

Since Peirce developed endoporeutic about thirty years before Tarski, he never related it to Tarski's approach. But he did relate it to the detailed model-theoretic analyses of medieval logicians such as (227). (229) used model-theoretic arguments to justify the rules of inference for his algebraic notation for predicate calculus. For existential graphs, (231) defined endoporeutic as an evaluation method that is logically equivalent to Tarski's.

That equivalence was not recognized until (211) showed that Peirce's endoporeutic could be viewed as a version of *game-theoretical semantics* by (213). (237) used a game-theoretical method to define the model theory for the first-order subset of conceptual graphs. For an introductory textbook on model theory, (205) adopted game-theoretical semantics because it is easier to explain than Tarski's original method. For evaluating NGMs, it is especially convenient because it can accommodate various extensions, such as import conditions and discourse constraints, while the evaluation progresses from one level of nesting to the next ((214)).

The flexibility of game-theoretical semantics allows it to accommodate the insights and mechanisms of *dynamic semantics*, which uses discourse information while determining the semantics of NL sentences ((218); (210); (209)). (242) characterized dynamic semantics by the slogan "You know the meaning of a sentence if you know the change it brings about in the information state of anyone who accepts the news conveyed by it." Dynamic semantics is complementary to Hintikka's game-theoretical semantics and Peirce's endoporeutic.

- Peirce developed the endoporeutic as a formalization of Ockham's method of evaluating the truth conditions of sentences in Latin, and Hintikka developed game-theoretical semantics as a simpler but more general method for evaluating truth conditions than Tarski's.
- Karttunen and Heim were addressing the problem of incorporating new information into a semantic representation during natural language discourse. They considered truth conditions to be an important, but solvable problem compared to the many unsolved problems of anaphoric references.
- The method of outside-in evaluation that characterizes both endoporeutic and game-theoretical semantics makes the evaluation procedure more amenable to the introduction of new information. As an example, the evaluation of Figure 9 in terms of Figure 10 allows information to be imported as the evaluation proceeds from one context to the next. The discourse constraints of dynamic semantics can also be enforced as each new context is entered.

More work is needed to reconcile and synthesize the various theories, but this brief summary sketches the outlines of how such a reconcilation could be formalized.

Although NGMs can accommodate many kinds of relationships that Tarski and Kripke never considered, they remain within the framework of first-order semantics. In principle, any NGM can be translated to a flat NGM, which can be used to evaluate denotations by Tarski's original approach. As an example, Figure 11 shows a flattened version of Figure 10. In order to preserve information about the nesting structure, the method of flattening attaches an extra argument to show the context of each circle

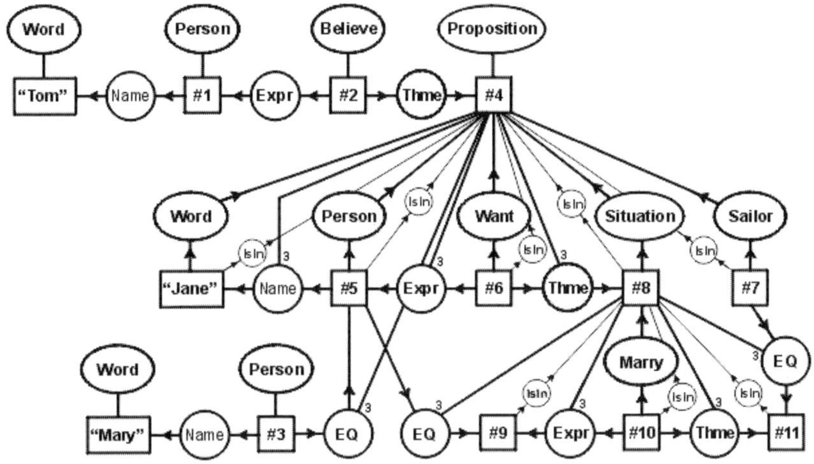

FIGURE 11. A flattened version of Figure 10.

and links each box to its containing context by a relation of type **IsIn**. Coreference links in the NGM are replaced by a three-argument equality relation **(EQ)**, in which the third argument shows the context in which two individuals are considered to be equal.

The conversion from Figure 10 to Figure 11 is similar to the translation from the CG notation with nested contexts to Shapiro's SNePS notation, in which nested contexts are replaced by *propositional nodes* to which the relations are attached. Both notations are capable of expressing logically equivalent information. Formally, any NGM G = (A,B,C,L,I) can be converted to a flat NGM F = (FA,FB,FC,FL,FI) by the following construction:

1. For every box *b* of G or of any NGM nested in G, let FB have a unique box *fb*, let label(*b*) be in FL, and let label(*fb*) = label(*b*).
2. For every circle *c* in G or in any NGM nested in G, let FC have a unique circle *fc*, let label(*c*) be in FL, and let label(*fc*) = label(*c*).
3. For every arc *a*=(*c*, *b*) in G or in any NGM nested in G, let FA have an arc *fa* = (*fc*,*fb*) where *fc* is the circle that corresponds to *c*, *fb* is the box that corresponds to *b*, and label(*fa*) = label(*a*).
4. Add the strings "IsIn" and "EQ" to the labels in FL. (If step #3 had already introduced either of those labels in FL, then append some string to the previous labels that is sufficient to distinguish them from all other labels in FL.)
5. For every box *fb* in FB whose corresponding box *b* contains a nested NGM H, the box *fb* shall not contain any nested NGM. In addition,

- For every box d of H whose corresponding box is fd in FB, add a circle e in FC with label(e) = "IsIn" and with two additional arcs in FA: (e,fd) with label 1 and (e,fb) with label 2.
- For every circle c of H whose corresponding circle is fc in FC, add an arc (fc,fb) to FA. If c has n arcs, let label((fc,fb)) = $n+1$.

6. Let the set FI be empty, and for every line of identity i in I, let H be the NGM whose boxes have a nonempty overlap with i and all other boxes of i are boxes of some NGM nested in H. Select some box b of H which is also in i and whose corresponding box in FB is fb. For every box d in i other than b whose corresponding box in FB is fd, add a circle c to FC for which label(c)="EQ", add an arc (c,fb) with label 1 to FA, add an arc (c,fd) with label 2 to FA, and if the box fd is linked to a box fx by a circle with the label "IsIn", add an arc (c,fx) with label 3 to FA.

The verbosity of this specification is typical of translations from graphs to text: graphs are easier to see or draw than to describe in words or in algebra.

The method used to map a nested graph model to a flat model can be generalized to a method for translating a formalism with nested contexts, such as conceptual graphs, to a formalism with propositional nodes but no nesting, such as SNePS. In effect, the nesting is an explicit representation of Tarski's stratified metalevels, in which higher levels are able to state propositions about both the syntax and semantics of propositions stated at any lower level. When two or more levels are flattened to a single level, additional arguments must be added to the relations in order to indicate which level they came from. The process of flattening demonstrates how a purely first-order model theory is supported: propositions are represented by nodes that represent individual entities of type **Proposition**. The flattened models correspond to a Tarski-style model, and the flattened languages are first-order logics, whose denotations can be evaluated by a Tarski-style method.

Although nested contexts do not increase the theoretical complexity beyond first-order logic, they simplify the language by eliminating the extra arguments needed to distinguish contexts in a flat model. The contexts also separate the metalevel propositions about a context from the object-level propositions within a context. That separation facilitates the introduction of Dunn's semantics into the langauge:

1. The modal operators $\Box$ and $\Diamond$ or the equivalent CG relations **Necs** and **Psbl** make metalevel assertions that the nested propositions they govern are provable from the laws or consistent with the laws.

2. The laws themselves, which are asserted in a metalevel outside the context governed by the modal operators, are all stated in FOL, and conventional theorem provers can be used to check the provability or consistency. (For undecidable logics, only some of the checking may be computable, but that is better than Kripke's primitive accessibility relation, which eliminates any possibility of checking.)
3. Formally, the laws, facts, and propositions governed by the modal operators are all stated in FOL, and conventional theorem provers can be used to check their provability or consistency.
4. Computationally, the separation between the metalevel and the object level allows the two kinds of reasoning to be performed independently, as illustrated by the example in Section 4 about Joe's belief in astrology.
5. Any kind of reasoning that is performed with modal operators defined by Kripke semantics can also be performed when the operators are defined in terms of laws and facts. But Dunn's semantics also makes it possible to perform metametalevel reasoning about the propositions considered as laws or facts. In particular, probabilities and heuristics can be used to select laws at the metametalevel, while logical deduction with those laws is used at the lower levels.

The import rules for copying information compensate for the possibly incomplete information in a context. To use the terms of Reiter (1978), a context represents an *open world*, in contrast to Hintikka's maximally consistent model sets, which represent *closed worlds*. Computationally, the infinite model sets contain far too much information to be comprehended or manipulated in any useful way. A context is a finite excerpt from a model set in the same sense that a situation is a finite excerpt from a possible world. Figure 12 shows mappings from a Kripke possible world w to a description of w as a Hintikka model set $\boldsymbol{M}$ or a finite excerpt from w as a Barwise and Perry situation s. Then $\boldsymbol{M}$ and s may be mapped to a McCarthy context $\boldsymbol{C}$.

From a possible world w, the mapping to the right extracts an excerpt as a situation s, which may be described by the propositions in a context $\boldsymbol{C}$. From the same world w, the downward mapping leads to a description of w as a model set $\boldsymbol{M}$, from which an equivalent excerpt would produce the same context $\boldsymbol{C}$. The symbol $\models$ represents semantic entailment: w entails M, and s entails C. The ultimate justification for the import rules is the preservation of the truth conditions that make Figure 12 a *commutative diagram*: the alternate routes through the diagram must lead to logically equivalent results.

The combined mappings in Figure 12 replace the mysterious possible worlds with finite, computable contexts. Hintikka's model sets support operations on well-defined symbols instead of imaginary worlds, but they

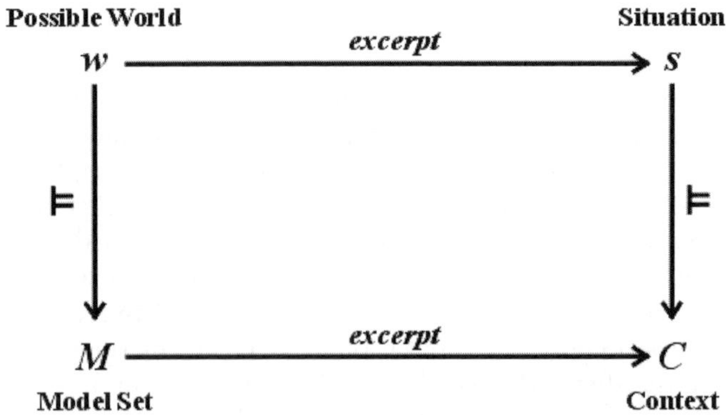

FIGURE 12. Ways of mapping possible worlds to contexts.

may still be infinite. Situations are finite, but like worlds they consist of physical or fictitious objects that are not computable. The contexts in the lower right of Figure 12 are the only things that can be represented and manipulated in a digital computer. Any theory of semantics that is stated in terms of possible worlds, model sets, or situations must ultimately be mapped to a theory of contexts in order to be computable.

The discussion so far has addressed the first four of the seven key questions on page 169. The next section addresses the last three questions, which involve the kinds of verbs that express mental attitudes, the ontological status of the entities they represent, the roles of the agents who have those attitudes, and the methods of reasoning about those attitudes.

7. THE INTENDED INTERPRETATION

Models and worlds have been interpreted in many different ways by people who have formulated theories about them. Some have used models as surrogates for worlds, but Lewis, among others, criticized such "ersatz worlds" as inadequate. In a paper that acknowledged conversations with Lewis, (224) explained why he objected to "the identification of possible worlds with models":

> ...two possible worlds may differ even though they may be indistinguishable in all respects expressible in a given language (even by open formulas). For instance, if the language refers only to physical predicates, then we may consider two possible worlds, consisting of exactly the same persons and physical objects, all of which have exactly the same physical properties and stand in exactly the same physical relations; then the two corresponding models for our physical language will be identical. But the two

> possible worlds may still differ, for example, in that in one everyone believes the proposition that snow is white, while in the other someone does not believe it.... This point might seem unimportant, but it looms large in any attempt to treat belief as a relation between persons and propositions.

Montague's objection does not hold for the NGM illustrated in Figure 10, Which includes entity **#2** of type **Believe** and entity **#6** of type **Want**. Such a model can explicitly represent a situation in which one person believes a proposition and another doesn't. But the last sentence by Montague indicates the crux of the problem: his models did not include entities of type **Believe**. Instead, he hoped to "treat belief as a [dyadic] relation between persons and propositions."

In that same paper, Montague outlined his method for reducing "four types of entities – experiences, events, tasks, obligations – to [dyadic] predicates." But he used those predicates in statements governed by modal operators such as *obligatory*:

> *Obligations* can probably best be regarded as the same sort of things as tasks and experiences, that is, as relations-in-intension between persons and moments; for instance, the obligation to give Smith a horse can be identified with the predicate expressed by 'x gives Smith a horse at t'. We should scrutinize, in this context also, the notion of partaking of a predicate. Notice that if R is an obligation, to say that x bears the relation-in-intension R to t is not to say that x *has the obligation* R at t, but rather that x *discharges* or *fulfills* the obligation R at t. But how could we say that x *has* at t *the obligation* R? This would amount to the assertion that it is *obligatory* at t that x *bear the relation-in-intension* R to some moment equal to or subsequent to t.

All of Montague's paraphrases are attempts to avoid saying or implying that there exist entities of type **Obligation**. To avoid that implication, he required any sentence with the noun *obligation* to be paraphrased by a sentence with the modal operator *obligatory*:

1. Jones has an obligation to give Smith a horse.
2. Obligatory(there exists a time t when Jones gives Smith a horse).

Only people who had been steeped in the mindset that underlies Montague's semantics could imagine how this syntactic transformation might have a semantic effect. As a mathematician, he hoped to transform his new problem to a previously solved problem without introducing any new assumptions. Therefore, he took the following ingenious, but circuitous route through a forest of notation decorated with subscripts, superscripts, and Greek letters:

1. The noun *obligation* had to be eliminated because it implied the existence of an unobservable entity of type **Obligation**.
2. Since Kripke had previously "solved" the problem of defining modal operators, Montague transformed the noun to an adverb that represents a modal operator.
3. Then Kripke's semantics could define the operator **Obligatory** in terms of possible worlds and the accessibility relation between worlds.
4. To evaluate the denotation of sentences for his model theory, Montague adopted Carnap's idea that the *intension* of a sentence could be defined as a function from possible worlds to truth values.
5. To construct those functions from simpler functions, (225) assigned a lambda expression to every grammar rule for his fragment of English. The parse tree for a sentence would then determine a combination of lambda expressions that would define the intension of a sentence in terms of simpler functions for each part of speech.
6. With this construction, Montague restricted the variables of his logic to refer only to physical objects, never to "experiences, events, tasks, obligations."

Montague's *tour de force* eliminated references to unobservable entities such as beliefs and obligations. Yet he pushed all the semantics associated with beliefs and obligations into the dubious possible worlds, the mysterious accessibility relation between worlds, and the magical functions that map possible worlds to truth values. Any of them is far more questionable than the existence of beliefs and obligations; the combination is a *reductio ad absurdum.*

Peirce had a much simpler and more realistic theory. For him, thoughts, beliefs, and obligations are signs. The types of signs are independent of any mind or brain, but the particular instances – or *tokens* as he called them – exist in the brains of individual people, not in an undefined accessibility relation between imaginary worlds. Those people can give evidence of their internal signs by using external signs, such as sentences, contracts, and handshakes. In his definition of *sign*, (230) emphasized its independence of any implementation in proteins or silicon:

> I define a sign as something, A, which brings something, B, its interpretant, into the same sort of correspondence with something, C, its object, as that in which itself stands to C. In this definition I make no more reference to anything like the human mind than I do when I define a line as the place within which a particle lies during a lapse of time. (p. 235)

In terms of Dunn's semantics, an obligation is a proposition used as a law that determines a certain kind of behavior. If Jones has an obligation to give Smith a horse, there exists some sign of that proposition — a contract on paper, sound waves in air, or some neural excitation in a brain. The semantics of the sign is independent of the medium, but critically dependent on the *triadic* relation, which adds an interpretant B to the dyad of sign A and object C. The interpretant is another sign, which is essential for determining the modality of how A relates to B.

In 1906, Peirce introduced colors into his existential graphs to distinguish various kinds of modality and intentionality. Figure 4, for example, used red to represent possibility in the EG for the sentence *You can lead a horse to water, but you can't make him drink.* To distinguish the *actual*, *modal*, and *intentional* contexts illustrated in Figure 8, three kinds of colors would be needed. Conveniently, the *heraldic tinctures*, which were used to paint coats of arms in the middle ages, were grouped in three classes: *metal*, *color*, and *fur*. Peirce adopted them for his three kinds of contexts, each of which corresponded to one of his three categories: Firstness (independent conception), Secondness (relative conception), and Thirdness (mediating conception).

1. Actuality is Firstness, because it is what it is, independent of anything else. Peirce used the metallic tincture *argent* (white background) for "the actual or true in a general or ordinary sense," and three other metals (*or, fer,* and *plomb*) for "the actual or true in some special sense."
2. Modality is Secondness, because it distinguishes the mode of a situation relative to what is actual: whenever the actual world changes, the possibilities must also change. Peirce used four heraldic colors to distinguish modalities: *azure* for logical possibility (dark blue) and subjective possibility (light blue); *gules* (red) for objective possibility; *vert* (green) for "what is in the interrogative mood"; and *purpure* (purple) for "freedom or ability."
3. Intentionality is Thirdness, because it depends on the mediation of some agent who distinguishes the intended situation from what is actual. Peirce used four heraldic furs for intentionality: *sable* (gray) for "the metaphysically, or rationally, or secondarily necessitated"; *ermine* (yellow) for "purpose or intention"; *vair* (brown) for "the commanded"; and *potent* (orange) for "the compelled."

Throughout his analyses, Peirce distinguished the logical operators, such as $\wedge$, $\sim$, and $\exists$, from the tinctures, which, he said, do not represent

> ...differences of the *predicates*, or *significations* of the graphs, but of the predetermined objects to which the graphs are intended to refer. Consequently, the Iconic idea of the System requires that they should be represented, not by differentiations of the Graphs themselves but by appropriate visible characters of the surfaces upon which the Graphs are marked.

In effect, Peirce did not consider the tinctures to be part of logic itself, but of the metalanguage for describing how logic applies to the universe of discourse:

> The nature of the universe or universes of discourse (for several may be referred to in a single assertion) in the rather unusual cases in which such precision is required, is denoted either by using modifications of the heraldic tinctures, marked in something like the usual manner in pale ink upon the surface, or by scribing the graphs in colored inks.

Peirce's later writings are fragmentary, incomplete, and mostly unpublished, but they are no more fragmentary and incomplete than most modern publications about contexts. In fact, Peirce was more consistent in distinguishing the syntax (oval enclosures), the semantics ("the universe or universes of discourse"), and the pragmatics (the tinctures that "denote" the "nature" of those universes).

Classifying contexts. Reasoning about modality requires a classification of the types of contexts, their relationships to one another, and the identification of certain propositions in a context as laws or facts. Any of the tinctured contexts may be nested inside or outside the ovals representing negation. When combined with negation in all possible ways, each tincture can represent a family of related modalities:

1. The first metallic tincture, argent, corresponds to the white background that Peirce used for his original existential graphs. When combined with existence and conjunction, negations on a white background support classical first-order logic about what is actually true or false "in an ordinary sense." Negations on the other metallic backgrounds support FOL for what is "actual in some special sense." A statement about the physical world, for example, would be actual in an ordinary sense. But Peirce also considered mathematical abstractions, such as Cantor's hierarchy of infinite sets, to be actual, but not in the same sense as ordinary physical entities.
2. In the algebraic notation, $\Diamond p$ means that p is possible. Then necessity $\Box p$ is defined as $\sim \Diamond \sim p$. Impossibility is represented as $\sim \Diamond p$ or equivalently $\Box \sim p$. Instead of the single symbol $\Diamond$, Peirce's five colors represent different versions of possibility; for each of them, there is a corresponding interpretation of necessity, impossibility, and contingency:
   - **Logical possibility**. A dark blue context, Peirce's equivalent of $\Diamond p$, would mean that p is consistent or not provably false. His version of $\Box p$, represented as dark blue between

two negations, would therefore mean that p is provable. Impossible $\sim \Diamond p$ would mean inconsistent or provably false.

- **Subjective possibility**. In light blue, $\Diamond p$ would mean that p is believable or not known to be false. $\Box p$ would mean that p is known or not believably false. This interpretation of $\Diamond$ and $\Box$ is called *epistemic logic*.
- **Objective possibility**. In red, $\Diamond p$ would mean that p is physically possible. As an example, Peirce noted that it was physically possible for him to raise his arm, even when he was not at the moment doing so. $\Box p$ would mean physical necessity according to the laws of nature.
- **Interrogative mood**. In green, $\Diamond p$ would mean that p is questioned, and $\Box p$ would mean that p is not questionably false. This interpretation of $\Diamond p$ corresponds to a proposition p in a Prolog goal or the where-clause of an SQL query.
- **Freedom**. In purple, $\Diamond p$ would mean that p is free or permissible; $\Box p$ would mean that p is obligatory or not permissibly false; $\sim \Diamond p$ would mean that p is not permissible or illegal; and $\Diamond \sim p$ would mean that p is permissibly false or optional. This interpretation of $\Diamond$ and $\Box$ is called *deontic logic*.

3. The heraldic furs represent various kinds of intentions, but Peirce did not explore the detailed interactions of the furs with negations or with each other. Don Roberts (234) suggested some combinations, such as negation with the tinctures gules and potent to represent *The quality of mercy is not strained.*

Although Peirce's three-way classification of contexts is useful, he did not work out their implications in detail. He wrote that the complete classification of "all the conceptions of logic" was "a labor for generations of analysts, not for one."

Multimodal reasoning. As the multiple axioms for modal logic indicate, there is no single version that is adequate for all applications. The complexities increase when different interpretations of modality are mixed, as in Peirce's five versions of possibility, which could be represented by colors or by subscripts, such as $\Diamond_1$, $\Diamond_2$, ..., $\Diamond_5$. Each of those modalities is derived from a different set of laws, which interact in various ways with the other laws:

- The combination $\Box_3 \Diamond_1 p$, for example, would mean that it is subjectively necessary that p is logically possible. In other words, someone must know that $\Diamond_1 p$.
- Since what is known must be true, the following theorem would hold for that combination of modalities: $\Box_3 \Diamond_1 p \supset \Diamond_1 p$.

Similar analysis would be required to derive the axioms and theorems for all possible combinations of the five kinds of possibility with the five kinds of necessity. Since subjective possibility depends on the subject, the number of combinations increases further when multiple agents interact.

By introducing contexts, McCarthy hoped to reduce the proliferation of modalities to a single mechanism of metalevel reasoning about the propositions that are true in a context. By supporting a more detailed representation than the operators $\Diamond$ and $\Box$, the dyadic entailment relation and the triadic legislation relation support metalevel reasoning about the laws, facts, and their implications. Following are some implications of Peirce's five kinds of possibility:

- **Logical possibility**. The only statements that are logically necessary are tautologies: those statements that are entailed by the empty set. No special lawgiver is needed for the empty set; alternatively, every agent may be assumed to legislate the empty set:

  $$\{\} = \{p\text{:Proposition} \mid (\forall a\text{:Agent})(\forall x\text{:Entity})\text{legislate}(a, p, x)\}.$$

  The empty set is the set of all propositions p that every agent a legislates as a law for every entity x.

- **Subjective possibility**. A proposition p is subjectively possible for an agent a if a does not know p to be false. The subjective laws for any agent a are all the propositions that a knows:

  $$\text{SubjectiveLaws}(a) = \{p\text{:Proposition} \mid \text{know}(a, p)\}.$$

  That principle of subjective possibility can be stated in the following axiom:

  $$(\forall a\text{:Agent})(\forall p\text{:Proposition})(\forall x\text{:Entity})\ (\text{legislate}(a, p, x) \equiv \text{know}(a,\ x \models p)).$$

  For any agent a, proposition p, and entity x, the agent a legislates p as a law for x if and only if a knows that x entails p.

- **Objective possibility**. The laws of nature define what is physically possible. The symbol *God* may be used as a place holder for the lawgiver:

  $$\text{LawsOfNature} = \{p\text{:Proposition} \mid (\forall x\text{:Entity})\text{legislate}(\text{God}, p, x)\}.$$

  If God is assumed to be omniscient, this set is the same as everything God knows or SubjectiveLaws(God). What is subjective for God is objective for everyone else.

- **Interrogative mood**. A proposition is not questioned if it is part of the common knowledge of the parties to a conversation. For two agents a and b, common knowledge can be defined as the intersection of their subjective knowledge or laws:

  $$\text{CommonKnowledge}(a, b) = \text{SubjectiveLaws}(a) \cap \text{SubjectiveLaws}(b).$$

- **Freedom.** Whatever is free or permissible is consistent with the laws, rules, regulations, ordnances, or policies of some lawgiver who has the authority to legislate what is obligatory for x:

  $$\text{Obligatory}(x) = \{p\text{:Proposition} \mid (\exists a\text{:Agent})(\text{authority}(a,x) \land \text{legislate}(a,p,x)\}.$$

  This interpretation, which defines deontic logic, makes it a weak version of modal logic since consistency is weaker than truth. The usual modal axioms $\Box p \supset p$ and $p \supset \Diamond p$ do not hold for deontic logic, since people can and do violate laws.

Reasoning at the metalevel of laws and facts is common practice in courts. In the United States, the Constitution is the supreme law of the land; any law or regulation of the U.S. government or any state, county, or city in the U.S. must be consistent with the U.S. Constitution. But the tautologies and laws of nature are established by an even higher authority. No one can be forced to obey a law that is logically or physically impossible.

To relate events to the agents who form plans and execute them, (206) distinguished three determining factors: *beliefs, desires,* and *intentions* (BDI). He insisted that all three are essential and that none of them can be reduced to the other two. Peirce would have agreed: the appetitive aspect of desire is a kind of Firstness; belief is a kind of Secondness that relates a proposition to a situation; and intention is a kind of Thirdness that relates an agent, a situation, and the agent's plan for action in the situation. To formalize Bratman's theory in Kripke-style model structures, (207) extended Kripke's triples to BDI *octuples* of the form $(\Theta,\text{P},\text{E},\text{Agnt},\text{T},\text{B},\text{G},\Phi)$:

1. Θ is a set of entities called *things*;
2. P is a set of entities called *people*;
3. E is a set of *event types*;
4. Agnt is a function defined over events, which specifies some entity in P as the *agent* of the event;
5. T is a set of possible worlds or *courses of events*, each of which is a function from a sequence Z of time points to event types in E;
6. $\text{B}(w_1,p,t,w_2)$ is a *belief accessibility relation*, which relates a course of events w_1, a person p, and a time point t to some course of events w_2 that is accessible from w_1 according to p's beliefs;
7. $\text{G}(w_1,p,t,w_2)$ is a *goal accessibility relation*, which relates a course of events w_1, a person p, and a time point t to some course of events w_2 that is accessible from w_1 according to p's goals;
8. Φ is an evaluation function similar to Kripke's Φ.

The list of features in the BDI octuples is a good summary of the kinds of information that any formalization of intentionality must accommodate. But it also demonstrates the limitations of Kripke-style models in comparison to the more general nested graph models:

- The multiplicity of Greek letters and subscripts tends to frighten nonmathemticians, but it is not a serious defect of the formalism. NGMs would represent logically equivalent information in a more readable form, but with no reduction in the total amount.
- A more serious limitation is the information that BDI octuples leave as undefined primitives: the belief accessibility relation B and the goal accessibility relation G. With Dunn's semantics, B and G would be replaced by selections of laws and facts, which explain why some courses of events are accessible from others.
- The sets Θ, P, and E constitute an ontology with only three concept types: **Thing**, **Person**, and **Event** (which is actually the supertype of an open-ended number of event types). A more realistic ontology would require a much richer collection of concept types, their interrelationships, and their associated axioms. Some such ontology is a prerequisite for constructing models, but the definition of the function Φ for evaluating denotations is independent of any particular ontology.
- The set of event types E would correspond to the set of verb senses in natural languages, which has a cardinality between 10^4 and 10^5. The function Agnt, which specifies the agent of an event type, is just one of several thematic roles that must be specified for each event type. In addition to the types and roles, an ontology must also specify the definitions and axioms for each type.
- The definitions and axioms of an ontology are the laws that enable Dunn's semantics to derive accessibility relations such as B and G instead of assuming them as undefined primitives.
- The axioms of the ontology and the discourse constraints of dynamic semantics determine the conditions for importing information from one context to another when denotations are evaluated.
- The formal definition of NGMs in Section 5 is general enough to accommodate any ontology for any domain of discourse, and the evaluation methods of Peirce and Hintikka provide a flexible model theory that can support dynamic semantics.

This comparison of BDI models with nested graph models summarizes the arguments presented in this paper: Kripke-style models even with the BDI extensions relegate some of the most significant semantics to undefined and undefinable accessibility relations; Dunn's semantics can use the axioms of an ontology as the laws that define the accessibility relations; Peirce-Kamp-McCarthy contexts combined with Tarski's metalevels can support metalevel reasoning about the selection of laws and facts; the outside-in evaluation method of Peirce's endoporeutic or Hintikka's game-theoretical semantics can accommodate the discourse constraints of dynamic semantics; and nested graph models are flexible enough to represent all of the above. NGMs, by themselves, cannot solve all the problems of semantics, but they can incorporate ongoing research from logic, linguistics, and philosophy into a computable framework.

21 Palmer Avenue
Croton-on-Hudson
NY 1052
USA

REFERENCES

[205] Jon Barwise and John Etchemendy. *Tarski's World.* CSLI Publications, Stanford, CA, 1993.

[206] Michael E. Bratman. *Intentions, Plans, and Practical Reason.* Harvard University Press, Cambridge, MA, 1987.

[207] Philip R. Cohen and Hector J. Levesque. Intention is choice with commitment. *Artificial Intelligence*, 42(3):213–261, 1990.

[208] J. Michael Dunn. A truth value semantics for modal logic. in H. Leblanc, ed., *Truth, Syntax and Modality*, North-Holland, Amsterdam, pp. 87-100, 1973.

[209] Jeroen Groenendijk and Martin Stokhof. Dynamic Predicate Logic. *Linguistics and Philosophy*, 14(1):39–100, 1991.

[210] Irene R. Heim. *The Semantics of Definite and Indefinite Noun Phrases.* PhD Dissertation, University of Massachusetts, Amherst. Published (1988) Garland, New York, 1982.

[211] Risto Hilpinen. On C. S. Peirce's theory of the proposition: Peirce as a precursor of game-theoretical semantics. *The Monist*, 65:182–88, 1982.

[212] Jaakko Hintikka. The modes of modality. *Acta Philosophica Fennica, Modal and Many-valued Logics*, pages 65–81, 1963.

[213] Jaakko Hintikka. *Logic, Language Games, and Information.* Clarendon Press, Oxford, 1973.

[214] Jaakko Hintikka and Jack Kulas. *The Game of Language: Studies in Game-Theoretical Semantics and its Applications.* D. Reidel, Dordrecht, 1985.

[215] G. E. Hughes and M. J. Cresswell. *An Introduction to Modal Logic.* Methuen, London, 1968.

[216] Hans Kamp. Events, discourse representations, and temporal references. *Langages*, 64:39–64, 1981.

[217] Hans Kamp and Uwe Reyle. *From Discourse to Logic.* Kluwer, Dordrecht, 1993.

[218] Lauri Karttunen. Discourse referents. in J. McCawley, ed., *Syntax and Semantics* vol. 7, Academic Press, New York, pp. 363-385, 1976.

[219] Saul A. Kripke. Semantical analysis of modal logic I. *Zeitschrift für mathematische Logik und Grundlagen der Mathematik*, 9:67–96, 1963.

[220] Saul A. Kripke. Semantical analysis of modal logic II: Non-normal modal propositional calculi. In J. W. Addison, Leon Henkin, & Alfred Tarski, *The Theory of Models*, North-Holland Publishing Co., Amsterdam, pp. 206-220, 1965.

[221] David K. Lewis. *On the Plurality of Worlds.* Basil Blackwell, Oxford, 1986.

[222] John McCarthy. Epistemological problems of artificial intelligence. *Proceedings of IJCAI-77*, reprinted in J. McCarthy, *Formalizing Common Sense*, Ablex, Norwood, NJ, 1977.

[223] John McCarthy. Notes on formalizing context. *Proc. IJCAI-93*, Chambéry, France, pp. 555-560, 1993.

[224] Richard Montague. On the nature of certain philosophical entities. originally published in *The Monist* **53** (1960), revised version in Montague (1974) pp. 148-187, 1967.

[225] Richard Montague. The proper treatment of quantification in ordinary english. reprinted in (226), pp. 247-270, 1970.

[226] Richard Montague. *Formal Philosophy.* Yale University Press, New Haven, 1974.

[227] William of Ockham. *Summa Logicae.* Johannes Higman, Paris, 1488. The edition owned by C. S. Peirce, 1323.

[228] Charles Sanders Peirce. On the algebra of logic. *American Journal of Mathematics*, 3:15–57, 1880.

[229] Charles Sanders Peirce. On the algebra of logic. *American Journal of Mathematics*, 7:180–202, 1885.

[230] Charles Sanders Peirce. *Logic, Considered as Semeiotic.* MS L75, edited by Joseph Ransdell, `http://members.door.net/arisbe/menu/LIBRARY/bycsp/L75/ver1/l75v1-01.htm`, 1902.

[231] Charles Sanders Peirce. Manuscript 514. with commentary by J. F. Sowa, available at `http://www.jfsowa.com/peirce/ms514.htm`, 1909.

[232] Arthur N. Prior. *Papers on Time and Tense.* revised edition ed. by P. Hasle, P. Øhrstrøm, T. Braüner, & B. J. Copeland, Oxford University Press, 2003, 1968.

[233] Willard Van Orman Quine. Responding to saul kripke. reprinted in Quine, *Theories and Things*, Harvard University Press, 1972.

[234] Don D. Roberts. *The Existential Graphs of Charles S. Peirce.* Mouton, The Hague, 1973.

[235] Stuart C. Shapiro. The SNePS semantic network processing system. in N. V. Findler, ed., *Associative Networks: Representation and Use of Knowledge by Computers*, Academic Press, New York, pp. 263-315, 1979.

[236] Stuart C. Shapiro and William J. Rapaport. The SNePS family. in F. Lehmann, ed., *Semantic Networks in Artificial Intelligence,* Pergamon Press, Oxford, 1992.

[237] John F. Sowa. *Conceptual Structures: Information Processing in Mind and Machine.* Addison-Wesley, Reading, MA, 1984.

[238] John F. Sowa. Syntax, semantics, and pragmatics of contexts. in Ellis et al. (1995) *Conceptual Structures: Applications, Implementation, and Theory,* Lecture Notes in #AI 954, Springer-Verlag, Berlin, pp. 1-15, 1995.

[239] John F. Sowa. *Knowledge Representation: Logical, Philosophical, and Computational Foundations.* Brooks/Cole Publishing Co., Pacific Grove, CA, 2000.

[240] Alfred Tarski. Pojecie prawdy w jezykach nauk dedukcynych. German trans. as "Der Wahrheitsbegriff in den formalisierten Sprachen," English trans. as "The concept of truth in formalized languages," in Tarski, *Logic, Semantics, Metamathematics*, second edition, Hackett Publishing Co., Indianapolis, pp. 152-278, 1933.

[241] Richmond H. Thomason. Review of *Formal Aspects of Context* edited by Bonzon et al. *Computational Linguistics*, 27(4):598–600, 2001.

[242] Frank C. Veltman. Defaults in Update Semantics. *Journal of Philosophical Logic*, 25:221–261, 1996.

RYSZARD WÓJCICKI

REFERENTIAL SEMANTICS

ABSTRACT

The task of this paper is to define the notion of referential semantics, to comment on its relevance to various epistemological issues and to prove a theorem that defines the class of logics whose logical constants are definable in terms of interpretations set forth by a referential semantics. The theorem I am going to prove extends from propositional to predicate languages, a result I presented in 1979 (see note on referential semantics in Section 16 below).

1. THE GENERAL IDEA OF REFERENTIAL SEMANTICS

One arrives at the idea of referential semantics by assuming that truth-values of sentences may depend upon "reference points," meant to be e.g. contexts in which sentences are uttered or possible worlds. Under the possible world interpretation of reference points, referential semantics collapses to possible world semantics. But this interpretation is but one of those that the idea of reference points might acquire. Throughout this paper by a reference point I shall mean a group of users of the analyzed language whose members all subscribe to the same truth-criteria. Groups of this kind will be called **reference communities**.

EXAMPLE 1. Suppose a language L serves as a means of communication for two reference communities r′ and r″. Under this assumption the pairs (0,0), (0,1), (1,0) and (1,1), 0 standing for **falsity** and 1 for **truth**, are all sequences of truth-values a sentence might acquire. The fact that instead of dividing sentences into true and false one might divide them into four "epistemic categories" allows one to define various logical concepts that are not definable within standard two-valued semantics. Suppose for instance, that two communities accept the same truth criteria for sentences of the form *It is a fact that* α (e.g. *It is a fact that the population of the city of New York is greater than that of Copenhagen*). Suppose moreover that those criteria define a sentence of the form *It is a fact that* α to be true iff α is true both under the truth conditions applied by r′ and those applied by r″. Let F stand for 'is a fact'. Then the truth table for the connective F would be the following

V.F. Hendricks, K.F. Jørgensen and S.A. Pedersen (eds.), Knowledge Contributors, 185–198.

α	F(α)
(1,1)	(1,1)
(1,0)	(0,0)
(0,1)	(0,0)
(0,0)	(0,0)

Table 1

For someone who prefers to interpret F by appealing to possible world semantics, F is the necessity connective (for more on that see Section 7). From the formal standpoint, the possible world semantics and the referential semantics are reducible to one another. From the philosophical standpoint the referential semantics has all the advantages of possible world semantics, at the same time being free of the metaphysical commitments of the latter.

The general idea of reference points and that of reference semantics should be sufficiently clear, so we may set to work.

2. LANGUAGE

In what follows by a **language** I shall mean a language L whose syntactical structure is essentially the same as that of a one-sorted first-order predicate language with identity. The **vocabulary** of L consists of the following familiar categories of symbols:

- **predicates** (symbols of relations),
- **symbols of functions**,
- **individual variables**,
- **proper names**,
- **identity symbol** =,
- **connectives** $\$'$, $\$''$,...
- **quantifiers** Q$'$, Q$''$,...

I shall assume that the proper names form a set numerous enough to ensure that each individual object in the intended universe of L has its proper name in L. Unconventional as it is, the assumption is not without precedent. Several examples of applying it are known (cf. e.g. (247).)

The familiar notions such as that of a free variable, bound variable, term, well-formed formula (**formula**, for short), sentence, atomic sentence, etc., etc. will be understood in the usual way. Thus e.g., α is a **sentence** of L, $\alpha \in$ Sent(L), iff α is a formula of L in which no free variable appears. A sentence α of L is **atomic,** $\alpha \in$ At(L), iff α contains neither connectives nor quantifiers.

The terms that contain no variables will be referred to as **names**. In other words a name is either a proper name of an expression that one may form by applying symbols of functions to either proper names or compound names that have been already formed. The set Name(L) of all names of L will be assumed to be arranged in a certain fixed way (e.g. in accordance to the alphabetic order) into the sequence

$$< n_1, n_2, n_3, \ldots >$$

without repetitions ($n_i = n_j$ only if i = j).

3. COMPONENTS OF REFERENTIAL SEMANTICS

Every **referential semantics** for L is defined to be determined by the following four components:

- The non-empty set R of the **reference points**.
- The set E_R of mappings from R into {0,1}. The elements of E_R will be referred to as **truth-evaluations**.
- The set $Mod_R(L)$ of mappings that assign to every atomic sentence a truth-evaluation. The elements of $Mod_R(L)$ will be referred to as **possible referential models** for L (**models** for short).
- The structure

  $$(\$'_R, \$''_R, ...; Q'_R, Q''_R ...),$$

  is referred to as the **referential matrix**, $Matr_R(L)$, for L. They are operations that assign truth evaluations to sequences (finite in case of the connectives and infinite in case of the quantifiers) of truth-evaluations. Their intended role, which might be defined only informally, is to fix the meanings of the connectives and the quantifiers of L corresponding to them.

The four components R, E_R, $Mod_R(L)$, $Matr_R(L)$, determine a **referential semantics** for L iff they satisfy conditions that will be stated in Section 6.

4. SUBSTITUTIONS

In order to complete the definition of referential semantics I need the notion of a "substitution." Informed of some ideas one can find in (246) (cf. note "structurality" in Section 17), I define a **substitution** to be an effectively defined composition of (not necessarily finitely many) the following operations:

- **Permutation of proper names**. An operation of this kind consists in replacing in every sentence α in Sent(L) every proper name n by the name $\tau(n)$, where τ is a permutation of the set of all proper names of L.
- **Predicate replacement**. Let $P(x_1,...,x_{\sigma(P)})$ be an atomic formula formed by a σ(P)–ary predicate P and $x_1,...,x_{\sigma(P)}$ pairwise different variables. Let $\Phi(x_1,...,x_{\sigma(P)})$ be any formula whatsoever with the same free variables as those in $P(x_1,...,x_{\sigma(P)})$. A **predicate replacement** is an operation that consists in replacing in

every sentence α in Sent(L) every part of the form P(ξ_1,..., $\xi_{\sigma(P)}$), if any, by $\Phi(\xi_1,..., \xi_{\sigma(P)})$.

- **Function replacement**. Let $\varphi(x_1,...,x_{\sigma(\varphi)}) = x$ be an atomic formula formed by a $\sigma(\varphi)$–ary, $\sigma(\varphi) \geq 0$, function symbol φ, and pairwise different variables $x_1,...,x_{\sigma(\varphi)}$, x. Let $\theta(x_1,...,x_{\sigma(P)})$ be a compound term with the same free variables as those appearing in $\varphi(x_1,...,x_{\sigma(\varphi)})$. A **function replacement** is an operation that consists in replacing in every sentence α in Sent(L) every part of the form $\varphi(\xi_1,..., \xi_{\sigma(\varphi)}) = \xi$, if any, by $\theta(\xi_1,..., \xi_{\sigma(\varphi)}) = \xi$.

5. SOME NOTATION

Let $\Phi(x)$ be a formula with x being its only free variable. Then

$$< \Phi(x) >$$

will stand for the infinite sequence $< \Phi(n_1), \Phi(n_2), \ldots >$, each $\Phi(n_i)$ being formed by replacing all free occurrences of x in $\Phi(x)$ by the name n_i from the sequence $< n_1, n_2, n_3, \ldots >$. Consequently, if s is a substitution then

$$\mathrm{s}< \Phi(x) > = <\mathrm{s}\Phi(n_1), \mathrm{s}\Phi(n_2), \ldots >$$

Now we are in a position to complete the definition of referential semantics.

6. THE DEFINITION COMPLETED

Let R, E_R, Mod_R(L), Matr_R(L) be as described in Section 3. Then they determine a **referential semantics** for L iff they satisfy the following two conditions:

(R1) For every model h̲ in Mod_R(L) there is exactly one mapping h: Sent(L) $\longrightarrow$ E_R called a (**possible referential**) **interpretation** for L such that both, the model and the interpretation, coincide on At(L).

(R2) For every interpretation h, the truth evaluations that h assigns to compound sentences are defined recursively by the following two equalities:

(R2a) For every k-ary connective \$ and all sentences $\alpha_1,...,\alpha_k$ of L,

$$\mathrm{h}\$(\alpha_1,...,\alpha_k) = \$_R(\mathrm{h}\alpha_1,...,\mathrm{h}\alpha_k)$$

(R2b) For every quantifier Q of L and every sentence of the form $\mathrm{Q}\Phi(x)$

$$\mathrm{h}(\mathrm{Qx}\Phi(\mathrm{x})) = \mathrm{Q}_H <\mathrm{h}\Phi(n_1), \mathrm{h}\Phi(n_2)... >$$

Given a referential semantics determined by R, E_R, Mod_R(L), and Matr_R(L), I shall denote by [R] the set of all possible interpretations that the semantics provides. By inspection of the conditions imposed on the components of a referential semantics, one easily realizes that [R] is definable in terms of R, E_R, Mod_R(L), Matr_R(L) and vice versa; each of the components is definable in terms of [R].

There are two ways to argue that the conditions that a referential semantics is postulated to satisfy are selected properly. To begin with, the quality of the definition should speak for itself, and it speaks for itself if the notion it introduces proves to be useful in dealing with problems of sufficiently large interest. On the other hand, one may examine the quality of the definition against the general principles the semantic analyses are expected to observe. I am going to do this in Section 8.

7. A FEW EXAMPLES

The following examples, supplementing the one known from Section 1 should facilitate familiarizing the chief ideas of referential semantics still before the adequacy of its definition is examined.

EXAMPLE 2. It is quite obvious that referential semantics may preserve the meanings that connectives and quantifiers have within two-valued logic. Thus e.g. in order for interpretations in [R] to render to the material implication, $\rightarrow$, its standard meaning, every interpretation h should assign 1 to $\alpha \rightarrow \beta$ at every point r except those at which it assigns 1 to α and 0 to β. If, for instance, R is a four-element set, the truth-table for $\rightarrow$ should include among others the following rows:

α	β	$\alpha \rightarrow \beta$
...	...	...
(1,0,1,1)	(1,0,0,1)	(1,1,0,1)
...	...	...
(1,0,0,1)	(1,0,0,1)	(1,1,1,1)
...	...	...
(1,0,0,1)	(0,0,0,0)	(0,1,1,0)
...	...	...

Table 2

Note that, in fact, what is customarily called the truth table for $\rightarrow$ is the truth table for $\rightarrow_R$.

The case of classical quantifiers is similar. Thus e.g., in order for [R] to render the existential quantifier $\exists$ its standard meaning every interpretation h should assign 1 to $\exists x\Phi(x)$ at every point r except those points at which the h assigns 0 to all formulas of the form $\Phi(n)$. The operation $\exists_R$ should be defined accordingly.

EXAMPLE 3. The truth-values that an interpretation assigns to a formula at a reference point r may depend upon the values the formula acquires under this interpretation at other points. Let us take another look at the truth table for F (see Section 1, Example 1) with F being interpreted as the necessity connective. The modal logician is likely to point out that the analysis was incomplete because it was ignoring the role of the accessibility relation. Let us dwell on this point.

Indeed suppose r″ is accessible from r′ but not vice versa. Then the truth table for F should be

α	F(α)
(1,1)	(1,1)
(1,0)	(0,0)
(0,1)	(0,1)
(0,0)	(0,0)

Table 3

The third row under the previous version of the truth-table was

(0, 1)	(0, 0)

If one switches from the possible world interpretation to one under which reference points are meant to be reference communities, the "accessibility relation" (the term becomes misleading in this case) might be understood as follows. The truth-criteria applied by a reference community might depend in various ways on those applied by other reference communities. In particular, the truth-value criterion for sentences of the form Fα accepted by r′ might require to treat Fα as true iff α is true both under the "inner criteria" – those accepted by r′ – and "outer criteria" – those accepted by r″. But there need not be any reciprocity in the r″ attitude towards the criteria applied by r′ and the truth criterion for Fα accepted by r″ might require to treat Fα as true iff α is true (i.e. true under the criteria accepted by r″). Truth table 1 was the truth table for F_R defined under the assumption that the truth-criteria for the sentences of the form Fα applied by the two communities are "symmetrical". The truth table 3 corresponds to the case when judgements of r′ are informed by those of r″ but not vice versa. The relation "is accessible" becomes the relation "is informed by".

8. FOUR PRINCIPLES OF LOGICAL ANALYSIS

Amongst various epistemological principles that underlie the development of modern logic the following are the most typical.

(P1) The symbols that form the vocabulary of the examined language divide into "descriptive" and "logical". The **descriptive** are predicate symbols, function symbols, proper names and variables. The **logical** are all the remaining ones, thus connectives, quantifiers and identity.

(P2) Logic is not in the position to offer any analysis whatsoever of the meanings of descriptive symbols. It might merely provide some general framework for such analyses.

(P3) Logic is not able to decide how numerous the set of objects is represented by the variables of the examined language, though logical considerations are carried out under the assumption that it is not empty.

(P4) The chief task of logic is to set the meanings of logical symbols.

One may find it difficult to subscribe to these assumptions without provisos. Logic underwent many changes from the time when those principles were taken for granted. But besides their historical role, they are still of considerable methodological value. The logical analyses in which they are respected preserve their paradigmatic role.

I am going to argue that as long as one accepts (P1) – (P4), one has to accept conditions (R1), (R2). To begin with note that postulates (P1) – (P4) explain why the definition of a referential semantics splits into the definition of $\mathrm{Mod}_R(\mathrm{L})$ and that of $\mathrm{Matr}_R(\mathrm{L})$. While $\mathrm{Matr}_R(\mathrm{L})$ provides the logical terms with definite meanings, $\mathrm{Mod}_R(\mathrm{L})$ is not supposed to fix the meaning of the descriptive terms. Its role is not to define how the descriptive terms are understood but merely to define how they might be understood.

Indeed, select any model $\underline{\mathrm{h}}$: $\mathrm{At}(\mathrm{L}) \longrightarrow \mathrm{E}_R$ in $\mathrm{Mod}_R(\mathrm{L})$. The referential semantics does not tell us whether $\underline{\mathrm{h}}$ is the "intended model" of L. In other words, it does not tell us whether the actual meanings of the descriptive words coincide with the meanings the model defines. Suppose they might be the same. Now select any substitution s. Might actual meanings also be such as those that the composition of s and $\underline{\mathrm{h}}$ defines, i.e. such that for every atomic sentence α, the "right" evaluation of this sentence is $\underline{\mathrm{h}}(\mathrm{s}\alpha)$? The theorist seeking to answer this and similar questions is bounded by two limitations. Firstly, any answer he might offer – (R1) being one of them – must be motivated by the intuitive idea of what is "logically possible" and what is not. Secondly any such answer must be stated in terms of those concepts that are available in the meta-language in which the analyses are carried out. Condition (R1) is all what one might say about $\mathrm{Mod}_R(\mathrm{L})$ if the tools for semantic analyses available in the meta-language reduce to the tools applied in syntactical analyses. The syntactical tools are the only tools I am using.

Semantic analyses that do not involve any meta-linguistic means other than those applied in syntactical analyses are not unusual. The most remarkable examples of them are perhaps the following (see also note "syntactical approach to semantic problems", Section 17). (1) Lindenbaum's methods of forming logical matrices by means of formulas of the analyzed calculi (numerous variants of this technique were developed – one of which will be applied in the proof of the Adequacy Theorem, see Section 16), (2) Tarski's early analysis of the notion of truth under the assumption that the analyzed language is part of meta-language, (3) Hintikka's conception of model sets.

There is one more point left to be discussed. I shall undertake it in Section 10.

9. LOGICAL CONSEQUENCES

The primary task of logic is to study logical consequence operations meant to be the consequence operations whose properties are exclusively determined by the meanings of logical symbols. Except the identity predicate, of which I have tacitly assumed that it should be understood in the "usual" way, the meanings of the other logical symbols of L are left completely unspecified. We cannot, therefore, tell logical consequences defined in L from non-logical ones. The only thing of which we can be sure is that a consequence operation C is not logical unless it is structural.

Indeed, logical consequence operations should be "structural" in the following sense. If C is logical then the answer to the question of whether $\alpha \in \mathrm{C(X)}$ should depend upon the "structure" of α and that of sentences in X and nothing more; it should depend on how these sentences are formed from atomic sentences by means of connectives and quantifiers. The formal counterpart of this loose definition is the following.

A consequence operation C defined in L is said to be **structural** iff for every sentence α, every set of sentences X and every substitution s, the following is satisfied:

$$\text{If } \alpha \in \mathrm{C(X)} \text{ then } \mathrm{s}\alpha \in \mathrm{C(sX)}$$

Note that the structurality condition imposed on logical consequence operations parallels the condition that requires the set $\mathrm{Mod}_R(\mathrm{L})$ of possible models for L to be closed under substitutions. The justification of the two is the same. Both the semantic conditions imposed on logical symbols and "deductive" ones should cover all "logically possible" meanings of descriptive symbols. By a **deductive** condition (property etc.) I mean a condition (or resp. property, etc.) defined in terms of properties of C.

10. A FEW COMMENTS ON THE PECULIAR STATUS OF THE IDENTITY PREDICATE

The identity predicate is the only logical symbol in the vocabulary of L whose intended meaning is known to us. What we do know suffices to make some judgments both about semantic systems and consequence operations. Thus e.g. it suffices to identify a system of referential semantics as "intensional" if there is an interpretation h such that for some terms n, m, h "classifies" $n = m$ as true at the reference point r ($\mathrm{h}(n = m)(\mathrm{r}) = 1$), and yet there is a pair of sentences $\alpha(n)$ and $\alpha(m)$ such that they are the same except that some occurrences of n in $\alpha(n)$ are replaced by m in $\alpha(m)$ and, nevertheless, h does not assign to them the same truth value at the point r. Also it suffices to identify a consequence operation C as "incomplete with respect to =" if $n = k \notin C(n = m, m = k)$. It suffices, however, neither for setting conditions that a system of semantics nor that a consequence operation should satisfy in order to meet all expectations one might address to them guided by the intended meaning of =.

The main reason why it is so is that L may happen to be intensional. If this is the case, neither semantic nor deductive properties of the identity symbol =, can be sufficiently well defined without examining how the meaning of = is related to the meanings of the remaining symbols of L.

From the deductive standpoint intensionality consists in that the rules of inference for sentences that involve the identity predicate depend upon the context in which the predicate appears. From the semantic standpoint (and the relevant semantics is that of possible worlds) this phenomenon largely remains a puzzle. Some modal logicians might disagree with this opinion, which might be exaggerated indeed. And yet I believe various aspects of intensionality are beyond what can adequately be accounted for by means of possible world analyses. The following concise remark is meant to illustrate the point.

As was argued by Kripke, under the conception of possible worlds which Kripke considered the right one, proper names should be treated as "rigid designators" (i.e., as expressions that stand for the same objects in every possible world). Should one keep treating proper names as rigid designators if one opts for referential semantics with reference points defined to be reference communities?

There is no compelling reason to do so. In fact, there is a good reason to decline from doing so. No assertions of the form $n = m$, except those of the form $n = n$, can be justified by appealing to purely logical criteria. Non-logical criteria, often empirical ones, that different reference communities apply to learn whether $n = m$ might vary from one community to another, regardless of whether n and m are proper or compound names. And if so, it might happen that two proper names n and m denote exactly the same object according to the truth criteria of the community r′ and they denote two different objects according to the truth criteria of r″. So at least one of these two names does not denote the same object at both r′ and r″.

Not forcing us to accept the theory of rigid designators, referential semantics opens a possibility to look at the phenomenon of intensionality from a perspective different from that offered by the possible world semantics. (See note "Rigid designators", Section 17).

11. GENERAL PROPERTIES OF CONSEQUENCE OPERATIONS

Besides structurality, all consequences I am going to consider are supposed to satisfy the following two familiar conditions:

(c1) $X \subseteq C(X) = C(C(X)$,
(c2) If $X \subseteq Y$ then $C(X) \subseteq C(Y)$.

They were set (see note "consequence operation in Section 17) by Tarski, at the time when he examined properties of "deductive systems" (248). Condition (c2) is known as the monotonicity postulate. Within the last few decades non-monotonic logics (i.e. consequence operations that do not satisfy (c2)) have been widely studied.

12. THE TRUTH PRESERVING CONSEQUENCE OPERATIONS

A familiar way of defining a consequence operation consists in defining it as an operation that applied to true sentences yields true conclusions. In the case of the referential semantics this general idea might justify several non-equivalent definitions. Let us dwell on this point.

An interpretation h will be said to **verify** (**falsify**) α at the reference point r iff the truth value that h assigns to α at the reference point r is 1 (is 0). If, for a set X of sentences, h verifies all sentences at a point r, h will be said to **verify** X at that point. Note that under this stipulation, the empty set of sentences is verified by every interpretation.

By saying that α is a consequence of (follows from) a set of sentences X one may mean, among others, one of the following:

- For every interpretation h and every reference point r, h verifies α at r whenever it verifies X. $Cn_{[R]}$ will denote the corresponding consequence operation.
- For every possible interpretation h, h verifies α at all reference points whenever at all reference points it verifies X.
- Let r_0 be a fixed reference point, e.g. the "actual world" in the set of all possible worlds. For every possible interpretation h, h verifies α at the point r_0 whenever at that point it verifies X.

In what follows only the first of the three consequences, thus $Cn_{[R]}$, will be of my interest. This should not suggest that alternative ways of defining a consequence operation are of lesser significance.

13. THE PROBLEM OF ADEQUACY

Hardly ever a semantic definition of a consequence operation is applied directly for judging whether a sentence is a consequence of a given set of premises or not. Rather, by appealing to it, one proves validity of various rules of inference in order to argue with the help of them. The question of whether all sentences that follow from a set X of premises (are semantic consequences of X) can be derived from X with the help of rules whose validity were demonstrated (are syntactical consequences of X) is known as a **completeness problem**. A set of valid rules of inference is said to be **complete** if the semantic and syntactic consequence operations coincide.

The problem of adequacy is opposite to that of completeness. In both cases a consequence operation C is given and the solution to the problem consists in defining a set of conditions that provide an alternative definition of C. However, in the case of a completeness problem, the conditions looked for are postulated to be valid inference rules. In the case of an adequacy problem they are postulated to be semantic postulates of the right kind.

14. SELF-EXTENSIONAL CONSEQUENCE OPERATIONS

Let C be a consequence operation defined on the set Sent(L) of sentences of L. Given any two k-element sequences $(\alpha_1,...,\alpha_k)$, $(\beta_1,...,\beta_k)$ of sentences of L, I shall say that they are C-**equivalent**, in symbols

$$(\alpha_1,...,\alpha_k) =_C (\beta_1,...,\beta_k)$$

iff $C(\alpha_1) = C(\beta_1),...,C(\alpha_k) = C(\beta_k)$.

Both the notion and the corresponding notation extend to sequences of sentences of the form $< \Phi(x) >$, $< \Psi(x) >$ (x being the only free variable in formulas $\Phi(x)$, $\Psi(x)$) as follows. We shall say that $< \Phi(x) >$, $< \Psi(x) >$ are C-equivalent, in symbols

$$< \Phi(x) > =_C < \Psi(x) >$$

iff $C(\Phi(n_i)) = C(\Psi(n_i))$, for all $i = 1,2,...$

We are now in a position to define the predicate version of the notion of a self-extensional consequence. The consequence C defined in L will be said to be **self-extensional** iff the following two conditions are satisfied:

(E1) Let $(\alpha_1,...,\alpha_k) =_C (\beta_1,...,\beta_k)$. Then for every k-ary connective \$, $\$(\alpha_1,...,\alpha_k) =_C \$(\beta_1,...,\beta_k)$.

(E2) Let $\Phi(x)$, $\Psi(x)$ be formulas of L in which x is the only free variable. If $< \Phi(x) >) =_C < \Psi(x) >$, then for every quantifier Q:

$$Qx\Phi(x) =_C Qx\Psi(x).$$

15. ADEQUACY THEOREM

THEOREM 1. Let C be a consequence defined on Sent(L). Then there is a referential semantics [R] for L such that $C = Cn_{[R]}$ iff C is both structural and self-extensional.

For the proof of this theorem see (251).

16. THE NEED FOR REFERENTIAL SEMANTICS

Proving the adequacy theorem surely was not the main task of this paper. What it was should be clear from numerous examples I have been producing, all of which meant to illustrate need for referential semantics. This is the point I want to argue now from a larger perspective.

Knowledge develops through critical assessment of alternative points of views, alternative often also in the sense that they are expressed in "different languages" meant to be languages based on different criteria of truth.

Recall that throughout this paper the differences that consist in applying different criteria of truth have been ascribed to different groups of users of the same language. They have not been treated as differences that result in splitting a language into different languages. An obvious way to settle this terminological divergence is to call a language with only one set of truth criteria assigned to it **homogeneous**. Logicians tend to focus their attention on homogeneous languages and to treat non-homogenous ones as a merging of homogeneous ones. Those for whom logic is a normative discipline warn that using non-homogenous languages hampers communication by yielding misunderstandings and confusions.

In spite of what is maintained both by logical purists, not to mention philosophers fond of "incommensurability thesis" (languages based on different criteria of truth are not translatable one to another), people using different criteria of truth might perfectly understand one another. They might understand properly what people belonging to other reference communities say and thus their views might be informed by views formed under truth-criteria different from those to which they subscribe. Consequently they might revise judgements and even revise the truth criteria on which they base them.

To admit that the phenomenon of communication based on non-homogeneous criteria of truth is not marginal but typical for human communication is to admit that we have to find out the right tools for studying the phenomenon. For obvious reasons referential semantics and various logics (consequence operations) defined with its help should be particularly useful. One may hardly propose any alternative. Some aspects of the process of inter-group communication (a group meant to be a reference group) can presumably be accounted for in terms of translations from one homogeneous language to another. But the hypothesis that the communication goes via such translations introduces into the picture a redundant element. In order to be produced, a translation needs an interpreter – someone who assists people who are not able to communicate directly. People belonging to different reference communities are able to communicate without such assistance.

Contrary to what I claimed at the beginning of Section 9, the primary task of logic (logic intended to be an applied not merely theoretical discipline) is not studying logical consequence operations but studying the way in which people reason. Logical consequence operations are thus means, not the ultimate goal of the enterprise. So what are the consequence operations that people use when they reason in non-homogeneous languages? What are the logical constants they use or perhaps what is the best way to account for the referential aspects of the familiar connectives and quantifiers that in homogeneous languages are best understood as two-valued?

I do not believe that these questions can be answered without numerous case studies. The right framework for such studies might be provided by investigations into the problems that arise when one wants to find out the right way of programming a machine to be able to undertake decision on the base of conflicting information.

The last obvious point: many-valued referential semantics, fuzzy referential semantics are entirely natural generalizations of two-valued one.

17. NOTES AND REFERENCES

(1) Consequence operation: Alfred Tarski presented results of his investigations into formal properties of the consequence operation in the following papers: 'Über einige fundamentale Begriffe der Metamathematik' (1930), Fundamentale Begriffe der Metodologie der Deductiven Wissenschaften' (1930), Grundzüge des Systemkalküls (1935). Their English versions are available in Tarski (1956).

(2) Referential semantics: I defined the notion of referential semantics for propositional languages and presented the proof of the propositional version of the adequacy theorem in a note 'Referential matrix semantics for propositional calculi' published in 1979. The result along with a discussion of formal links between the referential and possible world semantics can also be found in (249).

(3) Reference community: In Wójcicki (2003) I define a reference community as a group of people who set forth criteria of truth. From the point of view of topics discussed in this paper the difference between setting forth the criteria and just subscribing to them is inessential. The right one is the definition accepted in (250), however. It is motivated by much the same considerations as those that underlie Ludwik Fleck's (243) idea of "thought style." This paper is not the right occasion to compare Fleck's epistemology with not the same epistemological tenets I am accepting. The essential difference, however, might consist in that Fleck treats thought styles as closed to any outside information, while the judgments formed within different reference communities may be informed by judgments formed within other reference communities.

(4) Rigid designators: The conception of rigid designators is an essential part of Saul Kripke's (245) conception of possible worlds and possible world semantics. It was pursued further in the Putnam – Kripke theory of causal denotation.

(5) Structurality: The notion of structurality is one of the central notions applied in logical analyses of propositional calculi. The language of such a calculus can be identified with the algebra of its formulas (an idea of such treatment goes back to Lindenbaum and Tarski, cf. Tarski (1956)) and then substitutions are defined to be endomorphisms of thus understood languages. Under these stipulations the definition of a structural consequence operation of a propositional calculus does not differ from one for predicate languages given in Section 9. The predicate version of

the notion of structurality is informed by the analysis offered by W. A. Pogorzelski (see Pogorzelski, 1969).
(6) Syntactical approach to semantic problems: Adolf Lindenbaum's idea to define a logical matrix adequate for the set of all logically true formulas of a propositional calculus by using formulas of that calculus as elements of the matrix originated the technique of analyzing semantic properties of various logical systems with the help semantic concepts (notably semantic models) formed by expressions of the analyzed language. An attempt to reduce semantics to syntax was a part of Rudolf Carnap's research program. The chief semantic units of his analyses were "descriptions" defined to be sequences of atomic sentences and their negations. Another remarkable example of a syntactical approach to semantic problems is Jaakko Hintikka's (244) technique of analyzing semantic properties of logical calculi by means of 'model sets' meant to be sets of sentences. Carnap's and Hintikka's ideas were exploited in model theoretical analyses. Under the assumption that every individual object from the universe of the examined language has its proper name in that language, semantic models are represented by their "descriptions" understood in the way suggested by Carnap (see e.g. Robinson (every individual object having its name in the language – Robinson (247))).

Institute of Philosophy and Sociology
The Polish Academy of Sciences
Warsaw
Poland

REFERENCES

[243] Ludwik Fleck. *Entstehung und Entwicklung einer wissenschaftlichen Tatsache, Einführung in die Lehre vom Denkstil und Denkkolektiv.* Basel: Schwabe & Co.;, 1936. English transl.: *Genesis and Development of Scientific Fact*, The University of Chicago Press.
[244] J. Hintikka. *Models for Modalities, Selected Essays.* D. Reidel, 1968.
[245] S. Kripke. *Naming and Necessity.* Harvard University Press, 1980.
[246] W. A. Pogorzelski. *Klasyczny rachunek kwantyfikatorów.* PWN, Warszawa, 1981.
[247] A. Robinson. *Introduction to Model Theory and to the Metamathematics of Algebra.* North-Holland, 1963.
[248] A. Tarski. *Logics, Semantics Metamathematics; Papers from 1923 – 1928.* Clarendon Press, Oxford, 1956.
[249] R. Wójcicki. *Theory of Logical Calculi.* Kluwer Academic Publishers, Dordrecht, 1988.
[250] R. Wójcicki. Foundationalism, coherentism and foundherentism – the controversies from an alternative point of view, 2003. To appear in the volume devoted to Susan Haack.
[251] R. Wójcicki. A logic is referential iff it is selfextensional. *Studia Logica*, 73:323 – 335, 2003.

INDEX